TIM McCARVER'S
DIAMOND
GEMS

**Favorite Baseball
Stories from the
Legends of the Game**

Edited by TIM McCARVER

with

JIM MOSKOVITZ *and* DANNY PEARY

New York Chicago San Francisco Lisbon London Madrid Mexico City
Milan New Delhi San Juan Seoul Singapore Sydney Toronto

The *McGraw·Hill* Companies

Library of Congress Cataloging-in-Publication Data

Tim McCarver's diamond gems : favorite baseball stories from the legends of the game / edited
  by im McCarver ; with Jim Moskovitz and Danny Peary. — 1st ed.
       p.   cm.
     ISBN 978-0-07-154594-5 (alk. paper)
       1. Baseball players—United States—Anecdotes.   2. Baseball players—United States—
     Biography.   3. Baseball—United States—Anecdotes.   I. McCarver, Tim.   II. Moskovitz,
     Jim.   III. Peary, Danny, 1949–

     GV873.T56   2008
     796.3570922—dc22
     [B]   2007039633

1 2 3 4 5 6 7 8 9 10 11 12 13 14 15 16 17 18 19 20 21 22   FGR/FGR   0 9 8

ISBN 978-0-07-154594-5
MHID   0-07-154594-8

McGraw-Hill books are available at special quantity discounts to use as premiums and sales
promotions, or for use in corporate training programs. For more information, please write to the
Director of Special Sales, Professional Publishing, McGraw-Hill, Two Penn Plaza, New York, NY
10121-2298. Or contact your local bookstore.

This book is printed on acid-free paper.

To the marvelous people of the game past and present who weave the stories of the sport and life. And also to Kelly and Kathy, who have heroically and lovingly survived a rugged baseball life.

—Tim McCarver

To the two most important women in my life: my magnificent wife, Joyce, whose loving inspiration has opened unimagined dreams and opportunities; and my mother, Charlotte Moskovitz, who provided me with the strength to realize those dreams.

—Jim Moskovitz

To Julianna, Zoë, Suzanne, and Laura, four generations of feisty females, and in memory of Vic Power, Nellie Fox, Richie Ashburn, and Al Kozar, my baseball heroes.

—Danny Peary

CONTENTS

Contents

FOREWORD

George Will

Never having hit a triple, I can't say for sure, but Tim McCarver says it is true, so it must be: he says hitting a triple is better than having sex—and only a really rash person would question *any* of Tim's judgments touching on baseball. Besides, as the only catcher ever to lead either of the major leagues in triples (with thirteen in 1966), he has had a lot of opportunities—fifty-seven in his major-league career—to contemplate the comparison.

My baseball career was, to say no more, rather less distinguished. It reached its apogee—and ended, for that matter—more than half a century ago, when I turned thirteen and was no longer eligible to play Little League in Champaign, Illinois. There I exhibited mediocrity under pressure for the Mittendorf Funeral Home Panthers, whose color was, of course, black.

A few years ago, when I was inducted into the Little League Hall of Excellence, in Williamsport, Pennsylvania, the Little League officials made it clear—painfully clear; unnecessarily clear—that I was being honored for achievements after Little League. And not for athletic achievements of any sort. After Little League, my athletic achievements consisted of playing basketball briefly and badly for the University of Illinois High School, which was known in central Illinois athletic circles as Puny Uni.

My two fellow inductees that day in Williamsport were Kareem Abdul-Jabbar and Tom Selleck, who, before his acting career, had been a fine athlete at the University of Southern California. I said I was accepting the Hall of Excellence honor in the name of right fielders everywhere. You know who we are. We are the ones who were sent out to the position where we could do the least damage.

But even—maybe especially—a bad player can appreciate a good student of the game, which Tim has always been. We who could not play the game well could at least excel by trying to understand the game. For people like us, people like Tim are indispensable.

Long ago, catchers' equipment came to be called "the tools of ignorance," but catchers actually are—they must be—among the most cerebral players. From their vantage point in foul territory, they have all the unfolding action in front of them. As a catcher, Tim had a lot of experience not just calling games for his pitchers but also running games for his teams.

In an earlier book, the title of which is as effervescent as Tim is (*Oh, Baby, I Love It: Baseball Summers, Hot Pennant Races, Grand Salamis, Jellylegs, El Swervos, Dingers and Dunkers, Etc., Etc., Etc.*), he wrote: "In a manner of speaking, the top hitters in baseball don't hit off pitchers. They hit off catchers. It's the catcher who's in there, day after day, ordering up the pitches, and in most instances the pitchers don't shake off their catchers." All of this means that Tim knows the game, and as this volume demonstrates, he knows the questions to ask of those who have played it, or who are still playing.

With the catcher, umpire, and batter all sharing a small space on the field, conversations can break out around home plate. It is a good place for the gregarious—think of a talkative catcher named Yogi— and Tim certainly is that. Which is one reason why he is such an extraordinarily engaging television host.

Bruce Catton once said that baseball is the greatest conversation piece ever invented in America. That was quite a testimonial, considering that Catton was a distinguished historian of the Civil War, which has been a pretty durable conversation topic. To fans who follow baseball closely, this much is clear: if the Hall of Fame in Cooperstown had a wing devoted to baseball's best conversationalists, Tim would long ago have been enshrined in the first class.

While playing for the Phillies, Tim caught a famously taciturn Hall of Famer, Steve Carlton. Before that, while with the Cardinals, Tim caught Bob Gibson, the Hall of Famer who rarely balked but did once when McCarver started out to the mound after Gibson had already begun his motion to deliver the next pitch. Gibson was not amused to glance up and see his catcher approaching. Especially when the ferociously competitive Gibson was at work, he was not, shall we say, the chatty type. But McCarver always has been ebullient, which is why he is such a gifted interviewer. His unflagging enthusiasm for the game is infectious, and he has the indispensable gift of a fine conversationalist: he is a good listener.

Well, sure, who would not listen when the people talking are the guests Tim has had on the television program over the years? Readers of this delightful volume will be, in effect, listening in on fascinating conversations Tim has had with the likes of Henry Aaron, Ernie Banks, Johnny Bench, Yogi Berra, Wade Boggs, Tony Gwynn, Ralph Kiner, Stan Musial, and many others.

When baseball is discussed, numbers are always involved. But of all the most familiar baseball numbers—Ted Williams's .406 batting average in 1941, Joe DiMaggio's 56-game hitting streak the same year (the year Tim and I were born), Nolan Ryan's 5,714 career strikeouts, etc.—perhaps the number most difficult for fans to fully fathom is the humble number 162, the number of games each team plays in the long season.

The season requires sustained effort and a sturdy commitment to professional standards. That is why when you ask real baseball people to name the qualities they most admire in players, the quality most frequently named is consistency. That is why Stan Musial was considered a player's player: he got 3,630 hits, 1,815 at home and 1,815 on the road. Consistency is what makes Tim the broadcast equivalent of Stan the Man. Tim is always at the top of his game. Since he quit playing, his game has been the challenge of making the game—its past, present, and future—as intelligible and entertaining as possible for the rest of us.

The many millions of us who have enjoyed and benefited from Tim's three decades in broadcasting booths are in his debt. And with this book, our debt has grown. Fortunately, Tim is a kindly creditor. All he asks in payment is that we continue to join him in his enjoyment of baseball. So, turn this page and get to the good stuff—Tim and the unending conversation about the great game.

ACKNOWLEDGMENTS

This book has been more than a decade in the making, so there are numerous people my coeditors, Jim Moskovitz and Danny Peary, and I would like to thank.

Rob Wilson at Wilson Media superbly represented this book, along with Robert L. Rosen and Jennifer Unter at RLR Associates, Ltd. Bob and his colleagues Craig Foster, Gary Rosen, and Michael Klein at RLR have been essential to *The McCarver Show*'s birth and longevity, and we greatly appreciate their longtime friendship. Our appreciation also goes to Gail Lockhart, Barbara Hadzicosmas, and Scott Gould.

We have enjoyed our relationship with McGraw-Hill, and our deep gratitude goes to Ron Martirano for his enthusiasm for this book and his editing expertise. Even three editors can use help! Also at McGraw-Hill, several individuals deserve to be singled out: Judith McCarthy, Marisa L'Heureux, Craig Bolt, Eileen Lamadore, Ann Pryor, Tom Lau, and Joe Berkowitz.

We gratefully acknowledge Chevrolet for its powerful support of *The Tim McCarver Show*, now enjoying its ninth 52-week television season. Since November 1999, Brent Dewar, Ed Peper, Kim Kosak, Scott Metzger, Phil Caruso, Kelly O'Neill, Mike Hughes, James Ryan, John Roth, Brooke Baratz, and Brian Elwarner have been indispensable to the show's success. We also wish to thank Christine Coraci and Chris Murphy at GM Planworks.

Gregg Foster, Jeff Mitchell, Vinny Sinopoli, and Mary Ann Muro have been with us all the years and lead our show's production team, which is the best in sports television. We give much credit to Peter Bleckner, Dan Culleny, Joe Dechaves, Dan Stewart, Walter Cranston, Denise Balish, Jack Williams, Arie Hefter, Doug Schneider, Rich Schlomann, John Bell, Alex Schoenfeld, Greg Inkpen, Pete Forrest, Bill McDonald, Amy Faas, Grace Rosenkrantz, Pete Rodriguez, Frank Berman, Paul Chappell, Kerry Soloway, and all the other talented crew members who have helped put out our show over the years. Special thanks as well to Grant Norlin for his fine work with the show. We are lucky to work hand in hand with the outstanding NEP Image Group's Barry Katz, Ken Mochtak, Willie Sheehy, Betty DeCaires, and Debbie Baboolall.

Great thanks go to Richard von Kleist, a computer expert and poet, who designed and maintains the show's website and helps book travel. We also are grateful to our Canadian transcriber, Katherine White-Dolan.

Our partners at New York's luxurious Kimberly Hotel have been nonpareil and integral to the production of our show. Special thanks go to our great friends Marcia James, Jorge Garciadealba, and Sara Ayele.

Foremost, we thank all the gracious guests who have been on our show and are represented in this book.

INTRODUCTION

In 1999, when we decided to move *The Tim McCarver Show* from radio to television, my longtime friend Joe Torre was my lone guest on the pilot. When I asked him what he wanted to do after he retired from managing, he looked at me and said, "Be in your chair." I wonder if he remembers that remark nine years later. Until he decided not to return as manager last October, Joe remained on the Yankees' bench, and I've been comfortably perched in my interview chair the whole time. It's true that he collected more rings than I did since we made that pilot, but I'm proud to say that Chevrolet's *Tim McCarver Show* has had success as well, and 250 shows later, it is telecast nationwide in almost every market.

I believe that the show's popularity with viewers and guests alike is due to my telling whoever is sitting across from me three words: "It's your show." My primary goal each week is to make the guest so comfortable that he (or she) feels as free to talk as if he were sitting in his own living room and I was visiting. I never try to elicit any information, explanation, or story from guests that they might be reluctant to talk about. I simply want them to converse about what they feel at ease sharing. That in itself—as you will discover while reading this book— is terrific material that reveals a great deal about them and the sport they love. Of course, homework is essential, as "A" material is offered only to the prepared interviewer, but I'd also like to think that they *know* that I'm as genuinely interested in what they have to say as the avid viewers at home. It has been rewarding to learn as much as I do from each guest, including people I have known for years.

Often I'm asked if it's easier to interview someone I have never met or barely know or someone with whom I've been friends for years. There's no comparison. It is much harder to interview someone who I know inside out. For example, over a span covering more than forty-five years, my former Cardinals battery mate and friend Bob Gibson and I have talked about every conceivable baseball situation and gone through every human experience imaginable. So, each time he comes on the show, I worry that he won't want to open up about certain things because he assumes I already know everything he's going to say. Fortunately, Bob, like Joe Torre, Jim Palmer, and other longtime acquaintances, continues to surprise me with new revelations. It's also a joy to let viewers see the funny, intelligent, kind, multidimensional Bob Gibson I've known on a personal level, rather than the intimidating competitor they remember from his pitching days.

On my show, it has been exciting and enlightening to have the opportunity to interview athletes in all sports, from football and basketball to skating and snowboarding. But naturally, most guests have come from my sport, baseball. I've had the privilege of talking to the late Larry Doby about the discrimination he endured, Cal Ripken about what (actually, who) gave him the character and fortitude to succeed in what I believe was a "quest for perfection," Yogi Berra about being both a baseball and war hero, Lou Piniella about embarking on a baseball career after flunking a course in square dancing, Willie Mays about his "Catch," Mike Schmidt about being convinced by Pete Rose that he really was a great player, Earl Weaver and Jim Palmer about their peculiar relationship, and on and on. Even Sandy Koufax appeared on the radio show, a rare occurrence. I knew him well enough to know that he'd relax around me and that, when he's comfortable, there are few people as erudite about baseball. Koufax trying to find a third pitch to complement his devastating fastball and curve? I had no idea. For me, the beauty of the show is that such nuggets are unearthed with surprising regularity.

Diamond Gems is, I like to think, baseball history, first-person accounts from Hall of Famers and star players and managers that have never been printed before. I have included a treasure trove of personal stories, opinions, and professional insight from more than seventy current and retired baseball players and managers who have graced my show, including all the remarkable individuals I mentioned. As with Sandy Koufax, I try to make them all comfortable under the lights when they make their first and repeat appearances, because I know they have so much to say, as this volume confirms. Just as it is their show, this is their book.

ONE

FILLING OUT THE LINEUP CARD

EARL WEAVER
The Cardinals Were My First Love

My dad ran a dry-cleaning service in St. Louis, and we used to deliver the uniforms to the Cardinals and Browns. It was the late '30s, the days of the Gas House Gang—Pepper Martin, Ducky Medwick, Dizzy Dean, and Leo "the Lip" Durocher. Those guys had great nicknames, didn't they? I would go with my father into the clubhouse and see all the players' lockers. And I'd get to see a lot of games. When the Cardinals lost, I'd get mad at the manager because I thought I could do a better job. Billy Southworth was a good manager with good players, and his teams won 100 games a record three years in a row—I would become one of the only other managers to accomplish that. I went to Beaumont High School, which was about a ten-minute trolley ride and thirty- to forty-five minute walk from my house, and was about a ten- to fifteen-minute walk to Sportsman's Park. In 1944, when I was fourteen, the Cardinals and Browns faced each other in the World Series, so I'd skip my last class, walk over to the park, buy myself a ticket, and sit in the bleachers—so, I was able to see all the games.

I dreamed of playing second base for the Cardinals, and when I was seventeen, they signed me. I was in their system from 1948 to 1957 and never played an inning of major-league ball. But there were things I was proud of. I was the MVP in two of my first four seasons, and one year drove in over 100 runs, although I hit only two homers—my teammates were on base all the time. I'm proud of being in the Hall of Fame, but the one thing I'm really proud of is that I was put on the St. Louis Cardinals roster in 1952. Naturally, Red Schoendienst was going to be their second baseman for some time, and I didn't make the team, but I got to play exhibition games with Stan Musial and Enos Slaughter and be managed by Eddie Stanky. I even hit a home run off Bob Porterfield. When I was inducted into the Hall of Fame, I talked about that one spring training. They later came up with the box scores of sixteen of the eighteen games I played in, and I have them framed in my home. I was a very good Double-A player and a mediocre Triple-A player but just didn't have the tools to play major-league ball. However, I am so proud that I worked my way up through the Cardinals' system to get on their major-league roster that one spring.

I Was a Sore Loser

In my managerial career, I found that it was harder to lose than it was enjoyable to win. If the losses pile up, you're not going to stay in one town very long. I took full responsibility for our team winning or losing, because I wrote out the lineup card before every single game, and after the final out, the Win or Loss went to only me and the pitcher. Each and every loss really gnawed at me. The optimum season is when you win your division, you win the pennant, and you go on to win the World Series. The Orioles won a good number of divisions and pennants, but I experienced too many World Series losses. We won one in 1970, but it would really hurt when we lost.

2

It's such a long season, and every game means so much when you get down to late August and mid-September, when everything gets exciting. People would say, "What do you care if you lost a game on April 15, when you have a whole season to go?" Well, that one loss may be the one game you needed to win in order to win your division. In 1982, the year I retired for the first time, we lost by one game on the last day of the season—so, that game we lost in April could have been the game we needed. I didn't take any loss well. That's why I have said I want my tombstone to read: "The World's Worst Loser."

Underestimating the Mets

In 1969, we were rooting for the New York Mets to beat out the Chicago Cubs for the National League East title. They had a bigger ballpark, so we figured the World Series share would be bigger. But we didn't think we'd play them in the Series. Even after winning their division, they had to play the Braves in the NLCS, and Atlanta had a powerful team with Hank Aaron, Rico Carty, Orlando Cepeda, and Joe Torre. Our pitchers were all rooting for the Mets. All of a sudden it's the World Series and we're playing the Mets, because they swept Atlanta.

We had to go against Tom Seaver, Jerry Koosman, Gary Gentry, and Nolan Ryan. They pitched tremendous baseball. Those guys could put it on the corners. We were a little too anxious to show everyone in America how good we were, and we were chasing their pitches. All season long, Brooks Robinson and Frank Robinson were waiting for their pitches, but in the Series, even they were swinging at the pitcher's pitches. We won Game 1 and then lost the next four games. That was so disappointing. Sometimes things don't turn out the way you want them to.

The Orioles Won a Lot of Games

3

My first full year as manager of the Baltimore Orioles was 1969. That was the first year there was divisional play. We won 109 games that year, which I think was second most in American League history, behind only the Indians' 111 victories in 1954. And I said, "We won all those games, and we still have to play a best-of-5 series to make the World Series?" And I said that again after we won 108 games in 1970 and 101 games in 1971. Fortunately, we swept all three League Championship Series and got into the World Series each time. In addition to a strong lineup, we had such great defense with Brooks Robinson on third, Mark Belanger at short, Davey Johnson at second, and Paul Blair and Frank Robinson in the outfield. They helped our pitching staff, and the pitchers knew it. Even Jim Palmer didn't go after strikeouts. Palmer, Mike Cuellar, Dave McNally, and Pat Dobson all wanted batters to go after the first pitch, the "pitcher's pitch," and hit the ball to one of our guys. Very seldom did Cuellar or McNally get to 100 pitches in a complete game. Even Palmer's count was down to 115 to 120 pitches for nine innings. Pitching and defense went hand in hand when I managed Baltimore, which is why we won over 100 games five times and reached the ALCS six times.

I Say Yes, Palmer Says No

Brooks Robinson has been quoted as saying that Jim Palmer and I were two of the sharpest baseball minds that he'd ever been around but that we both thought we knew the game better than the other. I think that's a fair statement. Jim had knowledge of baseball and was a thinker. I can understand why he and everyone else doesn't want to manage, but I wonder why he never wanted to be a pitching coach and help young kids. I know that he goes to spring training with the Orioles, because he's doing some broadcasting, and takes time to talk to the young pitchers. He complains to me that they don't listen to him, so maybe that's why he doesn't want to coach. When he tells me they don't listen, I'm thinking, "Neither did you." There's a bobble-head doll with the two of us. There's one head, and Palmer's on one side, and I'm on the other. If you touch me, the bobble-head will go up and down, signifying *yes*, and if you touch him, the head will go from side to side, signifying *no*. We couldn't agree on anything, but we were together seventeen years, and it was wonderful having him on my team.

I Relied on Stats to Determine Matchups

In the old days, there were eight teams in each league, and then in the early '60s, that expanded to ten. Teams played each other so many times that you could remember who hit who and which pitchers always got certain batters on your team out. When baseball really expanded and there were many more players in the league and teams didn't play as often, you couldn't remember as well. In the minor leagues, I knew there were some pitchers I couldn't hit. And I heard pitchers say, "Oh, I can't get that hitter out no matter what I do." That stuck in my mind, and when I first managed with the Orioles, I asked a publicity guy named Bob Brown to go back and check how our hitters did against certain pitchers. And I discovered that there were some batter-pitcher matchups that were good and some that were bad. All of a sudden I realize that Boog Powell can't hit Mickey Lolich or Jim Kaat. Not many left-handed batters had much success against those two lefties, but Powell had gone something like 1-for-64 against Lolich. So, from then on, when we went against Lolich, Boog appreciated sitting on the bench, resting his feet. Most batters don't mind sitting out guys they have trouble with, just as some can't wait to grab a bat against pitchers they've hit in the past.

I would use stats when I made out my lineups and throughout the game to adjust to the other team's hitters and pitchers. I was probably the first manager to use statistics before the printouts. I guess I was ahead of my time, because years later, every manager was doing that.

Arguing with the Umpires

I didn't want my players to get thrown out of games, because I wanted them to come through in the ninth inning. So, I went out to argue a lot of times to protect my players. Also, I went out when I thought the umpires missed the play. That got so frequent that I had my infielders give me a yes or no with their heads so I'd know if the umpire had been right or wrong. That saved me a few of my almost one hundred ejections. I was probably the first guy to turn my cap around to argue with an umpire. There was a reason for it. Most of the umpires were over six feet tall, and I was just 5'7", and it seemed like every time we got into an argument, they'd lean down to talk to me and hit their forehead on the bill of my cap. Each time they hit the bill, the president of the American League would fine me for bumping the umpire. So, I turned my hat around to stop that and save me some money.

Don Zimmer

Minor-League Memories

When I tell players today about my minor-league experiences, they don't believe me. They don't believe that when I began my professional career fifty-two years ago, I made $140 a month. Not a day, not a week, but a whole month. For a full five-month season, I made $700 total! I just took a road trip with the Yankees, and we got $700 meal money.

Nineteen fifty was my first year in Class D, which is a division that doesn't exist anymore. We played in Hornell, New York, and if we played at night at home and had to play the Cardinals' farm team the next night in Hamilton, Canada, we were in for quite a trip. After the game, we might shower and grab a hamburger and be on the bus to Canada at midnight. We rode in a yellow school bus, not a Greyhound, and it had worn shock absorbers, so you'd sit up straight and feel every bounce. We'd drive all night and not get into Hamilton until about three in the afternoon. We'd go straight to the ballpark, play the game, and then get back on the yellow school bus and go check in at the hotel. When I tell players today about this, they look at me as if I were lying.

They also find it strange how I got married to Soot in the minor leagues, when I was playing in Elmira, New York, in the Eastern League. Ed Roebuck and I were living in a boardinghouse in separate rooms, and I hollered to him through the door, "I think I'm getting married, Eddie." And he yelled back, "I'm thinking about it, too!" Our general manager, Spencer Harris, overheard us talking and said, "I was over in Ft. Worth, Texas, and two of our players got married at home plate. Why don't you two get married at home plate?" It sounded OK to me. I said, "If I'm getting married, I may as well do it at the ballpark." Ed and I agreed to a double wedding, but he was Catholic, and his mommy and daddy didn't want him to get married at home plate. We did end up getting married the same day, but Ed got married in a church that afternoon. Being a pitcher, he got to go on a four-day honeymoon. I got married at 6:45 that evening, and a half hour later, I had to face 6'8" Gene Conley.

The Beaning

On July 7, 1953, I was hit in the head, and my career almost ended. I was having a good year, and Al Smith, Wally Post, and I were in a home-run duel. We all had about fifteen or sixteen homers, and then I caught fire, and I hit my twenty-third home run on July 5. We got on the train and went to Columbus, Ohio. The first night in Columbus, I went up to hit against Jim Kirk, a big kid who had great stuff but was a bit wild. His first pitch was high, and I said to the catcher, "I didn't see that ball good." There were some trees in the distance with bare limbs, and they were in my sight lines. The next pitch hit me on the left side of my head. We didn't wear helmets in those days, and I went down. Never in my wildest dreams did I think Kirk was throwing at me. I just didn't see the ball.

I remember lying at home plate and looking up at my manager, Clay Bryant, who used to pitch for the Chicago Cubs. I asked, "Am I bleeding?" He said, "Nooo, you're not bleeding." I don't remember getting in the ambulance. The next thing I remember was waking up in a hospital bed and thinking it was the next morning. I turned my head to the right and saw my wife, my mother, and my father. I had triple vision, so I had three wives, three mothers, and three fathers. I went to say something, but my speech center had been affected, and I couldn't talk. Soot came and sat on the side of the bed and said, "Take it easy, and I will explain what has happened."

She said that I had been in the hospital thirteen days. I had been operated on twice. They had put tantalum buttons in my skull, like a tapered cork fitting into a bottle. It was the same consistency of your bone, and I had three in my left side. They told my family that there would be a big improvement in three or four days, but nothing happened. So, they had to drill into the right side of my skull and put another button in there to relieve the pressure on the other side. And then they said I'd get better day by day. A lot of people say, "I heard you have a plate in your head!" And I'll just go along with it.

Ever since then, I get a sick feeling when I see a batter hit in the head. Fortunately, players wear helmets now, because I've seen players hit with fastballs who would have died if not for them. Or at least experienced what I did.

I Was the Real Hero of the 1955 World Series

I'm sick of hearing about how Johnny Podres pitched a five-hit shutout against the Yankees to win the seventh game of the 1955 World Series for Brooklyn. All anyone remembers is Podres, Podres, Podres. It's aggravating. What about me? I had as much to do with Brooklyn winning its only World Series as anyone.

Who started at second base? I did. At the time, I was platooning with Junior Gilliam at second, and I started the Series games when a lefty started for the Yankees, and Gilliam played in left field. And while I was in there in Game 7, we took a 1–0 lead. In the sixth inning, we had a man on third with one out, and I was the batter. Yankees manager Casey Stengel didn't want their left-handed starter Tommy Byrne to face me, so he brought in a right-hander, Bob Grim. So, Walter Alston took me out of the game and sent George "Shot Gun" Shuba up to pinch-hit. Because I was out of the game, in the bottom of the sixth, Alston had to move Junior Gilliam from left field to second base. And he sent Sandy Amoros out to left field.

Gilliam was right-handed and wore his glove on his left hand, while the left-handed Amoros wore his glove on his right hand. That's important because that inning, with us up 2–0, the Yankees put two

8

men on base, and Yogi Berra sliced what looked like a double into the left-field corner. But Amoros ran into the corner and, because his glove was on his right hand, was able to reach out and make a spectacular catch. He then doubled up a runner to end their threat. Gilliam couldn't have made that play, so it's fortunate he was at second base, or they would have tied the game. And I've never gotten any credit for that! Podres got the MVP for finishing the shutout, and no one talks about my contribution. I think it's terrible.

My Short Stay at Shortstop

From 1954 to 1957, I was a utility infielder for the Brooklyn Dodgers. I was considered a prospect at short, but we had Pee Wee Reese, and nobody was going to replace him. But Pee Wee's career was winding down, and in 1958, when the Dodgers moved to Los Angeles, I finally became the regular shortstop. In 1959, Pee Wee retired and was our third-base coach, and there was no doubt that I was the Dodgers' shortstop. And I couldn't buy a hit. I stunk up the place. So Walter Alston benched me and played Bobby Lillis. He was no better than I was, so Alston moved us back and forth.

Alston heard that at Spokane they had made a switch-hitter out of a shortstop named Maury Wills. So, they brought him to L.A. and sent Bobby Lillis out. I don't think Wills hit a ball past the pitcher in a week. So Alston came up to me and said, "I'm done experimenting. You are my starting shortstop even if I have to pinch-hit for you in the third inning."

That night, I came up to bat against Larry Jackson, of the Cardinals. Dusty Boggess, a big, nice guy, was behind the plate. I would swing at anything, but Jackson threw a pitch that would have hit me in the ankle if I didn't move. So I back up, and Boggess says, "Strike three!" I turn around and say things to him I can't repeat. And he says, "You're gone!" So I was kicked out of the first game that I was a regular. Wills went in and got two hits that game, and I don't have to tell you the rest of the story. We won a world championship that year, and Wills was our Most Valuable Player for the next few years.

9

Don't Blame Me for All the Mets' Losses in 1962

I was the first third baseman for the New York Mets in 1962. I'm not sure if that's a good thing, because we lost our first game 11–4 to the Cardinals and then lost eight more in a row. I just couldn't get any hits, and when we finally beat Pittsburgh, that's when I sat on the bench for the first time. We lost three more games, but I couldn't get any hits, and then when we beat Philadelphia, I didn't play in that game either.

We came up the steps in that old ballpark in Philadelphia, and we were whooping and hollering because we'd finally won a game. We get into the shower, and there's Casey Stengel standing in the middle of the clubhouse in his shorts, with his little, bony knees showing. He's looking at me, and then he winked at me. He said, "Come here for a minute." So, I get out of the shower and wrap a towel around myself and go over to Casey to see what he wanted. And he started saying, "Center field. You're really going to like it. It's the greatest thing that ever happened." Casey could talk and talk, and this went on for four or five minutes, and I had no idea what he was talking about. Finally, I say, "Case, what are you trying to tell me?" "Oh!" he said, "we just traded you to the Cincinnati Reds, and you can play center field." People ask me, "How was it to lose 120 games that year?" And I say, "Well, I'll take the blame for a few of those losses, but don't put me in all of them!"

Actually, it was a great thing for me, because I was going home to Cincinnati at a time my father had started to lose his health. We had two children at the time, so when the four of us came to Cincinnati, it was better than any medicine in the world for him. Of course, I never played an inning in center field.

My Revenge on Bucky Dent

Two or three years after Bucky Dent's homer beat Boston in the 1978 playoff when I was the manager, I came to the Yankees to be Billy Martin's third-base coach. I needed a place to live, and someone said,

"Bucky's got a beautiful place over in Jersey." So, I rented Bucky Dent's house. And when I got there, I discovered that on every wall in every room, there was a picture of Bucky Dent's tremendous swing when he hit that famous home run. I got tired of looking at that image every day. The next time I saw Bucky, I said, "I took your pictures and put them facing to the wall." He said, "You didn't!" I also told him, "You know you have that white shag carpeting through your house? Well, you know I chew tobacco and spit tobacco juice." He said, "You didn't!"

My Most Gratifying Moment in Baseball

In 1988, I became the manager of the Chicago Cubs, the fourth team I managed. We had a losing record and finished fourth in the National League East. The next year, we went to spring training and were terrible. Everybody in America picked us to finish last. If I had been a sportswriter or broadcaster, I would have picked us for last, too. We had won 5 or 6 games and lost about 22. When we left Arizona, we went to Minnesota to play a couple of exhibition games in the Metrodome. Jim Frey, our GM, and I went out to dinner, and he said, "Do you think there's any way we can win 81 games this year?" And I looked at him as if he were nuts. I said, "Jim, if we win 81 games, you and I will dance down Michigan Avenue."

As it turned out, after 35 games, our record was like 17–18. That wasn't too bad considering how we played in spring training. I'd managed in San Diego, Boston, and Texas, and I tell you, I never had a group of players execute or do the things needed to win games as well. We had some great players, like Andre Dawson, Mark Grace, Greg Maddux, Ryne Sandberg, and Rick Sutcliffe, but everybody was playing hard and contributing. Comes the All-Star Game, and we realize we have a chance to win our division! There was a race among the Cubs, the Mets, the Cardinals, and Montreal, which traded a bunch of young pitchers to acquire left-hander Mark Langston. At the end, we pulled away, winning 93 games to win our division by 6 games over the Mets. People ask me what my most gratifying season in baseball was. That's the season I pick.

11

Jack McKeon
Charlie Finley's Phone Calls

When I first started managing Oakland for Charlie Finley in 1977, he woke me up with a phone call, and we had our first conversation. He said, "McKeon, are you up?" I said, "No, I'm in bed, Charlie. It's six o'clock in the morning." His response to that was, "Dammit, don't you know that only whores make money in bed? Get up like the rest of us!" He could be demanding, but Charlie was a good man and a lot of fun to work with during my two years there. I think he pushed you to keep you sharp. There was nothing you did that was right with him, so you'd better have options B, C, and D in place to cover yourself.

He would call me in the dugout and talk about my lineup. The A's didn't have good players in those days, so it really didn't matter who I played. But he didn't demand I play one player and bench another; he would just "suggest." One morning, he woke me with a 6 A.M. call and said, "Get the bible!" I looked around the hotel room and said, "There's no Bible in here, Charlie." "No, McKeon, not that Bible. The *Baseball Register* is our bible." So, I took out the *Baseball Register*, and he told me, "Let's look at page 7." Matt Alexander. He said, "Look at his whole career record. You see that Alexander has hit five career homers. Now turn to page 323. Let's look at Jim Tyrone's whole career record. You see that Tyrone has nine homers. Let's go for power tonight!" So, despite his having only four more homers than Alexander, I put Tyrone in the lineup to provide "power" against Seattle. Rob Picciolo gets on, and we move him to second base. Tyrone then singles up the middle, and we score a run. Mike Norris pitches a one-hit shutout, and we win 1–0. At six the next morning, the phone rings. "McKeon, this is Finley. I didn't hear about the game last night. What happened?" So, I told him that we'd won 1–0, and then he asked me to tell him how we scored our run. When I mentioned Tyrone, he stopped me and said, "Tyrone! You're a genius for putting him in the lineup!"

A Promise Kept

I had lunch with Jeffrey Loria, the owner of the Florida Marlins, who was thinking of hiring me to manage the team. After lunch, I said, "Thanks, Jeffrey, for having me down here." He said, "You certainly aren't trying to impress me." He offered me the job, and when I took over for Jeff Torborg, we were ten games under .500. We started putting a little streak together. One night after a game, Jeffrey and I went out to eat. As we walked by his car, I said, "That's not a bad-looking car." He said, "It's a Mercedes." I said, "Yeah, I know; my wife has one. I've gotta get me one, one of these days." He said, "If we get into the playoffs, I'll give you that one." We were still about five games under at the time, so I didn't think anything of it. Then we started to win a little more. Another time we went out to eat, and he said, "As a matter of fact, I'll get you a better one." I forgot all about it, and all of a sudden we're in the playoffs. One day, he asked me my favorite color for a car. I didn't know why he was asking, but I told him. A few days later, he came to the clubhouse and said, "You got a minute? I want to show you something." So, we went out to the parking lot, and there was a beautiful black Mercedes that he bought for me.

TOMMY LASORDA
Life Lessons from My Father

I grew up in the Depression in Norristown, Pennsylvania. We had nothing. My dad was one of the really great people, and he taught me a lot about life. In fact, much of what I taught the players I managed was what I learned from him. Let me give you an example that I'd use with my players: He had a little piece of ground that he farmed, and we'd live off what he grew through the winter. He drove a truck in a stone quarry, and when he'd come home from work, he'd start digging and planting. One day when I was about fourteen, he said to me, "Do you see that empty milk bottle over there?" I said, "Yes, Pop." He

13

said, "Get it and bring it over here." I did as I was told. He said, "About a quarter of a mile away is a spring. I want you to go fill this bottle with water and bring it back. And don't break it, because it's the only bottle we have." And he slapped me! I rubbed my face and said, "Why did you do that, Pop?" He said, "If you break that bottle, it's too late to hit you." So, when I carried that bottle, there was nobody who was going to knock that out of my hands, because I was thinking that if he hit me before I broke it, how much worse it would be after I broke it. That taught me in managing that it's too late to do anything about the guy who just made the error, but you can do something to prevent a guy from making a future error.

Another example: My father sat at the end of the table and said, "You five boys should love each other and do everything you can to help each other. If you five guys got on one end of a rope and pulled together, you can pull half a town with you." Those were the very words I would use with my players. I said, "We've got twenty-five guys, a manager, a coaching staff, and an organization, and if we all got on one end of a rope and pulled together, we could pull the rest of the clubs with us. But if half get on one end and half on the other end, then we could pull all day long and only be pulling against ourselves." So, I passed along what my father told me.

Who Do You Have to Beat Out to Get a Job Around Here?

In 1955, I had a real good spring with the Dodgers and made the ball club. But in the middle of June, Buzzie Bavasi, Brooklyn's general manager, called me into his office. He said, "Tommy, I've got bad news." I said, "Did one of your relatives get sick?" He said, "No, I'm going to have to send you back to Triple-A." I said, "What? I won twenty games pitching there last year, Buzzie! What do I have to do to prove to you that I can pitch here?" He said, "Tommy, I have a tough job. I have to send down one player from this club. If you were sitting in my seat, who would you send?" Without hesitation, I replied, "Sandy Koufax!" True story. At the time, Sandy was a young left-hander who was too wild to pitch in a game, so he sat on the bench. Buzzie said, "Well, we can't send him down. It's a rule that if you give a guy more than a $4,000 bonus, he has to remain on the major-league team for two years. So, Koufax must stay, and you must go." Now I can walk around and honestly say that it took one of the greatest left-handers in history to send me off that Brooklyn club. After Koufax became a great pitcher, I'd tell Buzzie, "I still think you made a big mistake."

Dodgers' Fielding Woes

One day, I called outfielder Pedro Guerrero into my office. I said, "Pete, you've got to do me a big favor." He said, "Anything, Skip." I said, "You've got to play third base for me." He said, "I'll play anywhere you want, Skip." For the first month of the season, he couldn't catch a cold down there. Meanwhile my second baseman, Steve Sax, was having a terrible time making the easy throw to first base, so we were getting a lot of infield errors, and that was costing us big runs. So, we had a team meeting, and I said, "Pete, are you concentrating?" He said, "Yes, Skip." I said, "Well, tell me exactly what's going through your mind when you're playing third and a batter comes to the plate." He said, "Before the pitcher throws the ball, I get into position. Then I look up to the heavens and say, 'Dear God, please don't let him hit the ball to me.' And then I look up again and say, 'Don't let him hit it to Sax either!' "

Beauty Is in the Eye of the Beholder

In 1981, prior to Game 3 of the World Series, there was a press conference where the two managers presented their starting pitchers. Yankees manager Bob Lemon was there with Dave Righetti, and I was with Fernando Valenzuela, who had completed a sensational rookie season and was going to try to prevent New York from winning its third straight game. Bob said to me, "Your guy isn't really twenty-one years old." I said, "What do you mean? He's really only twenty-one years old." He said, "He's too ugly to be twenty-one years old." I said, "Well, when he wins, he looks to me just like Robert Redford." After the game, Fernando did look like Robert Redford, because he pitched a complete game and gave us the first of four straight victories as we won the title.

Kirk Gibson's Famous Home Run

In the 1988 NLCS against the Mets, Kirk Gibson won Game 4 with a twelfth-inning home run off Roger McDowell that evened the series, and then hit a three-run homer in Game 5 as we took the lead. We eventually won in seven games, but Gibson hurt himself diving for a ball, and it didn't look like he could play in the World Series against the Oakland A's. So, the biggest guy in our lineup was doubtful against a powerful team with Jose Canseco, Mark McGwire, Rickey Henderson, Don Baylor, Carney Lansford, Dave Parker, Dave Henderson, and others. Before Game 1 in Los Angeles, Gibson doesn't even come onto the field, not even for introductions. He was on the training table, and before every inning, I'd go in to ask how he was. And every time, he'd give me a double thumbs-down sign.

We came off the field after the A's hit in the top of the ninth inning, trailing 4–3. Tony La Russa brought in his ace closer, Dennis Eckersley, to replace Dave Stewart. Due up for us was Mike Scioscia, Jeff Hamilton, and Alfredo Griffin, with the pitcher's spot to follow if we got anyone on base. I told Mike Davis that he would hit for the pitcher if it got that far. Then the clubhouse guy told me that Gibson wanted to see me up the tunnel. I met Gibson up there, and he had put his uniform on. He said, "Skip, I think I can hit for you." I didn't wait around to discuss it with him, because I didn't want him to change his mind. I ran back to the dugout. Now I told Davis that I wanted him to pinch-hit for Alfredo Griffin.

Eckersley got out Scioscia and Hamilton, and we were down to our last out. Now Davis walks up to the plate. Gibson wanted to go out to the on-deck circle, but I said, "I don't want Tony to know you can hit." Instead, I sent Dave Anderson to the on-deck circle. He was a right-handed singles hitter who couldn't reach the wall. Ron Hassey, the A's catcher, sees Anderson and is thinking Eckersley can get him out without any trouble, while Davis, a left-handed batter who had hit twenty-five homers with Oakland the year before, was dangerous. So, Eckersley, who rarely walked anyone, pitched around Davis and put him on. They anticipated Anderson coming up to bat. But when Davis got the fourth ball, I said to Gibson, "OK, big boy, now get out there."

When Gibson emerged from the dugout, he electrified the whole stadium. The fans went absolutely wild, because they'd been listening to Vin Scully on their transistors and he'd been telling them every inning that there was no way Gibson could play. I got goose bumps from the fans' reaction. So, Gibson batted against Eckersley. I didn't want to have Davis steal, because I was afraid Tony would then walk Gibson intentionally and have Eckersley face Steve Sax, our right-handed leadoff hitter. I wanted Gibson to get his shot. I told my coach that we'd give Gibson two strikes to get his pitch to hit out of the ball-park, but if he doesn't do it, we'll have Davis steal second and play for the tie. When Gibson got two strikes, Davis stole second easily.

I knew that very few managers, for whatever reason, will give an intentional walk any batter if the pitcher already has two strikes on him. I don't know why. Tony didn't walk him. And with the count 3–2, Gibson jerked a slider into the right-field stands to give us a 5–4 victory. We'd go on to win the Series in five games. Gibson never batted again, but what he did in that at-bat was enough. After that, we never looked back. When I see the tape of that homer and hear the calls by Vin Scully and Jack Buck, I still get choked up.

My Team Was Family   17

Most managers believe that if you get close to your players, then you have trouble managing them. I believe the opposite. My philosophy was that the nearer I got to my players, the harder they'd play for me. I knew the names of every player's wife and children. What other manager knew the names of his players' children? I did that because I felt we were family. I hugged my players; I went out to eat with them. Al Campanis said, "You can't eat with the players." I said, "Why not?" He said, "When I was a player, I never ate with my manager." I said, "Maybe he didn't want to eat with you." My predecessor Walter Alston never ate with players in his twenty-three years as the Dodgers' manager. But just because it hasn't been done, doesn't mean it can't be done. I brought in a whole new philosophy.

Many major-league managers come from the minors and change. Instead of being the way that got him to the majors, he changes his style. But I didn't change. I hugged my players and ate with my players in the minors and had a lot of success. So, I wanted to do the exact same thing when I managed many of the same players in the majors. I got the same results.

JOE TORRE
My Quick Transition from Player to Manager

I went from Mets player to Mets manager overnight in May of '77. It was a little uneasy, because you're playing alongside players, and all of a sudden you're in charge. But during the time leading up to this, I was realizing I was one of the oldest players around, and people were coming to me and asking my advice. So, when the transition was made and I took over the reins of the New York Mets, it was exciting. I was very fortunate, because I never had to face the end of my playing career, because my managing career overlapped. I probably could have played another year or so and had wanted to, but when the managing opportunity came, it was like being a regular player all over again.

None of my former teammates on the Cardinals were surprised that I became a manager. Tim and I would sit on the bench discussing the game and half-jokingly talk about comanaging a major-league team someday. Bob Gibson used to accuse me of managing in St. Louis when we were teammates. He'd say, "Tell Red this; tell Red that," and I'd say, "Leave me alone, will you, please." When you're a catcher, you see the game a little bit differently, and you're probably next to the manager as far as being criticized or getting confided in. I don't want to say catchers are smarter than anybody else, but no one is more aware of all the things that go on in the field. It's the nature of the position.

Becoming the Manager of the Yankees

After I was fired as manager of the St. Louis Cardinals, I had run out of teams I'd played for—I already had managed the Mets and Braves—and I'd run out of friends in the game. So, I really didn't think there was any place for me to go as far as managing. And even when the Yankees contacted me, I wasn't expecting to manage. In October of '95, I interviewed to be *general manager*. Gene Michael interviewed me, because he was stepping down. My wife, Allie, was pregnant with our daughter Andrea and was due in December. So, I asked Gene, "Is there any vacation time?" And he said, "No." I said, "Then I can't take this job," and I left.

About ten days later, I got a call from Arthur Richmond, one of George's assistants or advisers, and he asked if I'd be interested in managing. And I said, "Sure." I tell you, it was a no-lose situation for me. I was getting an opportunity I never thought was going to present itself, in a city that I was very familiar with, and for an organization that you read so many things about. But when I found out that Davey Johnson, Tony La Russa, and Sparky Anderson were on the list of candidates, I didn't think I stood a chance. But Davey went to Cincinnati, Tony succeeded me in St. Louis, and Sparky said, "I'm not leaving home." So, that basically left me, and I jumped at the opportunity, even though my brother Frank said, "You gotta be crazy working for George Steinbrenner."

19

I said, "I need to find out if I can do this. And I know one thing: George is not going to be chintzy about spending money to get players." I had discovered that you can't compete with a limited budget in today's baseball environment. I felt winning was that important to me, and I wanted to see if I could do this job. It's been the greatest thing that ever happened to me.

Wearing the Ring

Tim and other former teammates thought I was a good manager with the Mets, Braves, and Cardinals, but I couldn't overcome self-doubts until I managed the Yankees. What helped me gain confidence was winning the ring. You never really think you've arrived until you've won a title. It was the missing part of my career as a player and manager, even though other people didn't look at me that way. I just felt that I had to prove myself to myself. That happened once we reached the 1996 World Series in my first year with the Yankees, and I saw I was able to do things under tremendous stress.

I hit .363 one year; I knocked in a lot of runs; I had many good years. But did my team ever get to the World Series? No. I would have loved to have played in one but never had that opportunity. So, I never knew if I could perform under that kind of pressure. I would drive myself that way. The ring is nice, but what it represents is the most important thing. How many times do we get the opportunity to show we are the best?

Even when I won the MVP and led the league in hitting, I said, "I'd trade this all in right now to be in a World Series." More than twenty years later, when I first managed the Yankees, I was saying the same thing. I told Derek Jeter, who was in his rookie year, about how I'd accomplished so much during my career but would give it all back in a heartbeat just to be *in* a World Series, just to be part of a team in the World Series. It wasn't to *win* a title, and certainly not three titles in four years, when you'd be given a choice of rings to wear. It took me thirty-nine years and 4,272 games to make it to the World Series in 1996. And we won. Now I've been in six World Series as a manager, and it's such an enormously satisfying feeling that *this is the only game that's on television now, folks.* There's nowhere to go after that. As a kid, I hated the Yankees for winning too much. I don't feel that way anymore.

20

The Passionate Red Sox Fans

In the city of Boston, everyone is passionate about their team. A few years back, I was coming down the hotel elevator before the last game of a Boston–New York series. Two floors down, a gentleman got on. I don't know if he really was a gentleman, but he got on with his lady friend. He looked at me and said, "You're Joe Torre, aren't you?" "Yeah." He said, "We're going to beat you tonight." "Well, I hope not." He was silent, and I knew something was coming. Just as we landed on the first floor, he said, "You know, if I had the choice of capturing Saddam Hussein or beating the Yankees . . ." As the door opened, he said, ". . . I'd pick beating the Yankees." And he walked out of the elevator and disappeared. That's how passionate the people are in Boston. They just want to rub your face in it.

But one day, I saw a different side of the Boston fans. I returned to managing two months to the day after my surgery for prostate cancer. And I did it at Fenway Park. The night before, I was having dinner with my wife, and since I was feeling better, we were discussing when I should go back to managing. She said, "Why don't you do it tomorrow?" So, I did. I went up to Boston for the game. Don Zimmer had been my acting manager, and he said, "Why don't you take the lineup card out?" I usually have a coach do that, but that night I walked to home plate. I got a standing ovation from the Red Sox fans. It was incredible. I doubt if any other Yankees manager experienced that. I was very moved.

The 2004 ALCS, *Yankees Versus Red Sox*

It's tough playing the Red Sox without feeling the energy of everything that goes on. They talk about the Yankees playing the Mets, but the Yankees–Red Sox rivalry goes back long before the Mets even existed. And in 2004, they were so good, as they were the year before when we beat them on Aaron Boone's home run in Game 7 of the ALCS. What made their offense so tough was that they didn't strike out and could hit from both sides of the plate. In Game 1, we beat Curt Schilling, and in Game 2, Jon Lieber pitched a great game, and we were ahead two–nothing. And Game 3 was a blowout, 19–8, though it didn't start out that way. That was Kevin Brown's game, and we didn't know how many innings he was going to pitch. It went back and forth, and I didn't feel comfortable even when we had a 6-run lead,

21

because the Red Sox could really turn it on. Then we got a safe lead, and I brought in Tom Gordon, who usually was Mariano Rivera's setup man, to pitch the ninth inning, because he had been a little jumpy in the previous game. I said to Mel Stottlemyre, "Let's bring him into this game, because it'll give him a little feel if he finishes. And hopefully he'll help us tomorrow night."

After Game 3, I told the players, "Guys, we've got a little more work to do." Everybody was so businesslike, especially Derek Jeter, who was reminding his teammates that even though they'd just kicked the heck out of those guys, it was not over. In Game 4, we had a lot of opportunities, and nothing materialized. It was frustrating. When we got to the bottom of the eighth inning with a 1-run lead, I said to Mel, "Rivera. We're going through the middle of the order in the eighth inning, so this is the save inning."

Mariano did get through the eighth inning, but he walked Kevin Millar to lead off the ninth, which was unusual, because he has pinpoint control. If I was going to second-guess myself, it would be that I didn't tell Mariano not to do anything fancy—*Go out there and just let it go*—because it looked like he was trying to make pitches. I probably didn't say anything because a couple of days earlier, he blew Millar away at home. I certainly did not want to get in his way. I don't want to say there was a change in momentum, but after the walk, they put Dave Roberts in to pinch-run, he stole second, there's a ground ball hit by Bill Mueller, and boom, the game is tied. We were lucky we didn't lose the game that inning, but Mariano got out of it with a man on third base and David Ortiz at the plate. Unfortunately, Ortiz would hurt us later.

When I had managed Ortiz in the 2004 All-Star Game, I said, "Do me a favor and do something against the National League that you do against me all the time, will you please?" And he got up and hit a home run. I said, "That's what I'm talking about." He was a good hitter when he was with Minnesota, but he's gotten so much stronger since then with Boston. And the Sox win that ball game on his 2-run homer in the twelfth inning.

Then we go to Game 5, and here I am with a two-game, 2-run lead in the eighth inning. And I bring Gordon into the game, and he has trouble getting out of his own way. He was throwing too many balls down the middle of the plate. I said to Flash, "Are you OK?" He said, "I feel fine, Skip. I'm just excited." He just could not channel all that excitement to his pitching. Ortiz took Gordon deep, and then I brought in Mariano in the eighth, which I didn't want to do. He gave up a sacrifice fly to Jason Varitek to tie the game, and the Sox won in the fourteenth inning on a single by Ortiz.

So, the Red Sox were now down only three games to two. They won the next game 4–2 behind Schilling and won Game 7 easily. Mariano, our big weapon, pitched only a meaningless inning in that game. It all showed how quickly things can turn around.

A *Lasting Memory of Mickey Mantle*

Although I first played for Milwaukee in 1960, I didn't have my first full spring training with the team until 1961. I was a catcher then, and Mickey Mantle stepped into the batter's box in the first inning of an exhibition game we played against the Yankees. And I got goose bumps, because I was squatting down and looking up, and he looked bigger than life. Later on in that game, I hit a home run over the right-center-field fence off Whitey Ford. The image I had was Mickey Mantle looking up at the ball going out of the ballpark. I never forgot that.

Fast-forward ten years. I won the National League's Most Valuable Player Award in '71, and after the season, I went from banquet to banquet. One banquet, I found myself sitting next to Mickey, and he reminded me of the home run I hit as a rookie in spring training. I said, "Wow!" because he remembered. The only reason I could come up with for why he had a lasting impression of that homer is that the Yankees had played the Braves in the World Series of '57 and '58, and my brother Frank had been on Milwaukee. Maybe it struck him that

23

I was Frank Torre's younger brother. That's probably why that homer stayed in his memory bank, but that he remembered it for any reason made me feel pretty good. When I tell Whitey the story of my homer, all he says is, "You hit one off me, too?"

Tony La Russa
Every Decision Is a Risk

As a manager, you try to figure out your best chance to win. There was a lot made of my decision not to pitch my best pitcher, Chris Carpenter, on the last day of the 2006 season although we needed a victory to clinch the NL Central title. But I thought that decision gave us the best chance to win. My pitching coach, Dave Duncan, and I were what-iffing the thing a week before the end of the season. *What if . . . ? What if . . . ?* We had Chris slotted to pitch the last day. But when it came down to that Saturday night, when we were going to play Sunday still having a magic number of one, it really wasn't that tough a call to hold back Chris. If we lost Sunday and ended up tied with Houston, I could pitch Carpenter on Monday versus the Giants in a makeup game. The alternative was to pitch him on Sunday and not have him available to start a best-of-five series and be available for the fifth game versus San Diego. We wouldn't have had nearly as good a chance to win. Houston lost to Atlanta on the last day, so my decision to hold back Carpenter paid off.

When you make decisions, they're all risks. You don't push buttons. Sometimes a manager sits on the bench and makes one or two decisions all game. At other times, like Game 2 of the NLCS against the Mets, you have to pay attention and make moves. As I was taught by the famous Cardinals instructor George Kissell, when you make decisions during a game, the game will come real quickly, and the way to slow it down is to stay ahead of it. Then you play the what-if game. So, if something happens, you are ready with your decision, not caught off guard. But, again, making any decision is the same as taking a chance. You might bring in the game's best closer, Dennis Eckersley, and he might give up a game-winning home run. But that's OK, because what you did as a manager was try to take the best chance you could. That's your responsibility. As Paul Richards told me long ago: "Trust your gut; don't cover your butt."

Faith in the Underdog

I can't say that I was as surprised as many other people in baseball that the Cardinals won the world title in 2006. Many people didn't think we had a chance, because we won only 83 games during the regular season. We couldn't ask, "How in the world can you doubt our club?" because we had fewer wins than any team ever to win a world title, and we'd had two 8-game losing streaks and a 7-game losing streak near the end of the season. But if you consider we were 0–23 in those three stretches, then the rest of the time we were 83–56, 27 games over .500. In fact, in April we set a franchise record for wins.

Normally, a championship team is relentlessly consistent and plays as well in September as it did in April, but we could explain why we had those bad streaks and knew we had potential. One reason we felt we were going to be really dangerous in the postseason was that Jim Edmonds and David Eckstein were finally healthy and ready to play. As a team, we thought we had a chance, because when you get to the postseason, every team has a chance. I learned from past experiences — painfully, those times we were first or second seeded and didn't win — that if a team is good enough to make it to October, it's good enough to win a Series. I told my players that baseball pays the team that plays the best.

After we won the title, I told my players that they would hear a lot of comments about the Tigers' losing the Series and about how we weren't really a deserving champion. But, I pointed out, we were the one team in the playoffs that played like a world champion. We beat the favored New York Mets in the NLCS when Adam Wainwright struck out Carlos Beltran looking with a curveball. Beltran saw the ball at the top of its arc when it was head high, so he froze, and the ball tumbled — as Roger Angell wrote — "like a bat down an elevator shaft." Throughout the postseason, we caught the ball all over the park, we had clutch hitting up and down the lineup, and both our starters and relievers did well. We played quality baseball and earned that championship.

Putting My Success into Proper Perspective

When I first became a manager, I asked Chuck Tanner for advice, and he said, "Always rent." But I've managed for twenty years now with only three teams, so I've never had to rent. I've never gotten carried away with my two thousand wins, because I have very good friends, Tom Kelly and Jim Leland, who started out at the same time as me but have maybe a thousand fewer wins. The only difference is that I've never been in anything but an ideal situation. I'm talking about ownership, front office, development, and being provided with good players. The Chicago White Sox and Oakland A's were that way, and it's been the same in St. Louis. I've had support at the top, and everyone's on the same page, and other managers will tell me how disjointed their organizations are.

I would never disrespect the jobs managers and their coaching staffs do, but if you have talent, as I've had, your job can be easy. In a long season, there are things we can do to help players—it can be mechanical or mental or physical—so, we do have a role. And we work very hard doing what Sparky Anderson told me our job was—"to create an atmosphere where the players can be productive and succeed." If you do that, their talent takes over.

On some teams, you have to work very hard, but how much do you have to do when you have teams like I had in Oakland? When your outfield is Rickey Henderson, Dave Henderson, and Jose Canseco; and you have infielders like Carney Lansford and Mark McGwire at the corners and Walt Weiss, Mike Bordick, and Tony Phillips up the middle; and your catchers are Terry Steinbach and Ron Hassey; and you have Dave Stewart, Bob Welch, Mike Moore, and Storm Davis in your rotation; and Rick Honeycutt is setting up Dennis Eckersley, you can push a button and take a nap.

Overcoming Two Devastating Deaths

Over the years, we've had winning seasons and losing seasons, ups and downs, and postseason successes and failures, but there was nothing tougher than 2002, when we had to deal with the deaths of longtime Cardinals broadcaster Jack Buck and our beloved pitching ace Darryl Kyle, who was found in his Chicago hotel room. We got hit hard with Jack's death, because he was one of the great Cardinals of all time and was such an influence on our play. And a few days later, Darryl, a wonderful husband and father and as good a teammate as you could have, died in the prime of his life.

You talk about a club being devastated. It beat us up. For days after, there was gloom in our clubhouse as everyone searched for how to handle it. With most challenges you face as a coach or manager, you can go back to lessons you've learned over the years, but as a staff, we really wrestled with what to do. If a player who you know is disturbed and depressed does something unlike him, or isn't Cardinal-like—maybe he doesn't hustle—do you jump on him? We struggled so hard for a couple of weeks. For that club to rebound and play as well as it did and win our division and beat the defending-champion Diamondbacks in the first round of the playoffs was remarkable. I had so much affection and respect for my players. I don't know if it was destiny, but from the day Darryl died, we won 57 games—which was the number on his uniform.

BOBBY VALENTINE
From the Ballroom to the Ballpark

I grew up in Stamford, Connecticut, where the culture of my little neighborhood included singing and dancing. My mom said, "Sports are great, but you need something else. You're either going to sing or dance." I couldn't sing, so at twelve, I started ballroom dancing. I loved it and won competitions by the time I was fourteen. My cousin Donny and I grew up together—he played the piano, and I danced.

Without a doubt, dancing helped me later on with baseball. The rhythm and coordination of dance and baseball are the same. Whether an athlete is turning the double play, winding up, or swinging at a 90 mph fastball, rhythm is a key.

Making the Best of a Bad Injury

When I have quiet moments, I think back on pivotal moments in my career, when I chose to do one thing over another. I'm very happy with how it all turned out. I had wonderful opportunities and made good choices—except for trying to catch a home-run ball hit by the A's Dick Green in 1973, and breaking my leg when my spike got stuck in the wall. That was a bad decision that cut down my speed and curtailed my career.

Without a doubt, though, that injury helped me with my managerial career. Sitting on the bench, you can see what happens to the smallest detail. When you're doing it, you have no idea what happens, because it happens too quickly. Great hitters have no idea what's happening when they swing their bats; great pitchers have no idea what happens when they throw the ball; and even a double-play combo will say, "We did that?" when you slow down the video for them to see. Sitting around, having a lot of energy, and still wanting to contribute, I began to tell other players to hold and swing their bats differently. I stopped playing when I was still fairly young, and I became a coach, on my way to becoming a manager.

28 *Managing in a Nutshell*

The epitaph that you see on most managers' tombstones is either "He Left the Pitcher in Too Long" or "He Took the Pitcher Out Too Soon." That's often been said about me in New York, particularly with Al Leiter. In fact, I let Leiter pitch in the ninth inning of the fifth game of the 2000 World Series, and I was criticized after we lost on a dribbler up the middle. That would have bothered me more earlier in my career, in the first five hundred or thousand games or so, but after you've been doing it a few thousand times, I understand that all I can do is the best I can, and when it's all over, I'll see how it's written.

A manager can't control everything. Most things are done by the players, prepared by the coaches, and reacted to by the press and the fans. That's the way it is. But I must say I like the whole gig. I like the preparation, I like watching the players perform and being with them as they do it, and I like being with the press and fans when it's over. I've always been an organizer since I had five gloves on the handles of my bicycle and would ride around the neighborhood recruiting players for a pickup game. It was, "Hey, Billy, I've got the gloves; meet you at the park!" I guess I'm still like that.

LOU PINIELLA
I Wanted to Play Baseball, Not Square Dance

I went to the University of Tampa on a basketball scholarship. I'd been a Catholic All-American in high school. One game, I missed four foul shots against Louisville, and my coach said, "All-American, my ass!" And I said, "Well, you're the one who recruited me!" I played baseball that spring and did quite well, and when I got home after taking my final exams, I realized I wasn't going to Harvard or Yale. Lo and behold, Spud Chandler, who was scouting for Cleveland, was sitting in his car in my driveway and said, "Have you had enough of school and would like to try baseball?" I said, "I'd love to try it, but you're going to have to convince my mom and my dad, because they're the ones who wanted me to go to school in the first place." So, he came in the house and did a nice job talking to my parents, and we were able to finagle him for a few thousand more bucks and come up with a contract that sent me to Selma, Alabama, when I was eighteen. It was for about $25,000 total. That included a progressive bonus, and Major League Baseball had a program then that gave me money to pay for the rest of my college. I used about three years of

29

that, but then I flunked square dancing. How about that? I'd stayed up all night studying for a biology exam and was too tired to go to the square dancing final. I figured they'd give me a C or D, but they flunked me. So, I decided that was the end of school. I lack a little over a semester in getting a college degree. Thank God that I haven't needed it.

Off-Season Jobs

Among my off-season jobs while playing baseball was landscaping down in Tampa. In fact, I landscaped Mr. Steinbrenner's first home. That was an experience! I had a lot of fun doing it. Mr. Steinbrenner said, "I'm going to get you in shape for spring training," and he did just that. I had other jobs—I sold women's clothing all over the Southeast. I used to drive to Atlanta, up to Birmingham, Alabama, down through the panhandle of Florida, and all the way up to Naples. So, I had a big territory. A lot of times, I'd leave my car at the Atlanta airport and fly home for the weekend. And I worked for Chris Evert when she had a sportswear line. That was my first year with the Yankees, after I'd been in the big leagues five years in Kansas City.

I'd sold bonds for Perry, Adams & Lewis, a municipal bond house in Kansas City. We sold quite a few of the bonds that financed Arrowhead Stadium and Royal Stadium. I needed the money. I'd been Rookie of the Year, I hit .300 three times, I made the All-Star team, but in my time there, the biggest salary I got was $50,000, which was considered a good salary in those days. I'd play in three World Series with the Yankees before I'd make $100,000.

Learning to Play the Outfield

There's no question that Bill Virdon is the guy who made me into a good outfielder. When you get to the majors, you think that you have to hit to stay there, so you put all your concentration into hitting a baseball. But when you play for the New York Yankees, you'd better play both sides of the ball. My first year on the Yankees, Bill Virdon said, "Son, you're going to be a project." He told me I needed a quicker first step and needed to read the ball off the bat better. And every day, he'd work with me for about forty minutes, hitting me balls. He'd start me in center field and work me over to left field and then to right field. And then he'd get close to me to help with my agility. He'd hit these line shots, and at the end of the day, I'd be bruised, and my knees and ankles hurt, but I tell you this: he made me concentrate, and my outfield play really got good. I think I was really close to leading the league in assists for a few years—I don't know if that's good or bad, because if you have a great arm, they don't run on you! I was never a speedy guy, but I learned to position myself better and learned to study the game more from a defensive posture and got really respectable out there. And what I learned really helped with my managing, because you have to know where your outfielders are.

Saving Baseball in Seattle

I arrived in Seattle in 1993, when you had to turn to the third or fourth page of the sports section to read about baseball. The Seahawks, the Sonics, University of Washington sports . . . no baseball. But in 1995, that city came alive baseball-wise. We drew over three million people in the Kingdome and made this miraculous run to beat the Angels for the division title, winning in a playoff when Randy Johnson beat their left-hander. Then we beat the Yankees in an exciting postseason series. That was fun. I still remember Edgar Martinez hitting the ball into the left-field corner and Junior racing around from third and winning that thing. And all heck broke loose in the city. And the end result was baseball was saved in Seattle. They got financing for a new ballpark, and there were really good teams for the rest of the time I was there. In 2001, we won 116 games. It was unbelievable. The Yankees had won 114 games in 1998, and I remember reading that won't be done again. Then we won 2 more games. It took a lot of personal discipline, a lot of pride, and a lot of good players to do that.

31

WILLIE RANDOLPH
The Trials of a Rookie Manager

There were a lot of things I learned as a rookie manager for the Mets in 2005. It was a crash course in the ups and downs of the game. We had some tough losses. In our first game, against Cincinnati, we were two outs away from a victory, and I'm sitting there thinking about that cigar I'm going to puff on. Then all of a sudden it's "Get the Rolaids Out! Oh, my stomach!" Joe Randa beat us with a homer. In fact, we lost our first five games in Cincinnati and Atlanta, and I was asking myself, "Do you really want to be a manager? Do you really want to do this?" I wondered if we could ever win. It was a big test for me, and players were watching to see how I was going to handle it. I'd been in the game a long time and had been through many ups and downs, so I knew that in such tough situations, it's best to revert back to what you know and just keep it steady. The players didn't panic, and we were able to win our last game in Atlanta and then five more in a row at home. That was a good lesson for my players—experiencing adversity can make you stronger. I was proud of that.

Ready to Move to the Next Level

As a player and a coach in New York, I watched how people handled themselves in this environment, but until you're in the fishbowl, you really don't know how you'll do managing here. I feel really good that in my first year, I passed the grade, in my mind. Dealing with the media was tough at times, but we didn't really have problems. I knew the fans' high expectations were going to be there—and I welcomed that, because our goal was to win, too. I benefited from past experiences, playing on two world-title teams and coaching on four more, and also being on teams that didn't do so well. Over the years, I had watched different New York managers go through good times and bad. And I had worked as a coach with Joe Torre, who I think is the best in the business at handling situations and players.

"Giving It Up"

I'm always looking for an edge to get better, and I teach my players to do the same thing. As a leader, you must keep learning things, and I've always been a student of the game. I was fortunate to be around some great, great teachers and coaches when I was a player. I tried to absorb knowledge when I sat down and talked to Bill White, or the great Willie Stargell, who gave me my kick start when I began my major-league career in Pittsburgh, or Thurman Munson and Roy White when I came over to play for the Yankees. I think we're part of a legacy, and there is a process I call "giving it up" about the passing on of baseball knowledge you accumulated through the years. The reason I wanted to manage and, before that, coach is that I wanted to "give it up" to young players to make them better players and, hopefully, winners.

TWO

THE CATCHERS

YOGI BERRA
"Blame Your Mother"

I grew up on the Hill, an Italian section of St. Louis. My father came from the old country and loved to watch soccer. We played a lot of soccer; me and my brothers, Joe Garagiola, and the other Italian kids from the Hill would play the Spaniards, the Germans, and the Irish. We also played baseball, but my father didn't pay any attention to that. He worked in a brickyard, and all four of his sons worked. Two of us worked in a shoe factory, one brother was a baker, and the other brother was a waiter. My three brothers all had a chance to play baseball professionally, but my father didn't know what baseball was, so he said, "Nothing doing. You have to work." Finally my three brothers said, "Dad, we're all working. Let him go play." I wasn't the best player in the family, but I was the only one he gave a chance. After I was playing with the Yankees, I'd always tease my father, "See, Pop, if you'd have let all your sons play ball, you'd be a millionaire." He said, "Blame your mother."

How I Got My Nickname

My mother and father didn't call me Yogi. They always called me Lawdy, which was short for Lawrence, which she had trouble pro-

35

nouncing. Some people called me that; others called me Larry. When I played American Legion ball, everybody got nicknames. We couldn't think of a good one for Joe Garagiola, so we just called him "Garage." Bobby Hofman, who later would play on the New York Giants, nicknamed me Yogi. The reason is that we usually didn't have a bench, and I'd sit on the ground with my arms and legs crossed. He thought I looked like a yogi. I didn't really pay attention when I was called Yogi, but the name stuck.

When I came to the major leagues, I signed autographs "Larry Berra." One day, the famous umpire Bill McGowan sent in a kid with three balls for me to sign. I signed them, and the kid ran out. A few minutes later, McGowan storms in and yells, "Who the hell is Larry Berra?" So, McGowan is the guy who got me to start signing my name "Yogi Berra."

How I Became a Yankee

I wanted to play with either the St. Louis Cardinals or St. Louis Browns, but when I was ready to sign at seventeen, the Browns wouldn't offer me any bonus, and the Cardinals didn't offer me enough. At the time, Branch Rickey was the head of the Cardinals' farm system but was getting ready to become the owner of the Brooklyn Dodgers. He told me that I was only good enough to make it to Triple-A and offered me only $250. My friend Joe Garagiola had signed with the Cardinals for $500, and I said I wanted that, too. I would have signed for $500, but the Cardinals wouldn't give it to me. What made me mad was that Al McGuire was a scout for the Cardinals, and he had seen me play in American Legion ball, and he begged them to sign me. But even those in charge after Rickey left wouldn't pay me the extra $250.

Leo Browne, a man in the American Legion, knew Yankees general manager George Weiss and called him on my behalf and said I was a good ballplayer and wanted a chance. So, then John Schulte came to see me. He was a bullpen catcher for the Yankees at one time and lived in St. Louis, and he said, "We'll give you the $500." I said,

"Good" and signed their contract. You know, I should have read that contract, because I didn't realize that for me to get the $500, I couldn't be cut my first year.

I went to spring training for the Yankees' Kansas City team in Excelsior Springs, Missouri, in 1943. I got a telegram from Branch Rickey. It said: "Report to Bear Mountain for spring training with the Dodgers." Bear Mountain, New York, is where the Dodgers had spring training during the war. I guess now that he was head of the Dodgers, he was willing to pay me $500. I called him and said, "It's too late; I'm already a New York Yankee."

I Joined the Navy

Not long into my professional baseball career, I joined the navy to fight in the war. I spent ten days as part of a six-man crew on a thirty-six-foot LCSS that provided machine-gun fire to support the army and marines who stormed the beach during the Normandy Invasion. Then after a few weeks resting in Italy—during my stay, I hitched up to Rome and was picked up by a childhood friend from the Hill on the way to the front!—I also was part of the invasion in southern France. When we got back, they sent everyone to psychiatrists. I was asked if I had been afraid, and I said, "No, I really wasn't. From where we were, it looked like the Fourth of July; it was beautiful. I'd never seen as many ships and planes in my life. In fact, I just stood on the boat with my arms folded, watching the bullets and smoke, and my captain had to tell me to get my head down." I wasn't scared, but it was upsetting seeing the men who had drowned in the water. And realizing what had happened there and how many soldiers had died, I felt lucky to be back.

37

I was then sent to the New London Submarine Base. I said, "Why am I being sent there? I didn't volunteer for no submarine." You had to volunteer for them to put you in a submarine. But I went there, and it turned out they were trying to start a baseball team there. Jim Gleason, who had been with the Reds and Cubs, was in charge of putting together the team. He was a lieutenant commander, and I walked into his office. He said, "What do you do?" I said, "I'm a ballplayer." He looked at me as if I were lying and said, "Who do you play for?" I said, "Norfolk, in the Piedmont League." He didn't believe me. He thought I was a boxer!

I Learned to Catch from the Best

I didn't start out as a catcher. In American Legion ball, I played outfield and a little infield. But when I went to Excelsior Springs, Missouri, for my first spring training in 1943, they thought I had a good arm and made me a catcher. My first two full years with the Yankees, in 1947 and 1948, I wasn't too good behind the plate. In fact, I played almost as much in the outfield. We had a lot of catchers—Aaron Robinson, Sherm Lollar, Gus Niarhos, Charlie Silvera, Ralph Houk—and gave away a few. I didn't care where I played, because the fun of baseball was hitting. I hit a lot better than I caught in those days.

In the 1947 World Series, I caught a few games and played right field in two others, including the opening game at Yankee Stadium. Bucky Harris sat me down in Game 3 at Ebbets Field because a couple of guys stole bases on me, but I got my only big hit that game, a pinch homer off Ralph Branca. It was the first pinch homer in World Series history.

In 1949, Casey Stengel became the Yankees' manager, and he really emphasized defense. He'd have the players work on cutoffs and other plays, and if we got it wrong, he'd keep us out there. He'd say, "You play defense; I'll tell you when you can hit." We had traded off the other catchers, so Casey wanted me to play every day, and to do that, I had to improve my defense. Stengel had Bill Dickey spend many hours working with me.

Dickey had been a great catcher, and he helped me in many ways. He didn't need to teach me how to call a game, but he taught me the fundamentals. He taught me how to block balls so they wouldn't get past me. He taught me how to keep my hand behind the glove and then bring it around like a cup in a relaxed fashion. He said, "Don't use a fist." With a relaxed hand, the pitch just glances off your fingers.

A lot of guys used a fist, and they'd always split their fingers. I had my finger split twice, and that was my first year. Because of Dickey, I never had another split finger. I never had a broken finger, even. He taught me how to block balls in the dirt with my chest protector.

He taught me how to throw to second. I always had a pretty good arm, but I was too slow with my release, so he got me to go into the pitch. He'd toss balls to me, and I got used to stepping forward, much like how an infielder charges the ball. I got the knack of going across home plate with my mitt, and if the batter swung, he wouldn't hit me. Dickey taught me footwork and got me to always start with my right foot. He explained that a curveball from a right-hander to a right-hander breaks away, so I would go with it, right foot first. I learned that when there was a fast runner on base, the easiest ball to throw is the inside pitch, because it pushes the batter off the plate. Since you know the hitter isn't going to stay there, and you'll have a clear path, you can cheat like heck and get off a quick throw. I didn't have to position myself inside. I don't know why so many catchers today move around and give away location, because I was taught to stay in the middle and to put my glove where I wanted the ball.

Dickey really worked my butt off that year, but it was great, and I became a good catcher. I owed everything to him.

I liked catching because I got to talk to players on the other team when they came up to home plate. I really loved it. I just talked to them before. I didn't distract them when the ball was on the way. I got down and gave the sign; that's all. Maybe I'd throw dirt on a couple of guys' shoes. I had a lot of fun.

The Best Center Fielder   39

When I'm asked who was a better center fielder, Joe DiMaggio or Mickey Mantle, I have to say DiMaggio. Remember that Mickey got hurt playing right field in the 1951 World Series against the Giants. Willie Mays hit a ball between DiMaggio and Mantle, and Mickey's feet got caught in the drainage ditch, and he hurt his leg pretty badly. So, when he replaced DiMaggio as our center fielder in 1952, he couldn't run like he used to. There's no telling how well he could have played center if he never got hurt. I didn't get to see Willie Mays play a lot, but of those I did see play center field, Joe was the best. I saw Joe for five years and never saw him slide for a ball. He didn't need to, because he caught up with everything and caught the ball chest high. He had a knack for getting exactly the right jump. He was a quiet guy who always ran to his position and did his job. Even when he tried to stretch a single into a double and we saw that he was going to be thrown out, he got there! He did everything right. I never saw him make a mistake!

Mickey Mantle Was a Great Teammate

Mickey Mantle was timid when he first came up, but after he felt comfortable, he was a lot of fun and a great teammate. He wasn't tall, but he had powerful forearms, and when he took off his shirt, you'd see all the muscles in his chest and back. He was built like a football player. Mickey is known for all his mammoth home runs, including two he hit into the trees out of Griffith Stadium, in Washington, off Camilo Pascual. I couldn't believe how far he hit them. He also hit a 565-foot homer there off Chuck Stobbs, and I remember another long homer off the Senators' Pedro Ramos. He almost hit a ball out of Yankee Stadium off Bill Fischer. It hit the top facade and would have gone out if it had been 10 feet to the left. There were many homers that went long distances. I used to tease him that while he was hitting those balls a hundred feet past the fences, I'd go into different parks and if it was 340 feet to the fence, I'd hit it 341 feet; and if it was 360 feet, I'd hit it 361 feet. I'd say to Mickey, "My homers count just the same as yours: only one run."

One game, Mickey struck out three or four times, and the fans booed him. And then he came into the locker room with his head down. My son Timmy, who was about eight or nine at the time, was at the park that day, and he went up to Mickey and said, "Mickey, you stink!" I had to give little Timmy a kick in the butt.

Mickey was best friends with Whitey Ford, and one day before Whitey pitched against Boston, Mickey said that he wanted to call the pitches. Whitey said, "Go ahead; talk to Yogi." So, while playing in center field, he stood up if he wanted Whitey to throw a fastball, bent over if he wanted a curve, and wiggled his glove if he wanted a changeup. Then I'd relay the signs to Whitey. So, we went right along with this, and after seven innings, Whitey had a shutout going. Then Mickey came into the dugout and told us, "I got you this far, but now you're on your own." Whitey completed the shutout. We had a lot of fun together.

Long Before There Was a Players' Union

George Weiss, the Yankees' general manager, gave me the extra $250 that convinced me to sign with the Yankees rather than the Cardinals, but he was notoriously cheap. Mickey Mantle always had trouble with him, because he'd do things like cut his salary after he batted .365. Early in my career, I was getting the minimum $5,000, but after I had a good year, I was expecting a nice raise. Weiss offered me only $8,000. I told him I wanted $10,000. He wrote me a letter that said, "You're lucky to be on the damn ball club!" I signed his contract. After we won five straight world titles and I'd been the MVP a couple of times, I was making $35,000 or $40,000. The most I ever made was $65,000.

Don Larsen's Perfect Game

41

My biggest thrill in baseball had to be catching Don Larsen's perfect game against Brooklyn in Game 5 of the 1956 World Series. It was perfect—you can't get much better than that. Larsen was really on that day. Anything I put down, he got over. He got three balls on a hitter only once, Pee Wee Reese in the first inning. Otherwise, he had no trouble. He wasn't even expecting to pitch that day. Our coach, Frank

Crosetti, would put the ball in the glove of the pitcher Casey Stengel wanted to pitch each game, and when Larsen got to his locker, he found the ball there. It was the same with Johnny Kucks, who had no idea he'd pitch in the final game of the World Series until he saw the ball in his glove. Larsen had no time to get nervous; he just pitched. After the final out, as everyone has seen over the years, I ran out and jumped on Larsen. I think that's the only time I ever did that after a game. I gave the ball to Larsen, the last pitch. My backup catcher, Charlie Silvera, says I gave him my jockstrap from that game, but I don't remember. The only thing I kept was my glove. I had it bronzed, and it's going in my museum in Montclair, New Jersey.

A Memorable Game with a Sad Ending

In Game 7 of the 1960 World Series against Pittsburgh, we were trailing 4–2 in the sixth inning when I came to bat with two men on to face forkballer Elroy Face, who was the Pirates' best reliever. I hit the ball deep to right field and thought it was going to go foul, but when I saw it was fair as it cleared the fence, I jumped in the air in excitement while running down the first-base line. That put us ahead 5–4.

We increased our lead to 7–4 in the top of the eighth inning. But in the bottom of the eighth, Hal Smith hit a three-run homer, and they scored five times, to go up 9–7. We scored twice, to tie it, in the top of the ninth inning. The play everyone still talks about was when Mantle was on first base and I hit a grounder off Harvey Haddix to the Pirates' first baseman, Dick Stuart. When a first baseman is holding a runner on, he waits for the pitch and always moves off the base and away from the line. But, my gosh, Stuart didn't move. I thought it was a hit down the line when it left the bat, but it went right to Stuart on the bag, and I was out. That took the force play off at second, and Stuart threw there for an easy tag play. But Mickey didn't run to second. Instead he slid safely back into first base. He was a very smart player.

In the bottom of the ninth, the Pirates won the Series when Bill Mazeroski hit a fastball by Ralph Terry over the left-field wall. I was playing left field and backed up to play the ball off the top of the wall.

I didn't think it would carry over it. If I did, I wouldn't have looked back; I would have just walked off the field. I was ready for the rebound, but it skimmed the ivy and disappeared. Afterward, I saw Mickey cry for the only time. We blew the Pirates out in the three games we won and thought we should have won the Series. That game, we had a lot of runs too, but that time, Pittsburgh had one more.

I Did a Good Job in 1964

I think I was prepared to manage the Yankees in 1964 without spending time in the minors managing. I didn't have any problem managing the players after having been their teammate for so long. All the players played for me. They could have taken a nosedive down the stretch, but we won the pennant on the next to last day of the season, so that must say something. I was fired after we lost the World Series to the Cardinals, but you have to remember that Whitey Ford hurt his shoulder in Game 1—in fact, that was his last game ever. He was always at his best in the World Series, so it was a big loss not having him for two more starts. Mantle was hurting, too, so he had to play right field, and Maris was in center. And Tony Kubek was out, which meant Phil Linz played shortstop for us. Despite all that, we still took the Cardinals the distance, seven games. So, I think I did a good job. It all worked out fine.

BOB UECKER

I Am Eternally Grateful to Have Been a Cardinal

In 1963, the Cardinals came close to winning the pennant. But they didn't win it without me, so they acquired me in a blockbuster trade for two players. I proved to be the missing ingredient in 1964, although some people point out that another newcomer, Lou Brock, played in about 150 more games than I did. The point is, we won the pennant in 1964, and I was there. I was making just a little under the minimum, but that was OK; I guess I should apologize to some of the players, because I sold a lot of their equipment so I could pick up another six or seven grand. That wasn't bad.

Kidding aside, how lucky can you get sometimes as a player? There are a lot of really, really good players who never get the opportunity to go to a World Series, let alone win one. But thanks to all of the great players on the 1964 St. Louis club—Boyer, White, Flood, Gibson, McCarver, Groat, Javier, Brock, and on and on—I had the opportunity to get a championship ring. No matter what, I always can say, "Hey, I was there, man. You can say whatever you want, but I was on the club."

I had a couple of great years in St. Louis. I got a ring, I played in the best baseball city in America, I played in the great old Sportsman's Park a couple of years before it was replaced, and I built lasting friendships with a lot of terrific guys—many who, like myself, became broadcasters. So I was fortunate to be traded to the Cardinals, because, I tell you, those were two of the greatest years of my life.

A Music Lesson

The 1964 World Series between the Yankees and Cardinals opened in Sportsman's Park, in St. Louis. Before Game 1, the Cardinals hired a couple of Dixieland bands to play in the outfield during batting practice. I was out there because I had taken my batting practice at about seven in the morning. Bing Devine had told me to get there early. He said, "Just suit up and shag, because you're not going to be playing." I said, "I don't care, because I want us to win this thing, too. So I'm comfortable with that." So I got my swings in that morning, and when the rest of my teammates started regular batting practice, I was standing in the outfield with Roger Craig, one of our pitchers. That's when I spotted the tuba.

One Dixieland group went on break, and the musicians put their instruments in the left-field corner. So I picked that tuba up. Since I spent most of my time as Tim McCarver's backup catcher talking to the fans in the bleachers, I had a lot of friends out there. So to entertain them, I put that tuba on, and I was messing around trying to blow it. Then I thought, "Hey, why not try to catch a fly ball in this thing?" So I took it out into the outfield, and I was standing there trying to catch balls in the large hole in the tuba. I didn't make any clean catches, which is why most outfielders prefer gloves to tubas, and by the time I finished, there were a lot of dents in that rim. I put that thing down again, and when those guys came back out on the field, man, the tuba player was irate. So after the Series, after we won a world title, I got a bill from the Cardinals for $250 to pay for the damages. Two hundred and fifty bucks, for that dumb tuba? I mean, the mouthpiece was like $2.25, so that big piece of brass really cost about fifty bucks.

Johnny Bench
There Was No Secret to My Catching

I was from Binger, Oklahoma, which was so small that when we once had a parade on the main street, everyone was in the cars, and no one was watching us pass by. There were 661 people, and my graduating class was 21, so getting to the majors was a long shot.

My father served two hitches during World War II, so he didn't realize his dream of playing professional baseball. He did get to play some semipro ball, and he'd tell stories of facing Satchel Paige and other great players. But since he didn't get to play in the majors, he wanted his kids to do it instead. I was his third son, and I wanted to fulfill his dream. I saw Mickey Mantle playing on TV, and the announcer said, "Here's the next big star from Oklahoma." I looked at my dad and asked, "You can be from Oklahoma and play in the major leagues? That's what I want to do!" He said that catching was the quickest way to get to the majors. So, I became a catcher, although I had no flexibility whatsoever. After signing with the Cincinnati Reds when I was seventeen years old, I went for my physical with the Tampa Tarpons, and the doctor said, "Touch your toes." I reached down to about my ankles, and he said, "Son, unless you get more flexibility, you're not going to be able to play."

45

I started out using the round catcher's mitt like everybody else. I got it from Jeff Torborg. It required that I use both hands, and I broke my thumb and split my thumb, so I thought it was crazy, because Randy Hundley was catching 150 games for the Cubs using a flexible mitt that allowed him to put his throwing hand behind his back. Even Elston Howard was using it a little bit. I said, "The only way I can stay in the lineup is if I use a one-handed glove and keep my throwing hand out of the way." So, I started using the one-handed glove, and I began backhanding balls in the dirt and did other things that came naturally. I tried to catch every ball. I had good reactions, plus I was blessed with my father's hands and had a strong arm, good footwork, and quick release, because as a kid, I practiced transferring the ball from glove to hand over and over and over.

What I'm most proud of in all my playoffs and World Series is that I went twenty-seven games without giving up a stolen base. That's the kind of thing that makes a difference in wins and losses. As a catcher, I had so much fun controlling a game with my arm. I also liked calling a game. It wasn't hard to win catching a Don Gullett or Tom Seaver, but to be able to get a win for a guy who didn't have great stuff is so satisfying. Gosh, you walked down to the clubhouse happier than he was, because you knew what a job you'd done that day.

The Strange Education of a Ballplayer

To prepare my arm for catching, my dad would have me throw from more than two hundred feet. I put a coffee can up on our shed, and I'd stand there and fire the ball at it. Then I'd back up and throw at the can, and then back up farther and throw at that can, over and over. I took every slat out of our shed, and my dad wouldn't say a word. I had a strong arm. I'd also work on hitting by knocking rocks from our driveway. I'd stand in the driveway and hit every rock, and the bat would split in half, and I'd keep hitting. My father would have to bring in a new load of gravel, but again, he never said a word.

We'd play tin-can in the backyard, and if you hit the can a couple of times in the air, there would be dents in it, and you could throw a curveball, screwball, or slider—and when it was knocked into the size of a pea, it was like a missile when you threw it. That was what our life was about: you worked in the fields, you played basketball, you played baseball, you played Home Run Derby down at the park.

I have no idea where I got my confidence. I really don't. I always was a couple of years ahead of the other kids. When I was fourteen, I was playing with seventeen- and eighteen-year-olds in American Legion ball. I just assumed I'd play major-league baseball. I think it's necessary to have an inner conceit that you have the ability to be better than the situation. My team was the most important thing, and I had to do whatever I could to help it win.

The Reds Had No Idea Who I Was

People don't know this, but while everyone knew I was a catcher, I pitched much more than I ever caught. As a pitcher in Little League, I was 75–3. I pitched for my high school team when we won the state championships. We had a kid who would catch but not play third, so when I wasn't on the mound, I had to play third. Then our American Legion team already had a catcher, so I had to play first and third. To catch, I had to go out of town. I think I caught only 17 games in Legion ball.

I got drafted by the Reds, and they had no clue who I was. In fact, it was the first free-agent draft, and some of the Reds' scouts were in a hotel room in Baltimore weighing their picks. Someone asked Jim McGlothlin, "What do you think of this kid Bench?" He said, "Aw, we're not that high on him" and walked out of the room. Everybody was saying, "Who's Bench?" Tony Robello and Bob Thurman had seen me play only twice, and I'd gone 1-for-8, but they'd liked the way I caught. They knew the Orioles were interested too, so the Reds drafted me in the second round.

My Plan to Nail Lou Brock

When I first came up, the Reds were playing the Cardinals in Cincinnati. And I was excited about showing off my arm to Lou Brock when

47

he got on base. He was the guy! Well, Brock got a double. He then took a big lead off second, and I'm thinking, "Maybe he hasn't heard of me. Maybe I'll just pick him off second base real quick. Maybe I'll just throw the ball through a car wash and not get it wet." Before the next pitch, I raise my eyebrows to the shortstop so he'll be ready. Lou took his big lead again. I came up firing and threw a rocket to second base. Lou just walked over to third base, looking at me as if there was nothing at all to be done.

Somehow Ted Williams Guessed Right

In spring training 1969, I wanted a ball signed by Ted Williams. I had played only one year with the Reds and didn't have the nerve to get it myself, so I asked Roy Sievers to go over and ask for it. Roy said sure and got the ball autographed and returned it to me. I didn't read it until I was going back to the dugout. I saw that he wrote, "To Johnny Bench, a sure Hall of Famer." And I'm looking around wondering if I'm on "Candid Camera." I was thinking, "Ted Williams actually knows who I am?"

Years later, I hosted "The Baseball Bunch" and had Ted on as a guest. The night before, we were having dinner, and he sat up and asked demandingly, "What do you think makes the curveball curve?" I said, "I think it's the rotation of the earth as it goes around the ball," and I turned away really quickly. It was near the end of dinner, and I didn't say another word. The next morning, I went to pick him up to take him to do the show. He hadn't even closed the car door when he yelled, "What do you mean, the rotation of the earth? Son of a bitch, you had me up all night!" That's the way he was.

48

Far and Away My Fondest Memory

My greatest moment in baseball was winning the 1975 World Series over the Boston Red Sox. Being Rookie of the Year, being the MVP, and doing all that other stuff is great, but you have to call other people to have a party. You walk into that locker room after you win, and there are all twenty-five players, all the coaches, the trainers, the equipment man, and you're all world champions. People who had great careers say they don't miss winning a championship, but I don't think there's any greater moment in any man's life than to be part of that. That ring is important! I was blessed to have two world championships, in '75 and '76.

I Never Realized My Promise

When I was young, everything was magical. I didn't think anyone could get me out. In 1970, when I was just twenty-two and won my first MVP, I actually looked breaking ball first, because I didn't think anyone could throw a fastball by me. In 1972, I won my second MVP. But they'd found a spot on my lung, and two days after I turned twenty-five, I had lung surgery. I had the first staple surgery in history. They cut muscle, they cut bone, nerves were affected, and it all changed after that. I never was the same. I was disappointed that I didn't do the things I really wanted to do in baseball. I did a lot, but I missed carrying the ball club, being so dominant, being the one at the plate who made the difference. I lost a little of that edge, because I knew I wasn't as quick. There were balls I wasn't getting to and throws that were just a little off. It wasn't about numbers. I wanted to win more; I wanted to do more.

GARY CARTER
Making a Name for Myself in New York 49

Opening Day at Shea Stadium in 1985 was a special day that I'll never forget, because it was my first game as a New York Met, and I homered to win the game in the tenth inning against the Cardinals. It was a cold day, and I got hit in the left elbow by a Joaquin Andujar fastball, and that was still biting me as the game progressed. It stiffened up and was hurting, but I needed to make an impression. I knew I was being counted on, because the Mets had traded four players to Montreal for me, and I was being called "the last piece of the puzzle."

So, there I was in New York City, in front of a sellout home crowd with a lot of expectations. We went into extra innings, and I came up against Neil Allen, a former Met who had a big curveball. He missed with the first pitch, and I just sat on the next one. When I first hit it, I thought it had a chance to go out, but I saw from the video later that it was just about a wall-scraper that Lonnie Smith might have caught if he got over quickly. I rounded the bases, and all my teammates were waiting at home plate, and the feeling of exuberance was overwhelming. After everybody settled down and I walked toward the dugout, I heard the fans who were filing out chanting my name: "Gary! Gary! Gary!" That was the greatest feeling, coming to New York and hearing those fans chanting my name.

Later I was on "Kiner's Korner," and Ralph Kiner forgot my name. He introduced me as "Gary Cooper." I was known as "the Kid," but never Gary Cooper, but that was OK, because *The Pride of the Yankees*, in which Gary Cooper played Lou Gehrig, is one of my all-time favorite movies. After the season, I signed a glossy photo to Ralph, "Gary Cooper Carter."

The Improbable Rally

I didn't want to be the answer to a trivia question: Who made the last out of the 1986 World Series? Wally Backman and Keith Hernandez made outs to lead off the bottom of the ninth of Game 6. We were down two runs, and three games to two, and were on the verge of being eliminated. But I went up to the plate with a great deal of confidence. My base hit to left field was a start. Then the pressure was on Kevin Mitchell, and he lines one into left center field off Calvin Schiraldi. Then Ray Knight battles. With two strikes, he breaks his bat and hits the ball over second-baseman Marty Barrett's head. I score and shake Mookie Wilson's hand and say, "OK, Mook, now it's on you."

Then Bob Stanley threw a wild pitch, and when Mitchell scored, I said, "Hallelujah, we're tied up! We're back in this thing again."

Then Mookie hit the ball down the first-base line that went through Bill Buckner's legs as Knight scored the winning run, a play that will be remembered forever. Buddy Harrelson, our third-base coach, was so excited, he almost beat Ray to home plate. There was jubilation that we were going on to Game 7. We came back to win that game, too.

IVAN RODRIGUEZ
Why I Can Throw Out Runners

I'm not afraid to make a mistake. Nobody's perfect, so I'll be very aggressive and risk throwing the ball away if a runner is too far off the base or trying to steal. I just try to do everything the best that I can. I think my height helps me. I'm only 5'10", and that helps me move my feet quicker than a taller catcher can. A catcher who is 6'1" or taller will say it's harder for him to get his feet in the right place to throw the ball, because his body is bigger and heavier, and there is more for him to do.

I want my legs to be strong and quick, so I do a lot with weights and a lot of running. I'll also work with coaches in spring training and before games to make sure I put my feet in the right place as quick as possible. What helps is that when I was a kid, I was a third baseman, so I needed to be quick going to each side. When I switched to catcher, I was quick. I still can move to the sides quickly, catch the ball, and make a strong throw.

What I do is anticipate what the runner might do in every situation. I'll be thinking ahead in the count, getting ready in case the runner will try to steal on a particular pitch. I'm always ready to throw, not waiting. I lead with my left foot, and my right foot comes quickly behind it. There are catchers who have different approaches. Lance Parrish and I worked a lot on throwing. When he played, he didn't move his back foot. He'd catch the ball and throw it without moving forward. For me, that's not the best way. I'm not too tall, so I can go forward and attack the ball and throw in the same motion. I go forward but always catch the ball behind the plate. I receive it first and then move my feet and then throw it, rather than go out to get it on top of

51

the plate. When I catch it, I'm ready to throw it to first, second, or third base. The players on other teams know that I can throw to any base at any time, so they have to watch out!

Paul Lo Duca
My Mother Helped Me with My Hitting

I was born in Brooklyn but grew up in Arizona, on the west side of Phoenix. My father always had two jobs—he ran restaurants, he had a cleaning business, he hustled a lot to support the family—and he always needed our one car, so I never really had a chance to go to a hitting cage. My mother used to lie around in a lawn chair with huge sun blockers on. One day when I was twelve or thirteen, she said, "Why don't I throw you some pinto beans, and you try to hit them?" So, beginning that day, she'd take these little white beans and throw them to me. And I'd swing a wooden bat and try to hit two or three hundred a day—unless she'd quit earlier after getting hit by a bean in the face. We had bean sprouts popping up all over our backyard. I got so good that I wouldn't miss any, even when they'd blow in the wind. It helped my hand-eye coordination, and when I played real baseball, I was a good contact hitter.

"I'm Going to Do It"

I was the *Sporting News*'s College Player of the Year as a junior at Arizona State, and we went to the College World Series, yet the Dodgers didn't draft me until the twenty-fifth round. I thought I was going to be drafted higher, but maybe it was because I didn't have a set position. I wasn't going to sign. I was a day away from going back to summer school, but I just said, "I'm going to do it." I was in a Denny's restaurant in Vero Beach when the Dodgers offered me a contract. My mom was my agent, and she was the stiff one. She negotiated my contract with Eddie Bane, who had scouted me. They ended up giving me a $20,000 bonus plus money for me to finish school.

Captain Red Ass

It was neat when *Sports Illustrated* did a cover story on the 2006 Mets. There were five of us on the cover, and the picture turned out unbelievable. The photographer was sort of a clown, and he had us dying from laughter. He told me to make a funny face. They titled the article "Welcome to Rip City"—meaning we all rip on each other in good fun in the clubhouse—and attributed it to "Captain Red Ass," which is the nickname Billy Wagner gave to me. I didn't think they could put that name on a publication! I got a million phone messages after that saying, "Call me back, Captain Red Ass." I don't know where Billy came up with that name, though I do get the red ass every once in a while. Sometimes my emotions get the best of me, and I get thrown out of way too many games. I take the game seriously. I don't want to lose, even in exhibition games. That's why I always get bugged by players who don't care about playing in the All-Star Game. In every clubhouse I've been in, guys playing checkers or cards or chess get upset when they lose and take it personally. That's how I am. I think that's the attitude you should have to play this game.

THREE

THE FIRST BASEMEN

TONY PEREZ
I Wanted to Play Baseball

I grew up in the small town of Ciego de Avila, in Camagüey, a province in Cuba. There were about three thousand people who lived there, and the boys played baseball all the time. We played anywhere we could—usually we had no gloves, used any piece of wood we could find as a bat, and made balls out of cigarette cartons. But it was fun. When I was a teenager, I stopped going to school so I could make money. I worked with my father in the sugar-cane factory, putting the company brand on sugar sacks and filling them with sugar. My shift was 3 A.M. to 11 A.M. I didn't like the work or the noise made by the machines in the factory, which you could hear at home when you tried to sleep. I would tell my mother and the rest of my family that I was going to be a ballplayer and get out of there. I was 6′2″ and weighed about 150 pounds, and my mother told me ballplayers were big and strong, and I was too skinny.

How Times Had Changed

When the Reds signed me to my first professional contract, I got nothing but $2.50 to pay for a visa. Twenty years later, when I was thirty-seven, I signed a three-year free-agent contract with the Boston Red Sox with a $250,000.00 bonus. How could that happen? How could the money in baseball have changed so much? The decimal point had moved over!

Leaving My Country to Play Baseball

I was one of the last players to get out of Cuba. The Revolution happened in 1959, and I signed with the Reds in 1960. It wasn't hard to get a visa to go to America, because the relationship between the United States and Cuba was still OK. In 1961, there was a meeting with the government and all the professional players, and they asked who wanted to stay to help with the aftermath of the Revolution and who wanted to go to America to play baseball. Only a few stayed.

I returned to Cuba in 1962 because I broke my leg playing in Rocky Mountain, North Carolina, and was out for the season. My mother worried my career was over and I'd never be able to come back to see her. It was OK to go back in '62, but when I tried to leave for the United States in 1963, it was difficult. I didn't get out till May or June and missed a lot of the minor-league season, before I was scheduled to play with Cincinnati. I didn't go back to Cuba anymore. The only exception was in 1972, when my father was very ill and I got permission from both governments to visit Cuba. After being away ten years, I spent about twenty days with my family, who missed me but understood why I left to play the sport I loved. It was good to be able to see my father before he passed away.

Pete Rose Should Be in the Hall of Fame

Of course Pete Rose should be in the Hall of Fame. I've said all along, if they don't want him in baseball, if they don't want him to manage or coach, it's OK, but they should vote him in for what he did as a player. When I was inducted into the Hall of Fame, I saw a lot of Pete's memorabilia in Cooperstown. If they're going to put his stuff there in the museum, why won't they let Pete come in?

Keith Hernandez

Experience Helped Me to Become a Gold Glover

I always knew I could field, but it was a matter of honing it down and becoming smarter. And that came with experience. Like with the 3-6-3 double play—my dad always said to keep the pitcher out of that play. It's a tough play because the shortstop has to throw to a moving target—the pitcher coming over from the mound. One day, I was holding the runner on first, and a ground ball was hit to me. I threw the ball to second base and found myself ten feet from first. I moved out of the way of the shortstop's throw to the pitcher covering first, and suddenly it came to me: "Wait a minute! After the ball is out of my hand, I can get back to first base in time." Before games, I started practicing the play. Whether I was playing back or holding a runner on, I would pick up the grounder, make an unhurried throw to second base, and, when I saw the ball five feet out of my hand, bust my fanny back to first base. That kept the pitcher out of the play. I got better with that play as I gained experience.

It was the same with bunt plays, where I became more aggressive as time went on and got to the ball so quickly that I was able to throw out the runner being moved up. I always felt that if I didn't get the lead runner on a bunt play, I'd failed. With experience, I knew what bunters would do. For instance, with men on first and second, they'd bunt toward third base. Bunting toward first was the way to beat me on that play, but nobody ever did it, because the "rule" is that they should bunt to the third baseman. With men on first and second, I didn't have to hold the runner on first and could charge in and try to pick up the bunt on the third-base side and gun it over to third base. If they made a good bunt down the line, I couldn't get to the ball to make that play, but pitchers and the majority of other hitters can't bunt that well.

The play I was proudest of was when I'd be playing back with a slow runner on second base. On a sharply hit grounder, I'd throw him out at third base. If I charged the ball, I'd pick it up and decide if I had time to get the runner at third or if I should run to first and get the unassisted putout. What helped me on all my throws was that I had a good arm. In fact, I was the lead cutoff man on doubles down the right-field line for the Mets. Usually the first baseman trails the sec-

57

ond baseman down the line, but I had a stronger arm than our second baseman, Wally Backman, so he trailed me.

Ron Fairly Taught Me Two Things About Fielding

When Ron Fairly was a teammate of mine on the Cardinals in the mid-'70s, he was disappointed not to get much playing time at first base, where I played, or in the outfield. Still, he took the time to teach me a few things about playing first base, and I'll always remember how much he helped me. One important thing he taught me was how to break in my big first-baseman's glove properly. You play catch to build a pocket, tighten the two sets of laces, and, after improving the pocket, tighten the laces again. Then soak the glove in lukewarm water; put one ball in the web and another in the palm of your hand; fold the long part of your glove over; tape it; and then hang the glove from a coat hanger. When the top part of the glove, above your fingers, is made stronger and shaped inward, it becomes easier to scoop up grounders and low throws. So, Ron helped me a lot with the glove.

Ron also taught me how to cheat at first base. He said to never cheat unless it's going to be a close play, because you don't want to get a reputation among umpires of being a cheater. He said that on a boom-boom play, when the ball gets to be around five feet in front of you, just extend out to it. Your foot will be pulled about six inches off the bag, but act like your heel was on the bag. Cheating is all about timing, and he said to just catch the ball in one smooth, deceptive motion, and come up ready to toss the ball around the infield. If you look like you're ready to move to the next play, you're telling the umpire that the throw beat the runner and your heel was on the bag. So, he'll be inclined to call the batter out at first.

58

Becoming a Leader

Frank Cashen was the general manager of the Mets when I came to New York from St. Louis. He would later say that that he knew what kind of player I was but didn't know if I was a leader. Neither did I. In St. Louis, I learned from Lou Brock, who was our silent leader. Bob Gibson was our other leader, and he was more inclined to get in your face. I was just trying to get my feet wet my first few years with the Cards. And when I was the National League's co-MVP with Willie Stargell, I didn't realize that I'd reached that level where my teammates were looking up to me. People told me that later. When Whitey Herzog became our manager, I read in the paper where he said, "I don't need any leaders on this club. I'm the leader." So, he never encouraged me to become a leader.

I was traded to the Mets in 1983, and in 1984 at spring training, we had a lot of young players like Darryl Strawberry and Dwight Gooden who were becoming stars with the media. Cashen pulled me aside and said, "We want you to handle the press to take the burden off the other players." So, as a veteran on a team of mostly young players, I immediately was looked on to provide leadership. I grew into a verbal, emotional leader as we evolved into a championship team.

The Mets Fell Short in 1988

In 1988, we lost the NLCS in seven games to the Dodgers, and it was like a nail in the coffin on the Mets' chances to win another championship with all those great players. Many people think that team was better than our 1986 title team, but I don't agree. We were a solid squad, but we weren't as tight a unit. There was less camaraderie and more inner turmoil on the team, the not-always friendly presence of the New York tabloid press, and younger players like Darryl Strawberry stepping out and wanting to spread their wings. And Gary Carter and I were still having good years, but we were ebbing a little bit. Still, we might have won the whole thing if we didn't lose Bobby Ojeda in late September when he almost sliced off the top of a finger on his pitching hand with electric hedge clippers. If we had Ojeda to pitch against the Dodgers, it might have been a different story.

It also might have been different if David Cone, who had a 20–3 record that year despite pitching the first month in the bullpen, hadn't written a story in the *New York Daily News* in which he called Orel Hershiser's performance in Game 1 "lucky" and ripped Dodgers closer Jay Howell for throwing a "high-school breaking ball." Actually, Coney hadn't written that story. *Daily News* sportswriter Bob Klapisch had ghostwritten it. Naturally, Tommy Lasorda hung up the article in the Dodgers' locker room to fire up his players before Cone's start in Game 2. Coney was a very sensitive guy, and he was upset. I was concerned he'd have a hard time pitching, so at batting practice I said to Ojeda, "Bob, go in and check on David; see if he's all right." He was another pitcher, so I thought he would be able to calm him down, but I should have gone in. To this day, I regret not going in to talk to Cone. Not that I would have made a difference, but I should have been the one to talk to him.

Cone went out there and got shellacked. They were all over him. He lasted an inning and a third and gave up five runs. I went to Klapisch after the game. I said, "What side are you on? I mean, aren't you pulling for us? You're a beat writer. Were you that wed to that story? You gotta write that trash?" He said, "Well, they assigned me the story." I said, "Did you have to write it?"

Cone beat the Dodgers easily in Game 6 to tie up the series. But Hershiser shut us out in Game 7, and it was over. There were a few losses that series that should have played out differently. Game 2 was the first.

DON MATTINGLY
How I Got My Power

60   I began in the minors at Oneonta, New York, near Cooperstown. They had dial-a-bus, where you'd call them up, and for a quarter, they'd send a bus to your house to pick you up. I had been drafted in the nineteenth round but had the opportunity to stay in the lineup because in addition to being a first baseman, I gladly played left and right field. In my three years in the minors, I hit over .300, but I was a Punch-and-Judy hitter, a 180-pound singles hitter who hit a lot of balls the other way.

When the Yankees called me up and I got to Yankee Stadium, I never felt I had to learn to pull the ball to take advantage of the short porch in right field, but Lou Piniella was the first guy to teach me how to put backspin on the ball to hit it farther. In the minor leagues, I had occasional pop and thought the ball was going out, but it would come down right at the wall. I was a top-hand guy. Lou really taught me to get back a little bit, use the weight shift, and hit down into the ball to give it backspin.

To me, the baseball swing is like chopping down a tree. You get the bat up, and then you swing downward—you think you swing downward all the way, but if you look at the bat as it goes through the zone, you will see it's level. If the front hand leads the bat down to the ball, it will leave it level in the strike zone. Guys who are able to keep the inside pitch fair when they hit it get down into the ball, and the backspin lifts it. Doing this gave me extra pop, plus I got bigger and stronger as I got older.

I Played the Game with Respect

I had a lot of injuries late in my career, and my numbers were lower, but the fans at Yankee Stadium never turned against me, because they knew I was making the same effort. I pretty much wanted to bring it every day. I think there's really only one way to play, and that's the right way. You prepare yourself and give the effort with everything you have. People come to see you play, and you have teammates counting on you, and they deserve your best effort. Sometimes it's not enough and it doesn't get the job done, but they still deserve that.

The one thing for me, playing in New York—and that pretty much sums me up as a player and how I look at things—is that I really didn't care about anything else off the field. I was married the whole time I was in New York; I had kids; I liked to go home and hang out with them. I wasn't interested in being in the limelight, or going downtown, or being seen in the papers or in commercials. I wanted people to think of me only for how I played the game on the field. So, I kept it simple; I played ball and kept the rest of my life private and

61

normal. Kirby Puckett gave me the nickname "Donnie Baseball," and that was appropriate, because that's pretty much all I did. I didn't have a lot of hobbies—I pretty much played the game and went home.

Winning the Batting Title

The last week of 1984, when my teammate Dave Winfield and I battled for the batting title, was a lot of fun. It was a no-lose situation for me, because that was the first year I was up all season with the Yankees and playing every day. I was basically a rookie. I was hitting over .330 going into the last week, and as a young player who'd probably bat .330 in a season in the big leagues, I was feeling pretty good about everything. It was a lot tougher on Dave, because he was a veteran who had gotten big money as a free agent to come to New York, so everyone expected him to win the batting title and rooted for the underdog. Even though I was the crowd favorite, he treated me so good during that period and never made me feel uncomfortable. He handled everything great. On the last day, Dave was up by a point or two. My last at-bat was against reliever Willie Hernandez, who was the league MVP for the Tigers as they won the championship that year. He wore me out all year. Hernandez was a lefty with a nasty slider, and I looked for the slider and got it. I hit it toward the second baseman, who moved quickly to his left. It could very easily have been a groundout, but it took a funny hop and jumped over his glove for my fourth hit of the game. So, I won the batting title.

62 CARLOS DELGADO
Choosing the Right Sport

I played baseball in Puerto Rico from the time I was five years old. But when I was about thirteen or fourteen and went to middle school, I got a little tired of baseball. I started playing volleyball all the time. My father, who is called "Big Carlos" because he's taller than me and weighs over three hundred pounds, was not thrilled. One day, he looked at me and asked, "How many Puerto Ricans do you see play-ing professional volleyball?" I had to say, "Not many." The following year, I went back to baseball. I grew and became stronger, and a year and a half later, I signed a professional baseball contract with the Toronto Blue Jays.

A Desire to Speak English

I took advanced English classes in high school in Puerto Rico. I have my dad to thank for that. I was a catcher then, and he pointed out that if I signed a professional baseball contract, it would be beneficial to be able to talk to my pitchers, to be on the same page with them when I called a game. Most kids in Puerto Rico learn the basics of English in school, but in my last year of high school, I bore down and really learned the language. When I was in Toronto's minor-league sys-tem, I started picking up slang and baseball terms. A lot of Latino play-ers are afraid to speak English because they don't want to embarrass themselves, but if you don't embarrass yourself a few times, you're never going to learn. I was never afraid to learn, because two languages are better than one. I still make mistakes, but I try to learn something every day.

A Game to Remember—but I Don't

September 25, 2003, was a special night for me. Against Tampa Bay, I became the fifteenth major leaguer to hit four home runs in a game. I never would have guessed that I'd have a big game, because after bat-ting practice I was feeling sick. I said to Toronto's trainer, "I think I'm getting a cold. Can I have some medicine?" I swallowed a couple of pills and then took a nap. When I woke up, I wasn't feeling any bet-ter. I almost decided not to play, and when I suited up, I told myself not to do too much.

The next thing I know, I'm playing in the game, and first at-bat: home run. And second at-bat: another home run. I remembered almost nothing from the third at-bat on. I don't remember running the bases after my third and fourth home runs. I don't remember flipping the bat after my fourth homer, which caused my teammates to give me a lot of grief!

On all four homers, the pitches seemed to be down the middle and in slow motion, easy pitches to hit with a lot of backspin. Later I watched the tape of the homers, and all four pitches were down or away, never in the middle of the plate. But at the time, they looked perfect to me. I still can't explain it.

FOUR

SECOND TO NO ONE:
ON JACKIE ROBINSON

RALPH BRANCA
Jackie Robinson Breaks the Color Barrier

I still marvel that Branch Rickey picked Jackie Robinson to integrate major-league baseball, because there were better African American ballplayers. But Branch knew he needed someone with the character to turn the other cheek and stand up to all the criticism that he knew would go on. I guess he looked back to Jackie's army record, where he was court-martialed for not going to the back of a bus and was acquitted for that. Rickey's choosing him was the key to the success of breaking the color barrier.

I grew up on a street that was the League of Nations, so it was second nature for me to accept Jackie Robinson as a teammate on the Brooklyn Dodgers in 1947. Other than our captain, Pee Wee Reese, who was from Kentucky yet put his arm around Jackie's shoulder to make him feel welcome, it was the guys from the South who had difficulty adjusting to an African American teammate. Dixie Walker, who was from Alabama, and the other Southerners came from a part of the country where there was segregation and a different set of mores. They voiced their resentment, passed around a petition, and threatened not to play if Robinson was a Dodger. But our owner, Branch

Rickey, made it clear that Robinson was staying, and he traded Walker and the others the following year. Dixie actually came around by August '47, because he realized Jackie was making a big contribution in our run to the pennant.

Jackie had a tough time, and there was a lot of angst. There was taunting every place we went from the stands and opposing dugouts, and Jackie had to play first base, a strange position, to protect him from runners who slid into second with their spikes high. Like Rickey had instructed, Jackie turned the other cheek and avoided conflict with anyone. He just stood his ground and tried to do his job. His secret weapon when he went home at night was his wife, Rachel, who calmed him down and helped him keep his anger in check. Also, Rickey wisely had two black writers—Sam Lacy, from the *Baltimore Sun*, and Wendell Smith, from the *Pittsburgh Courier*—travel with Jackie on the road all season so he wouldn't be so lonely.

Under the circumstances, Jackie played extremely well. He hit .297, led the league in stolen bases, and was chosen the first Rookie of the Year, an award that now bears his name. Jackie continued to turn the other cheek for two more years, though some people say it was only through the 1948 season. Being close to Jackie, I knew that was totally out of character for him, because he was feisty and outspoken and would tangle with anybody if he knew he was right. But with Rachel's encouragement, he did it.

It's well documented how much what Jackie did affected blacks across America. I could see how much they appreciated Jackie just by how they flocked to Ebbets Field and other ballparks to see him play. And white America could see that you can't judge a man by the color of his skin. Sociologically, all America changed, the whole world changed, because of Jackie. Did Jackie win? No, he triumphed.

Larry Doby

Jackie Robinson and I Had Similar Experiences

I have said that the only difference between what I went through and what Jackie Robinson went through in 1947 is that Jackie deservedly got all the publicity, because he made it possible for me to be part of it. You didn't hear much of what I was going through, because the media didn't want to repeat the whole story. I sincerely believe that. I'm not knocking the media for writing only about Jackie having a hard time, because there's no need to write about me having a tough time when it's assumed that I'm going through the same situation. In fact, one of the reasons I admired Jackie is that from my own experiences, I knew what he was going through without Jackie having to tell me.

The treatment isn't going to be different just because he's in the National League and I'm in the American League. It wasn't going to be easy for either of us. We weren't going to stay in certain hotels or eat in certain restaurants. Jackie and I had no need to talk about that stuff, so we'd talk most about the players on various teams who were on rosters only so they could be bench jockeys. He'd tell me which players were riding him, and I'd tell him the players who gave me a tough time.

RALPH KINER

The Greatest Competitor I Ever Saw

Jackie Robinson grew up in Pasadena, California, and I grew up nearby in Alhambra. I played fast-pitch softball against him. In my mind, he was the greatest athlete to ever play major-league baseball. He was a great football player, a great basketball player, and a great track star. Baseball was his worst sport! Yet, he's in the Hall of Fame. He was certainly the greatest competitor I ever saw.

What an ordeal he went through, at a time when bench jockeying was serious and racial epithets were common. Jackie didn't draw the huge crowds the baseball history book says he did as a rookie, but fans were giving him a hard time wherever he went. I remember when Jackie first played in Pittsburgh in 1947. Hank Greenberg was on our team that season, and he walked down to first base, Jackie's position that year, to give him some encouragement before the game. He told him that he'd experienced prejudice as a Jewish player when he broke

67

in with the Tigers in the 1930s. He said, "It's tough, but hang in there." I'm sure that helped Jackie, because most opposing players weren't friendly or supportive. I'm sure that bonded the two of them.

Jackie and I were respectful of each other when we played but didn't really talk very much, because it was a time when players from different teams were discouraged from fraternizing. I do remember that after I homered in the ninth inning to tie the 1950 All-Star Game, Jackie was the second player, after Stan Musial, to shake my hand after I crossed home plate.

Robin Roberts
Jackie Robinson Was Much More than a Great Player

I faced Jackie Robinson more than any other pitcher. I never missed the Dodgers, pitching seven or eight times a year against them in Philadelphia and Brooklyn. After we beat them in the final game of the 1950 season to win the pennant, I was exhausted, having pitched three times in five days. I was sitting by my locker, really whipped, when I felt someone tug on my shoulder. It was Jackie, who came into our clubhouse and went to every guy and shook his hand. I'm thinking, "If I'd have lost, would I have gone over to the Dodgers' clubhouse?"

For him to do that just shows you what kind of person he was. He was a marvelous player and a tough competitor who anyone would love to have on his team. But he also was a beautiful person. I really enjoyed competing against him, although he lit me up as much as I got him out. When he was being honored by Major League Baseball, I was hoping that his being a solid person came across more than his exploits on the field. He was willing to go through so much so other black players would have an opportunity to play professional baseball.

He came up in 1947, and he experienced terrible abuse. The Phillies got on him more than any team, and the manager, Ben Chapman, was the worst of all. But he beat up on the Phillies so badly that in 1948, when I was a rookie, there was a fine if anyone got on Jackie. You couldn't believe the days he'd have against us. Once he went

7-for-8 in a doubleheader in Ebbets Field. The Dodgers were a good team, but Jackie was something special. I was upset that Major League Baseball didn't keep him in some capacity after he retired.

When Jackie Robinson Took Me Deep

A big game I'll always remember was the final game of the 1951 season at Connie Mack Stadium, when we played the Dodgers, who needed a victory to tie the Giants in the pennant race. I had pitched Saturday, but Eddie Sawyer brought me into the game in the eighth inning, which is when Brooklyn scored three times to tie the score, 8–8. In the top of the eleventh inning, the Dodgers had the go-ahead run on second with two outs. Jackie Robinson was up, with Roy Campanella next. Sawyer came to the mound. When he came out to the mound, you were usually gone; it wasn't to chitchat. But this time, he said, "Who would you rather pitch to, Robinson or Campanella?" I said, "It doesn't matter to me, Skip." He said, "It doesn't matter to me, either." And he ran off the field! People had thought there was a big strategy session going on out there. I got Jackie out that time. And then in the fourteenth inning, he hit a home run to win the game. That allowed them to have the playoff with the Giants, which they lost on Bobby Thomson's famous home run.

HANK AARON
The Value of Jackie Robinson

Aside from what he contributed socially by breaking baseball's color barrier, Jackie Robinson was a tremendously gifted athlete who could do things that ordinary athletes could not do. For instance, Jackie Robinson was the best base runner I ever saw, not only when stealing bases but also taking the extra base. He had such great instincts, and if you made any kind of mistake on him in the outfield, like double-pumping or not throwing the ball correctly, he would take advantage of that. What he brought to the Dodgers reminds me so much of a

69

Michael Jordan. He made everybody around him play just a little bit better and a lot harder than they could play. Even in batting practice, he could make his teammates bear down and perform beyond their peaks.

Frank Robinson
Jackie Did It the Hard Way so We'd Have It Easy

I ended my Hall of Fame induction speech in 1982 by thanking Jackie Robinson and the other black players who came before me for opening the door for me and all the black players who have played since. It can't be overstated how much easier Jackie made it for all us African Americans who followed him. But at times, we do take him a little bit for granted for that very reason—it has become easier. And it will be easier for the players coming along five years from now. You can't simplify what this man did, what he had to go through, and the sacrifices he made for us to come later and be successful.

Willie Mays
I'm Indebted to Jackie Robinson

I have been quoted as saying, "Every time I look at my checkbook, I see Jackie Robinson." Before 1947, I had three guys I could talk about in the major leagues—Ted Williams, Stan Musial, and Joe DiMaggio—but from then on, I had Jackie. When Jackie played for Brooklyn that year, I knew I had a chance to play in the majors, too. All I had to do was keep playing, keep playing, and wait for my chance. And I did. When I became a New York Giant in 1951 and saw the money I was making, I said to myself, "Boy, when I see Jackie, I'm going to thank him, even though he's not going to know what I'm talking about. I'm going to thank him because he took such a beating for two years without saying anything—he just played ball so I could play ball."

FIVE

THE THIRD BASEMEN

MIKE SCHMIDT
Early Home Runs off a Particular Catcher

The Phillies selected me in the second round of the 1971 draft and sent me to Reading, in the Eastern League, which was Double-A. In 1972, I spent the full year with Eugene in the Pacific Coast League, Triple-A, and came up to the Phillies at the end of their year for a cup of coffee. I hit my first and only home run that year off Balor Moore, of Montreal. He had a little streak of scoreless innings going at the time, and we ended up winning the game and giving him some earned runs as a result of my home run. His catcher was someone who'd play a major role in the early part of my career and a major role in the later years. His name was Tim McCarver, and I think he felt sorry for me, because he called for a fastball right down the middle.

The following year, 1973, I made the Phillies but separated my shoulder at the end of spring training. So, I had to stay in Clearwater and miss the first week of the season. I came back, and the first game I played was against the Cardinals. The pitcher was Scipio Spinks, and believe it or not, Tim was catching, because he had been traded back to his first team in the winter. I'm sure Tim remembers this, because with two outs, I dropped down a bunt single for my first hit of the year. He didn't like that too much and was all over me. We topped that series off the next day when I hit a Sunday-afternoon home run to beat

Bob Gibson 2–1. Tim could see that I could take a low-and-away fast-ball and wrap it around the left-field foul pole, so from then on, when I hit against the Cardinals, he had his pitchers throw inside.

One Swing Turned Me into a Confident Hitter

I batted .196 in 1973, my first full season with the Phillies. I've been told that is the lowest average ever for a future Hall of Famer. Our final series of the year was in St. Louis, and I was hitting a solid .201 going in. We had to face Rick Wise and Bob Gibson, and that darn Cesar Tovar, who I was platooning with, refused to play. So, they made me play against Gibson, and I dropped under .200. It was discouraging. I knew what my weaknesses were, but I wasn't sure that I'd ever correct them.

I played my second straight winter down in Puerto Rico, and my manager, Bobby Wine, the onetime Phillies shortstop, helped me tremendously. I was always the kind of guy who needed a positive experience, so that I could lock in on that good feeling, and I had something good happen to me down in Puerto Rico. We were play-ing in the Puerto Rican World Series against Tommy Lasorda's team, and Pedro Borbon was pitching for him. Out of the clear blue, I thought I'd go up to home plate and take a nice little easy swing. Sounds simple, but I never had done that in my life. I'd always felt like I had to swing really hard to hit the ball very far, and when you swing hard, the left shoulder comes flying out, and you're vulnerable to the breaking ball. That's why I never was a very good hitter. Borbon threw me a fastball, and I moved the bat as soft, easy, and slow as I could move it, and the ball went off the left-field wall.

A whole new world of execution as a hitter opened up to me with that one swing of the bat. I finally realized that I didn't have to be quick and try to swing hard and jerky, because nice and easy worked much better. I carried that sense of swinging easy at that ball for about four years after that, and it just kind of put everything into place. If I could just convince myself on a 2-and-0 fastball to just swing easy at it, my shoulder stayed in and I could hit to all fields. I rode that feeling and got the needed confidence boost in order to play the game at a high level. And teammates like Dick Allen, Gary Maddox, Tim, and Pete Rose all seemed to help me out a lot in that sense. They all said a lot of positive things to me, and I guess I was the kind of guy that needed that.

I Wished Philadelphia Fans Appreciated Me More

It's unfortunate that when I was young, I was so sensitive to let the booing of the Philadelphia fans hurt me and affect how I played. At times, it made me play too hard and try to do too much. Looking back, most of that was my fault, but you know how tough the Phillies fans can be with a sensitive player. They didn't bother Tug McGraw, Pete Rose, Greg Luzinski, or Bob Boone, but for some reason the vocal minority bothered me. I was an intense player, and probably nobody worked as hard behind the scenes to maintain a level of play at the top of the game. What disappointed me the most is that I didn't feel the people in the stands knew I was working that hard on my game. I was told I had this aloofness about me on the field; maybe it was the way I walked or wore my uniform, or just the presence I had on the field. Maybe I had the outward appearance of being cocky and overly confident, but internally I was never very sure of myself from the day I first walked onto my first professional baseball field at Reading, Pennsylvania. I had a good way of masking my insecurities as a baseball player. People may have thought things came too easy for me, because of how I carried myself, so they expected more out of me. It was different with a Rose, Luzinski, or Larry Bowa, because they carried themselves differently on the field and looked like they were working all the time.

I got dirty on the field, but I was labeled as someone who didn't want to get dirty, who never dived for balls. Graig Nettles, who was a great third baseman, dove for every ball. Maybe I didn't dive for every ball because of my bad knees or because I had a quicker first step and played a little deeper, so I didn't have to dive as often. But I did my share of diving. I wanted to be "Dirty" Mike Schmidt my whole

73

career, but I never could get that label. Pete Rose wanted to be like me, but I wanted to be like Pete and get dirty. I wanted to be like Lenny Dykstra and have tobacco stains all over my uniform, because the fans loved that. I would have given anything to be the hero to the fans in Philadelphia, and they had no idea how hard I was working to be that guy.

Do I think they realize that now? I think there eventually was a good feeling between the city, its fans, and me *after* I had finished most of my career and got to the 500-homer plateau and started having my name associated with some of the all-time greats. I think people finally started to look at me in a different light. Today I think I'm appreciated enough when I go back to Philadelphia. I'm quite happy with my position in Philadelphia sports history. But looking back, I probably would have given up some of my accomplishments to have been more appreciated by the fans in Philadelphia. If I had it to do all over, I would have made sure to have more fun playing the game.

My Two Goals as a Player

There were two things that I strove to be as a player. First of all, I wanted to be known as "a gamer." Pete Rose was probably the ultimate gamer. That's probably the best thing that can be said about a player. He plays hard; he'll do what he needs to do to help win that game that day—take out a runner, break up a double play, slide hard into home, knock a guy over, play hurt, play the whole game even if it goes seventeen innings, do whatever it takes. And then show up the next day ready to play again, even if Nolan Ryan is pitching. I obviously was not a Cal Ripken in terms of being in the lineup every day, but I was in there over 150 games a season and gave it my all every game, even every at-bat. So, maybe I was a gamer, even if no one called me that.

The other thing I wanted to be was a complete hitter. I don't know that I ever achieved that. In the years when I won the MVP Awards, a power hitter could have "a good year" if he hit 35 home runs, drove in 100 to 110 runs, and hit .285. After having started my major-league career as a .196 hitter who had no idea how to hit to right field and probably didn't even belong in the big leagues, my goal and challenge was to become a hitter who could use the whole field and could be a tough out in the middle of a rally. That meant I couldn't strike out 150 times a year. I could see striking out 75 or 80 times a year, while driving in my 100 to 120 runs and hitting 30 to 40 home runs. But my batting average and consistency at the plate needed to be developed. I worked on that my whole career, and I don't know if I ever really achieved it. It was just my nature to be dissatisfied. I could hit a home run and come back to the dugout and be pissed off that I'd hooked it to the left instead of homering to right. I can't help it. That's just the way I am.

My Friend Pete Rose

Pete Rose wrote a blurb for my book, *Clearing the Bases*. That's pretty good, because it's hard getting Pete to read a book. Pete was one of my best friends when I played. When he came to the Phillies in 1979, he didn't just tell *me* how good I was on a daily basis, but told similar things to everyone on the team. That's the way he was, just a wonderful teammate. He really made the game fun for me and the other players. I'd played against him for so many years and couldn't stand him. He was an intimidating player who knew how to play the game.

Shoot, it's really hard to pinpoint exactly what it was that he brought to us. I guess he taught us that gamer mentality, but more than anything, he brought to us his big-game experience with the Big Red Machine. We'd won divisions; the Reds had won World Series. You have to understand, this is a hitter who hit singles and occasional doubles, but everyone knew he had the ability to change the ebb and flow of a big series. It was just his makeup. It was the way he intimidated the opposition. He did it to us, in the playoffs over several years. We hated it. But he sort of befriended Larry Bowa and Greg Luzinski, and when he became a free agent, I think a big reason he came to the Phillies was that he liked them and saw potential in me and others to be his friends. He just wanted to be a part of our team and bring it that element that we were missing. He was right, because the Phillies finally won their first world title in 1980.

I have a kinship to Pete Rose, and when I was inducted into the Hall of Fame, I felt a need to say some things about him while standing in front of all the people at the ceremony, because of how much he meant to me and my career. I'm not sure that I would have ever risen to Hall of Fame stature, or that my career would have been catapulted to where it was starting in 1979 and '80, if Pete hadn't chosen to come to the Phillies. So, I really felt that I owed him. I also know how much the Hall of Fame and being back in baseball would mean to Pete Rose in his life.

Pete's situation today is unfortunate. I was talking to someone the other day about Pete, and he used the word *purgatory* to describe the state where Pete finds himself. The commissioner's office has failed to make any kind of a call on Pete. In his 2003 book, he devoted a chapter that went into detail about the reinstatement process that he learned about when he admitted to Commissioner Selig that he did in fact gamble, after fourteen years of denying it. Years later and he's still dangling out there, and they've failed to find time to tell Pete whether they're going to reinstate him or refuse to do so. It's an injustice, because he needs to go on with his life knowing what baseball's position is on him, one way or the other.

WADE BOGGS
Meeting Ted Williams

At eighteen, I went to my first spring training in Winter Haven. My roommate and I were in a line at a movie, getting ready to go in, when I turned around and saw that Ted Williams was two people behind us. I went, "Oh, my gosh!" It was like John Wayne walking through the saloon doors. And I said, "I gotta meet him!" So, I walked up to him and said, "Excuse me, Mr. Williams." "Yeah, kid?" And I started shaking. I said, "Mr. Williams, I'm a member of the Boston Red Sox. I just signed in June." He goes, "Can you hit, kid?" I said, "Yes, sir, I can hit." He goes, "Show me your stance; show me where you hold your hands." So, all the people file into the movie theater, and we are still out on the sidewalk. I'm demonstrating my stance, and he's talking about hitting and where to hold my hands and various things like that.

Years later, the Red Sox were playing on "Game of the Week," and I came up to the plate. We were in Boston, and Ted was visiting the booth, talking to Curt Gowdy and Tony Kubek. The NBC crew had gotten hold of a picture of me when I was eighteen months old and was in the backyard swinging a bat. Without telling Ted it was a picture of me, they asked Ted during the telecast, "What do you think of this kid's swing?" And Ted said, "Well, I think this kid probably has a future in baseball with a swing like that." Then they said, "Well, Mr. Williams, he's up at the plate right now." By that time, I'd already won a couple of batting titles, and he snapped, "See, I told you that kid could hit." I loved Ted to death.

I Wondered if I'd Ever Be Called Up to the Majors

In 1981, eight or nine minor leaguers were being called up to the Red Sox at the end of our season. Joe Morgan, our manager at Pawtucket, was calling each and every player into his office. So, I'm slowly packing my bags, hoping he'd call me into his office and say I was going to Boston rather than home for the winter in Tampa. The last guy comes out, and there was a void of inactivity; nobody was going in or out. So, I passed Joe's office and yelled, "See you in spring training, Skip." And he said, "OK, Boggsy, see you in March." So, I knew I wasn't being called up.

Joe had told me earlier in the season that the organization felt I wasn't good enough defensively to play third base and that, after the season, I needed to learn to play first base in the Winter Leagues. At the time, I said, "OK," but I thought the Sox would bring me up after I'd broken eleven hitting records in the International League for a left-handed hitter at Pawtucket. Instead, guys who hit .230 and .240 were going by me as if I were tied to a post. Because I didn't get the call, I knew I had to work on something, so I went down to Puerto Rico to

77

learn first base. Ironically, the third baseman there broke his ankle, so I moved back to third base. I ended up batting .379 playing third the whole time. If you ever played on a field in Puerto Rico, Venezuela, or the Dominican Republic, you know how rocky it is, and that sured up my hands and helped me learn to field the position.

So, in December I was added to the forty-man roster for the first time and was going to go to spring training with the big club for the first time. Nobody called me to tell me this. I found this out from my father, who read it in the paper. I go to spring training for the first time. I walk into the clubhouse, and the first person I bump into is Yaz. I couldn't believe it. I'd never met any big-league player in the six years I'd been in the organization, including the two years I was at Pawtucket. Dwight Evans walks in, followed by Rick Miller, Jerry Remy, Mike Torrez, and Dennis Eckersley. In Winter Haven, I used to stay at a Howard Johnson's and look at the Holiday Inn across the street and see these guys getting out of their big fancy cars. Now I was getting dressed with all these guys, and I was like a kid in a candy store.

The Biggest Disappointment

I always felt deep down in my heart that I'd win a world title in Boston, because of some of the great teams we had. We were up three games to two and were leading the Mets by two runs in Game 6 of the 1986 World Series as we headed into the bottom of the tenth inning. We had kids in the clubhouse popping the champagne. When there were two outs and two strikes on Gary Carter, the third-base umpire, Harry Wendlestadt, said, "Boggsy, flip me your hat. I collect all winning third-basemen's hats in the World Series."

I said, "Harry, the game's not over yet."

He said, "Look at the scoreboard!"

I look over my left shoulder and see that on the Mets' scoreboard, it said: "Congratulations Boston Red Sox 1986 World Champions." And I said, "Oh, my goodness!"

And the next thing I knew, I was walking off the field, and we had lost. Carter, Kevin Mitchell, and Ray Knight got hits, and Mookie Wilson hit the ball that went through Bill Buckner's legs, and in that entire sequence I never touched the ball. I was just standing at third base, watching. And after the four batters, Harry Wendlestadt said to me, "Well, I guess I'll see you tomorrow night." And I said, "Yeah, see you tomorrow night." It all happened so fast. And we had to play the next night and lost.

Blanking Out on a Black Horse

To this day, I have no idea how I ended up on a police horse and rode around Yankee Stadium at the conclusion of the 1996 World Series. I have no memory of it. I do remember jumping on the pile and we Yankees collectively saying, "Let's take a victory lap." There were no fans on the field. It was amazing: fifty-six thousand fans were just standing by their seats. We were waiting to be trounced by all the fans, but they just stood there clapping, so we decided to take our lap. And the next thing I know, I'm in left center field on the back of the horse. To this day, I have no idea—and I've never wanted to look at the video—how I got on that horse. Police horses are huge, and you can't just hop on the back of one like you'd do in the wild, wild west. So, a couple of months later, you find out that the horse is doing autograph shows and making lots of money. It was just one of those nights!

The Burden of Being Superstitious

I can honestly say that my life is a lot simpler now than it used to be. Having eighty to eighty-five superstitions made days pretty difficult. It was not only that it was time-consuming, but also there weren't enough hours in a day to go through them all. Coincidentally, I'm the only guy in the Hall of Fame who has on his plaque, "The most superstitious baseball player."

It started with me as it does with many Little Leaguers: if I had a good day, I'd wear the same socks or T-shirt the next game. It evolved from there: when I'd have a good game, I'd start doing the same things,

79

and it would be like *Groundhog Day* every day. I'd get three hits, and I'd say, "Wow! So, I'm going to do the same things the next time." Then I'd get two or three hits and do the same thing the time after that.

In the years I was winning the batting titles, it seemed like every day was the same day. I'd wake up at the same time; I would get dressed at the same time; I'd eat chicken every day; I'd leave for the ballpark at the same time; I'd do the same routine at the ballpark every game. I'd keep my bats in the same place and take ground balls at the same time every day. And thank God, Johnny Pesky would know the exact time I wanted the balls hit to me. I never told Johnny how many balls to hit, but someone once went behind the stands before five games and counted, and it turned out that in four of those five days, I stopped him after having caught exactly one hundred grounders. I'd sense that I'd had enough and tell Johnny, "Three more" and then stop and feel I was at the spot I needed to be.

I would run out on the field eighteen minutes before a game. So, for a 7:35 game I'd run out on the field at 7:17. We were playing in Toronto once, and at 7:16, I got ready to run out of the dugout. And I'm waiting and waiting, but the clock wouldn't move. Then it changed to 7:18. All the Blue Jays players started laughing. Fortunately, I got two hits that night, so it didn't affect me too much.

I Could Hit

It didn't matter if I took one or two strikes, because I knew that if I swung the bat, I was going to make contact. That's one of the reasons I didn't want to get in the box and swing at the first pitch. I liked to pick out a pitch and felt that the longer I was in the box, the better the chance the pitcher would make a mistake. If I got seven, eight, nine, or ten pitches, I had the winning hand.

Defenses didn't know how to play me. I drove Yankees shortstop Wayne Tolleson nuts. We had a four-game series, and before the final game, Tolleson called me over and said, "I have to ask you a question. Do you watch me?" I said, "Wherever you go." He said, "It seems like if I move to the right to the hole, you hit it up the middle, but if I move to the middle, you hit it in the hole." I said, "You finally figured me out."

The best was Ray Miller. He told me that he figured me out and that I had no chance of getting a hit that day. I asked, "What are you going to do?" He said, "You'll see." We were in Minnesota, and when I came to bat, while the pitcher waited for a sign, the second baseman and shortstop were behind second base, one behind the other. When the pitcher wound up, one of them would run to his position, and the other would stand there. I went 5-for-5 that night. I'd just hit it into the position of the one who didn't move. After that, Ray Miller tipped his hat to me and said, "OK, we won't do that anymore."

Scott Brosius
Seeing My First Major-League Game

I grew up in Portland, Oregon. We never got up to Seattle to watch games. I never saw a major-league game in person until my second year in professional baseball when I was playing in Madison, Wisconsin. We went to Milwaukee County Stadium, and I saw the Brewers play the Twins, because our team was going to play against Milwaukee's A-ball team in the second game. I thought Milwaukee County Stadium was the greatest ballpark in the world. I was looking around, saying about everything, "Wow, look at this!" I was a total fan. I ate a brat, a nice pregame meal for me, and then went down to watch batting practice and said, "I gotta get a ball. I gotta catch a home-run ball." So, I went down to the left-field foul pole, and Tim Laudner, Minnesota's catcher, hit a ball down the line that caught me in my hands. I got my ball. There were all these kids around me, and people were yelling, "Give it to a kid!" But I said, "It's my first game, too!" I put it in my pocket and walked away. I still have that ball.

Start Spreading the News

When I learned that Oakland had traded me to the New York Yankees for Kenny Rogers, I said, "Are you kidding me?" My last year in Oakland wasn't a good year. Anything that could go wrong did: I wasn't healthy, I didn't play well, I was a bit unlucky—you name it. So, I pretty much knew I'd be playing someplace else. I heard rumblings the year before that I'd be traded, and the New York Mets were one of the teams mentioned before the '97 season. I honestly didn't like going to New York as a visiting player, so I called my agent and said, "Do what you can to squelch the deal, because I don't want to play in New York." So, I had an ongoing joke with my agent about being traded to New York.

After the '97 season, I heard a lot of rumblings that there was almost a done deal with the Angels. In December or January, I was with my family in Disneyland, so I thought it would be perfect to be traded to the Angels then. I was the last person to hear about the trade that did happen, because we didn't have a phone on, and I didn't pick up a paper for two days. I finally got a call from my agent at the hotel. Jennifer picked up the phone, and when I walked in, she was white as a ghost. So, I get on the phone and say, "I guess the trade happened." And he said, "Yes." "So, where am I going?" And he starts humming the beginning of "New York, New York." I thought he was joking, but he kept singing. He told me I was going to the Yankees, which startled me, because they'd never been mentioned in trade rumors.

After we hung up, I sat there with Jennifer, and there was stunned silence for about two minutes. I was a guy from a little town in Oregon with twenty thousand people, who had trouble spending three days visiting New York, so how was I going to survive a full year? Then I said, "I'm going to the Yankees!" And I was fired up. I called my dad and said, "Guess what: I was traded to the Yankees!" And he said, "I knew that. I saw it in the papers this morning." So, I was literally the last guy to know.

Fulfilling a Dream

I still get chills when I think of the 1998 season, my first year with the Yankees. What happened was better than I could have scripted it. Batting eighth or ninth, I drove in ninety-eight runs, but I've always felt RBIs are a team statistic. I'm not someone who hits thirty or forty home runs every year, so the only way I can come close to a hundred RBIs is if the guys in front of me were doing their jobs, too, and there were a bunch of guys on base when I batted. It was a year when offensively we were real good, which is a good reason we won 114 games. I was the product of a lot of guys doing real good. I'd rather be a number nine hitter on a great team than a five or six hitter on a poor team.

Getting the MVP of the World Series sweep of San Diego wasn't embarrassing to me, but I thought of it as just the icing on the cake, an added bonus that wasn't what I set out to win. The excitement came from just hugging all the guys on the field. You dream your whole life of just getting to the World Series. I remember being asked by a reporter after the Series, "Did you in your wildest dreams ever imagine this?" And I said, "Yes!" Every day in my backyard, my friends from the neighborhood and I would play ball and pretend to be whoever was in the World Series that year. We'd all try to hit home runs to win the Series, or make a great play against the fence to pull back home runs and save the Series. We even did our own commentaries. So, I didn't see playing in the '98 World Series as pressure, but a great opportunity to fulfill a dream. When you're going through it, you're so locked in and focused and working hard to be ready to play the games that you can't take in everything. Someday I might sit back and say, "Wow, look what really happened." That's when I can appreciate it all.

CHIPPER JONES
Dealing with Pressures to Produce

83

We've all got our pressures. Obviously, I've had them since day one of my professional career. Being the number one pick in the first round, everything you do is put under the microscope. But I learned very early on in my career that pressure can't come from outside—it comes from inside, what you put on yourself. I've always been pretty good at tuning things out and not taking press clippings very seriously, and just going out and having fun, playing the game and doing the things that have made me successful my whole career. I realize that as one of the players who have been here longest, there is added pressure on me in that role, but everyone on the Braves feels pressure for the team to produce, and shares the criticism and burden when it doesn't.

We play for an organization where it's not about how you play in the regular season, but how far you go in the postseason. That's how the success of your team and season is measured. The one thing the Atlanta Braves have to hang their hat on is their string of divisional titles. We won one World Series in 1995, which is more than a lot of teams have won, but otherwise it's the fourteen consecutive divisional titles that make everyone proud. Still, there's not a guy in our club- house who wouldn't trade one of those divisional titles for a World Series victory. I'd gladly finish second in the division if we could pull a Florida Marlins and rally in the second half of the season and win the wild card and be the hottest team going into the postseason and ultimately win the World Series. To really punctuate this run would give John Smoltz, Andruw Jones, and myself, who have been with Atlanta through most of the run, that validation we'd like.

We don't let it rankle us that we haven't won more titles, because that's just the nature of baseball, and we're of the belief that if we keep giving ourselves opportunities, one of these days we're going to be the hottest team in baseball going into the playoffs. We're going to get the bounces and breaks, and we're going to win another one. It hasn't hap- pened in quite some time, but for guys like John, Andruw, and myself, who have nothing left to prove as individuals, the only thing to keep playing for is that brass ring at the end of the rainbow.

I Love New York

When I come to New York, nobody calls me Chipper! At Shea Sta- dium, they've been known to chant, "Larry! Larry!" mockingly—when they're not booing me. I don't mind, because it means they remem- ber something I've done in the past to beat their team. I don't think Mets fans are vindictive toward me, as they might have been early in my career. Whenever I run into them when I'm out and about, they make sure to let me know they're Mets fans, but they're always very respectful and friendly. They'll compliment me and say, "We still love to hate you when you're performing." I understand. I long for fans who avidly follow their teams. I named my third son Shea because I've had a lot of success at Shea Stadium, including hitting my first major-league home run there, into the right-field stands. I'd spent all 1994, which was supposed to be my rookie season, on the disabled list, and we'd had a strike into the '95 season, so that homer was a long time coming. After I got back to the dugout, I went down into the tunnel and got emotional—I actually started crying. There was such a big weight off my shoulders. I'd finally arrived! That was my first of many great Shea memories.

If I Only Got to Hit

Of all our October failures, 1996 is the one that really sticks with me. It was my second year, and we go into New York as defending champions, and in the first two games of the World Series we drill them. Here I am, twenty-four years old, thinking, "I'm going to be in the big leagues two years and have two World Series titles. Life's pretty good!" But the Yankees, true to form and like true champions, didn't quit. David Cone pitches a gem in Game 3, and in Game 4, Jim Leyritz hits a big homer, and they rally from a 6–0 deficit. With that lead, we're thinking we'd have a 3–1 lead and John Smoltz on the hill in Game 5, so it was looking good. The Yankees got a big break when Jermaine Dye ran into the right-field umpire, Tim Welke, trying to catch Derek Jeter's foul ball. Jeter got new life and a hit, and the Yankees rallied. If you're not in a playoff, you don't even have an umpire down the right-field line! It was just one of those crazy, crazy, crazy postseason things that get overlooked that cost us a needed victory.

So it was 2–2 going into Game 5, and John and Andy Pettitte got locked into one of the greatest pitching battles you'll ever see. The Yankees scored the only run of the game in the fourth inning; it was an unearned run. Then we lost Game 6, and the Series was over. I was on deck when the game ended with us trailing 3–2, and I've been quoted as saying that if I had the opportunity, there was no doubt in my mind I would have gotten a big hit. That's part of being a brash young kid. That's how I was raised, to anticipate a moment when I'd get a hit to win a World Series game. So much of hitting is mental, so if you go to the plate believing you're going to get "that hit," then sometimes you will. If you go up to the plate struggling, and Mariano Rivera or John Wetteland is on the mound, chances are you aren't going to get a hit. I was feeling awfully good in that Series and was swinging the bat really well, and I'd faced Wetteland a few times and had a pretty good gauge on him, and I wasn't intimidated by the situation. I really wanted that one last opportunity, but I never got it.

When I Agreed to Move from Third to Left Field

My move from third base to left field was the result of the Braves' going through some tough economic times. At the time, I was making big outfield money, and it was going to be a lot cheaper to go out and get a quality third baseman than a quality outfielder. Quality outfielders demand a lot more money than quality third basemen. Vinny Castilla was on the market, and our general manager, John Schuerholz, called me and asked if I'd be willing to move to the outfield to sign him. It was a tough decision, because I'd made the All-Star team at third for three or four years in a row and was fairly confident in my ability there. But I agreed because I thought getting Vinny would make us a better ball club. And I was right, because we had successful years with him at third. But the fact of the matter is I never felt comfortable out in left.

86   At third base, I was into every pitch, because if you're not ready, you're likely to be wearing the ball. I perform best when I'm mentally in tune with everything that is going on. Out there in left, man, there's a lot of downtime, a lot of talking to myself and whistling, so I really didn't enjoy it. Plus I had a hard time staying healthy out there—and, in that one year, keeping my hamstring in one piece. After Vinny left, I finally went to Bobby Cox and said, "Look, if you want to keep

me in the lineup every day and healthy, you have to get me out of the outfield." He asked me if I wanted to play third or first, and I told him that third was my natural position and where I wanted to play. Bobby made it happen, and now I'm back home and feel great.

DAVID WRIGHT
The Lowly Rookie

When I was first brought up by the Mets in 2004, a lot of veteran players took care of me. Guys would take me to dinner, and Cliff Floyd even bought me my first suit in the big leagues. Joe McEwing said he felt an obligation to look after me because when he came to the majors, John Mayberry looked after him. I was treated so well by Cliff, Joe, Mike Cameron, and the other veterans that it was worth everything they put me through.

Part of the rookie hazing was to carry the veterans' luggage through La Guardia Airport when we had road trips. I was pretty much the only rookie at one time, and Mike Cameron would have me get up in front of the bus and perform karaoke. Also there was the annual "Rookie Dress-Up Day," where they put me in an outfit called "Strawberry Shortcake." I wore a red miniskirt with a tank top, a big red wig, and high white boots as they paraded us through the airport. We flew to Atlanta that day, and they dropped us off about five blocks from the hotel, so that we had to walk the rest of the way. Of course, a lot people who drove past us honked their horns. That's something I can't wait to do to the younger players someday.

Looking Up to Derek Jeter

Playing in New York, I've had the opportunity to learn from the likes of Derek Jeter, who has been great to me since day one. Every time I get the chance to see him, he comes over and congratulates me or gives me a piece of advice. If there's one player who you're going to look up to as far as on-field ability, as far as leadership, and as far as the way he carries himself, it is Derek Jeter. He's a proven winner, a guy I have the utmost respect for and would pay good money to see play on a daily basis.

All I Need Is Detergent and a Band-Aid

I like making diving stops at third base, and I don't shy away from diving into the stands for a foul ball. If I get banged up but I make the play, it's worth it. Why not? Playing black-and-blue is how I earn my money. I've always played that way, and I don't mind cuts and bruises. My mother used to yell at me for getting my uniform dirty in Little League, and now the Mets' equipment manager, Charlie Samuels, yells at me for the same thing. I still like to go out there and get the uniform dirty playing hard, which is the right way to play.

SIX

THE SHORTSTOPS

ERNIE BANKS
Why I Wanted to Play Two

Why was I always so happy? That's just the way life is for me. I come
from a large family—I was the second child and first boy—and I was
just overjoyed doing things in life: in school, playing baseball and
football, all of that. And then I came to the Cubs, who played day
games, with the fans close to the field, and I was just overjoyed by that.
Wrigley Field and the baseball diamond was my whole life. It was
where I could make my own decisions on when to swing, when to run,
when to talk and not to talk—it was different when I went home! I had
a wife, and let's just say I couldn't wait to get to the park to be at ease
and in control of my life, to be friendly and socialize with people, and
to be competitive. I would get up at 7 A.M. and couldn't wait to get to
the ballpark. I'd be driving to the park on Lake Shore Drive singing
"Bring out those lazy, crazy days of summer." It was just so much fun
being there. Then after the game, I'd go home and change into
another person.

My whole game was built around being relaxed. I'd relax at the
plate, moving my fingers as if I were playing the piano. I wanted to hit
the ball somewhere and feel my body was *in* the ball. I know it sounds
unusual, but I wanted to feel myself taking a ride on the ball. At
Wrigley Field, I'd see the fans in the bleachers, and I'd want to hit a

baseball to a kid out there to give him a thrill. I'd always think of that when I came to the plate. When I did that, we were both happy.

My Business Model

When I was the first black Ford dealer in the country, Cubs owner P. K. Wrigley wanted to buy the first car from me. His hobby was fixing up cars. He asked for a station wagon, and I was overwhelmed by that gesture. We became connected, and I learned a lot about business and life from him. He really didn't like the media much, so when he came to games, he sat in the bleachers, and nobody knew he was there. I was told that in 1945, the Cubs were in the World Series and he came to the park with about $40,000 worth of tickets in his pocket, and they wouldn't let him in. Another usher recognized him and said to the guy who wouldn't let him in, "Don't you know who that is? That's Mr. Wrigley!" He was low key, and that's how I wanted to be in business. I say, *You have to get the dough and go and stay low like a pro.*

Leo and Me

My philosophy when someone didn't like me or resented me—as was the case with Leo Durocher, when he managed the Cubs beginning in 1966—was to kill them with kindness. So, I'd always sit beside Leo on the bench or in the airplane. When he looked around, he'd always see me. Leo didn't like to play me all the time, and one day in Palm Springs, I wasn't in the lineup. But I still came out early, and when I passed the dugout, I saw Leo sitting with his good friend Frank Sinatra. I started singing "Strangers in the Night," which was a popular song at the time, and Frank convinced Leo that he should play me. I hit two home runs, including the game winner.

One day, we were playing in New York. John Boccabella started at first base for us because Leo had announced he was the team's starter for the rest of the season, and I was on the bench. But John got hurt on a play at first base. Leo went out to see how he was, and meanwhile

I started warming up. Leo looked around for a replacement, and I was the only one warming up, so he put me in. And I hit a home run that game, too.

Leo's feelings toward me changed, and he made an apology to me at our camp in Arizona. I really respected him a lot, because late in my career, he really inspired me to play better, to reach inside and focus and concentrate. And I did and had over one hundred RBIs and played really well at forty-one years of age. It wasn't difficult for me to think the best of Leo. When you lit a fire on my heels and told me I wasn't playing well and put pressure on me, it made me play better. Leo was constantly on me in person and in the papers. I never asked him why. Later on that year, he got married and invited me to his wedding, and we became friendlier. Later on, I was asked to recruit players for an old-timers game in Denver, and I called Leo up to ask him to manage the team. Leo said, "I don't want to do it. I don't want the media around me . . ." I interrupted him and said, "Leo, I need you to manage." So, he came, and we won before a big crowd in Denver. So, we patched things up toward the end of my career.

My 500th Home Run

I had a slim build but was able to hit a lot of home runs because I had strong wrists and hands. As a kid, I made an effort to strengthen them. I used to squeeze balls, hit tennis balls off the wall, and play handball. I felt my hands and wrists were what gave me a slight edge. I could be fooled on a pitch, but my hands were always back, so I could come around at the right time. I ended my career in 1971 with 512 homers, which at the time was the sixth or seventh most in history.

91

I hit my 500th homer the year before at Wrigley Field off Pat Jarvis of the Atlanta Braves. That morning, my daughter kept telling me, "Dad, get this over with so we can get the media off of our backs!" I said, "OK, I'm going to do it today. It will be quick." So, I went to the park, and in the first inning, he threw me an inside fastball, and I hit it over the left-field fence. I didn't think it was going out, because I hit it on the line, very low. Rounding the bases, I felt happiness. I was thinking of all the fans who watch baseball and how it would bring them as much joy as it would bring me. It was a great thrill. I'm still proud to be part of the 500 Home Run Club. It's a great legacy for all of us. One thing it shows is stamina, because you have to play a long time to hit that many home runs.

I Didn't Play in a World Series, but . . .

I played nineteen seasons in the majors but never played in a World Series. Nineteen sixty-nine was my last chance to get into the post-season. I always thought about that after I retired. I'd dream about it, and when I walked down the street, I would say, "Gosh, why did that happen to me?" Then one day, all of a sudden I remembered that at the beginning of my career, the only thing I wanted to do was to get my kids an education. I had twin boys and a girl, and I wanted them all to go to college. And *that* was my World Series—just playing hard and saving money to send my kids to college so they could get a degree, to have a more prosperous life. I would tell them, "Listen, it's not the gold—home runs, the World Series—that counts, but the digging, the working hard and going after the gold. That's what matters in life." They'd look at me with wide eyes and say, "But Dad, you never worked a day in your life! You were saying, 'Let's *play* two.'" And I'd correct them, "I did work, so you could go to college. Long and hard."

BUCKY DENT
Realizing My Dream to Be a New York Yankee

92

Growing up in Florida, I watched New York Yankees games on TV. I became a huge Yankees fan and loved Mickey Mantle. But I didn't get the chance to go to any major-league games down there. In fact, the first major-league game I saw in person was in Milwaukee, and I was on the Chicago White Sox. You can imagine my excitement.

I met George Steinbrenner when I was a rookie playing for the White Sox. I went to a Bulls game, and the guy I went with said, "Do you know who's sitting in front of you?" I said I didn't, and he said, "That's George Steinbrenner, the owner of the Yankees. Do you want to meet him?" I said that I did, and he tapped him on the shoulder. He turned around and said to me, "I know who you are. I've been try-ing to get you!"

A few years later, he called to tell me he'd traded for me and I was a Yankee. I was thrilled. Getting traded to the Yankees was my dream. My only regret is that I didn't get a chance to play in the old Yankee Stadium. When I first played for the White Sox, the Yankees played two years at Shea Stadium while they renovated Yankee Stadium. But there was still a lot of Yankees tradition, and I loved the teams I was on. We had a great mixture of characters in those championship years—Catfish Hunter, Ron Guidry, Lou Piniella, Graig Nettles, Mickey Rivers, Sparky Lyle, Thurman Munson, Reggie Jackson, Chris Chambliss, Roy White, Willie Randolph.

Willie's first year with the Yankees was 1976, the year before I got there. He was a tremendous second baseman. People still ask if we talked a lot on the field in the six years we played together, and the answer is no. We just knew what each other would do, without hav-ing to discuss anything. We just flowed together. We got along great, but off the field we talked about other things than baseball. Sometimes it was blown up that there were players on those Yankees teams who didn't get along and there was dissension, but on the field, they played, and they were fun to play with. Even when we played in a World Series or against Boston in the one-game playoff in 1978, when it was more intense, Lou and Catfish were still getting on everybody, and players were still clowning around. I just loved playing in New York.   93

My Claim to Fame and Infamy

I think somebody reminds me of the homer I hit off Boston's Mike Torrez to give the Yankees the lead in the one-game playoff on October 2, 1978, about every thirty seconds. That's what it has seemed like during all the years since we beat the Red Sox. I do some work with a company in Boston and go back there all the time, and what is fascinating is that all the people there seem to know where they were when I homered. It was two great teams who were rivals coming down to a one-game playoff, and all these people know where they were and what happened.

Boston got off to a great start and played about .750 baseball well into the season. Meanwhile, we had some injuries. Catfish Hunter was hurt, Mickey Rivers was hurt, and I missed forty games after fouling a ball off in spring training and getting a blood clot. They were fourteen games ahead in late July, but not once did we give up. We felt we could catch them. It helped that there was a newspaper strike in New York, so nothing negative was being written about us. Also, Bob Lemon replaced Billy Martin as manager, and we had fewer distractions and no more controversy surrounding Billy and Reggie, Reggie and Thurman, and George Steinbrenner. Bob settled us down. He said, "You were champions last year; just go and play like them." So, we relaxed and just focused on playing baseball and winning. As we were getting all our players back, our goal became to pick up one game a week.

The big series that people forget was up in Boston in September after we had cut their lead to four games. We knew we needed to win at least three of the four games, and we blew them out in all four games in what became known as the "Boston Massacre." Then we beat them at home two out of three. Boston had to win its last six games to tie us at the end of the season, but we came from behind to win the playoff.

When we went to Boston, I was using Mickey Rivers's bat, his model. During batting practice, I cracked it right under the trademark, a hairline fracture that I couldn't really see. I fouled Torrez's first pitch off my foot. I moved away from the plate because my foot was killing me, and the batboy ran and told me I was using the cracked bat and handed me another one. I didn't think much about it, because my foot hurt.

Who knows if the ball would have gone anywhere if I hit it with a cracked bat. Torrez was pitching a great game and had gotten me to pop up twice—I had just missed putting good wood on the ball. We had wasted a few scoring opportunities, and now I came up with Chris Chambliss and Roy White on base in the seventh. The whole time I was in the on-deck circle, he didn't throw any warm-up pitches, so that was the first pitch he threw in a while. I just stepped up to the plate and hit the next pitch for a three-run home run. I was just trying to hit it hard, and I golfed it out of there. I didn't see the ball go out, because there was a shadow out there, and I didn't know until I rounded first base that the ball went into the net.

We still wouldn't have won the game, 5–4, if Lou Piniella didn't make two great plays in right field. Early on, Fred Lynn hooked a slider, and Lou caught it in the corner. Normally, he wouldn't have been playing Lynn to pull Guidry, but he didn't have his best stuff, so Lou moved over a couple of feet, which enabled him to make the catch. It was a crystal clear day, and it was very hard to see in the outfield. In the ninth inning, he stopped a ball he didn't even see from getting behind him and prevented Rick Burleson from going to third base. If he'd gone to third, the Sox then would have tied the game on Jim Rice's fly to center field. But it was an out, not a sacrifice fly. And we still weren't out of the woods, because they got men on first and third with Carl Yastrzemski up. He'd homered earlier against Guidry, and here was Goose Gossage throwing him a fastball right down the middle! I was standing out there at short, and I couldn't believe it! Fortunately, he just missed it and popped it up for the final out of what was the most intense, pressure-packed game I ever played in.

It doesn't bother me that people know me for only one thing despite my long career, because it was such a big moment. But there are other parts to my career that I really enjoyed and remember as much: playing in my first All-Star Game; being traded to the Yankees, who I always wanted to play for; the guys I played with; the thrill of being chosen MVP of the World Series that year when we beat the Dodgers. But of course the homer was a big moment for me, too. Every kid dreams about hitting a big homer in a big game, and it happened to me.

Ozzie Smith
Me Time

I ask kids today when they have any "me time." That's when you're alone and you go out and spend time throwing the ball against the steps or a wall, and catch it as it comes off at all the different angles. Growing up in Los Angeles, I did those things to develop my skills. Also, I used to throw the ball over the house and run to the other side to try to catch it. Just think about that: sitting down and throwing the ball over the roof and believing you are fast enough to get there before it comes down. I never got there, but ultimately it was that type of determination that made me the player I became. I wasn't a big guy, so I realized early on that for me to receive the same recognition, I'd have to work twice as hard.

My Gloves

When I was young, my first glove was a brown paper bag. Talk about creativity: I'd put the bag on my left hand, form a pocket in there, and roll it down on my hand. And I'd play with a tennis ball. That's how much I loved the game. Then when I was twelve or thirteen, when I was really getting into the game, I finally got a glove with a name on it. The glove had Stan Musial's name inscribed on it. It was the old six-finger, and I used that glove until the pocket wore out and it started to split. When I signed professionally with San Diego in 1977, I sent it to a leather shop to get it fixed, but I was told it wasn't worth the money it would cost to fix it. The old six-finger glove, which had been used primarily by outfielders, had been discontinued, but Rawlings ended up reintroducing it. And I would use the six-finger for the majority of my career. I changed my glove often, particularly in St. Louis. How often I did that depended on how hot it was in St. Louis

96

and how much I sweated during the hot summers, playing on that Astroturf. A glove can get waterlogged and be worthless, because it's all about feel. Sometimes I'd put on a glove and it didn't feel right. I didn't want my glove to be soft, because all I was basically doing as I caught a ball in the glove and moved it to my throwing hand was slowing the ball down and changing direction. It didn't stay in my glove long.

How I Avoided Collisions

I made a lot of catches running with my back to the infield yet was able to avoid collisions with outfielders. It wasn't because of luck. It was because of good communication. I covered so much ground that I told the outfielders that if we were both running after a ball and were not going to stop, "always remember to go to your right, because I'll be going to my right; if we do collide, the only thing that we'll hit will be our arms."

The Crowds Flipped for My Flips

When I was a kid, we lived across the street from a wood factory, and I learned how to do flips in a sawdust pit. We got these great big tire inner tubes, and two guys would hold down the ends, and that would be our springboard; or we'd take a plank and put it between two stacks of wood and use it as a diving board. From that point, it was just about having the nerve to turn your body in the air. It was those little, creative things we did as kids that helped us develop our personalities.

The two people who got me to do the flips on the field in the major leagues were my San Diego Padres teammate Gene Tenace and Andy Strasberg, who was the PR guy. It happened in 1978, when I finished second to Bob Horner in the Rookie of the Year voting but San Diego didn't have a very good year. Gene knew I could do flips and wanted me to do it for his girls sometime that year, but I was never able to do it until the final day of the season. That was Fan Appreci-

97

ation Day, when they had fifty thousand fans in the stands and the Chicken entertaining them, and they thought my doing a flip on the way to my position would add to the excitement. And it did. So, I was asked to do the flip again the following year on Opening Day. That's how it began, and I did it my entire career, with the Padres and Cardinals, and I always seemed to get a big reaction from the fans. Now when I look at the videos, I see that as I got older, I was getting lower and lower to the ground.

Whitey Herzog

After the 1981 season, the Cardinals wanted to trade their shortstop, Garry Templeton, to the Padres to acquire me. But I had a no-trade clause in my contract, which was unusual for a three-year player, and I wasn't sure I wanted to go to St. Louis. I remember when Whitey Herzog, the Cardinals' manager, came out to California and was sitting in my agent's living room. He told me, "Hey, if you come play for the St. Louis Cardinals, there is no reason we can't win it all." And he said, "Better than that, if you come play for us, we can agree to go to arbitration. You can submit whatever figure you want, we'll put in a figure, and whoever's figure is chosen, we'll shake hands and move on. And if you don't like it in St. Louis after one year, you can become a free agent." So, it was a no-brainer for me to come over. And sure enough, I loved playing in St. Louis, and we won the World Series in '82. I came back the following year, and when it came time to negotiate a contract, I went in, and Whitey and I talked numbers, and within ten minutes I walked out with a contract of about $1.1 million. It was the fastest contract I ever did.

98

We had great Cardinals teams, offensively and defensively, under Whitey Herzog. Everybody knew his role; we didn't have any players worrying about playing time, because Whitey utilized everyone. If there was anything you were unhappy about or unclear about, he'd tell you what he thought, because he was ruthlessly honest. We might not like what he said, but as players, having somebody telling you the truth is what you should want. If nothing else, it forced all of us to look in the mirror and ask, "Am I who I think I am?" He had just two rules: Be on time, and give 100 percent. So, I thought it was easy and fun to play for Whitey all those years.

CAL RIPKEN JR.
I Stubbornly Did My Job, and the Result Was "the Streak"

When I was a kid, Dad used to plow out the neighborhood. One day the tractor wouldn't start, so he used the crank to get it going. It slipped off the fitting and hit him in the head, opening up a big gash. He put an oily rag on it, and I took him back to the house. I had just gotten my driver's license, and I thought for sure I had to take him to the hospital. But he butterfly-bandaged it up and kind of cleaned it out, and then he went back out, started the tractor, and finished plowing out the neighborhood. He never did go to the hospital. When I tell this story, I go, "Can you imagine if I came in with a little turf toe or a hamstring pull or something like that and said I couldn't play?" Dad's expectation was much higher than that. When he started something that he thought needed to be done, he did it to the end.

People always described my dad as stubborn. When you describe someone as stubborn, people immediately think it's a negative characteristic, but I guess I changed the definition a little bit. When I think of Dad, I see it as a positive trait that lends itself to a sense of purpose. As long as your motives and intentions are right, then the stubbornness that it requires to get something done is a constructive thing. I know that for me to accomplish the consecutive-game streak, I had to be stubborn. I owe that to my dad.

In our family, if you approached the game in the honest, pure way Dad taught us, then you had to be strong and stand up when other people around you were weak. Dad always told me, "Your job is to be a baseball player. Even if you're tired, your job is to come to the ballpark and put yourself in the hands of a manager. The manager decides which members of your team have a chance to beat the other team

99

that day, and if the manager writes *you* in the lineup, then you try to respond as best you can." So, if you want to blame somebody for the streak, Baltimore managers Earl Weaver, Joe Altobelli, and Frank Robinson were the ones who wrote my name in the lineup. I just kept playing for 2,632 straight games. I played virtually free of serious injuries. I did have a lot of nagging injuries that somehow I could play through. It ended with back surgery, and now there are days that if I'm out playing too long or fly from coast to coast, I start to flare up, but I still am well enough to play basketball pretty regularly. And there's less stress in my life than when I felt I had to go out there and play every day. Overall, there are no bad effects from the streak.

2,632 Games and 22 Minutes

I broke Lou Gehrig's consecutive-game record on September 5, 1995, in the fifth inning, when our game against Toronto became official. And the Baltimore fans kept clapping. I was saying, "OK, thank you," and I was telling myself, "Let's get the game going, because this is unfair to the other players on the team; they've got to sit and watch." But Rafael Palmeiro and Bobby Bonilla were pushing me down the line and saying, "Look, we're not going to get this game started unless you run around the ballpark."

So, I started running and kept thinking, "Well, let me get this out of the way." And I ran all the way around the ballpark, and toward the end I said, "You know, I could care less about the game. This is such a wonderful moment." What happened is that there was an outpouring of love in my direction from the fifty thousand fans in the stadium. I started to shake hands, and it suddenly became very personal. I started recognizing people's faces, and I knew their names. And I ended up right in front of my family, celebrating with my wife, Kelly, and kids, Rachel and Ryan. Recently, I saw all of this on TV while flipping through stations. My kids were only six and two and looked like babies. It's been more than ten years since that happened, and my daughter remembers some of it; my boy, not too much. Whenever I see the tape of us standing there together, it is a great reminder of a wonderful celebration.

My Part in Bringing the Fans Back to Baseball

After the strike in 1994, I think a lot of fans were looking for something good in baseball. That's why they responded so much to my streak. There's this warm feeling that comes over us when we think of baseball years ago. We love to link the different time frames in baseball history through statistical analysis and those sorts of things. When my streak came along, it started to bring Lou Gehrig's accomplishments back into focus. So when fans heard about Gehrig, they got that warm feeling about baseball "when it was a game," so to speak. The fans just naturally came back to baseball in 1995. I don't think it was about me personally. The way it all unfolded was more of a celebration of baseball, and I happened to be in the right place at the right time.

Changing Positions

I was signed as a shortstop-pitcher. Luckily enough, I was given the choice to go into the draft as either. I chose to play every day, and I gave up pitching. It's kind of ironic that in the minors, I began as a shortstop, made a lot of errors, and, when there was an injury, moved to third. In my developmental phase, third was a lot easier, and I started to really blossom as a hitter, so they left me there. They developed me as a third baseman, and when I got to the big leagues, I played third for a while. I actually started the consecutive-game streak at third base. Then Earl Weaver just decided he was going to put me over at shortstop, and I played there for fifteen years. My fielding improved, and the numbers of errors decreased to the point I was making fewer than ten a year. In one year, I set the record with only three errors.

101

Going to third base late in my career was not foreign to me, because I'd played there early in my career. I was familiar with the position, but after you've done something else for fifteen years and go back, you have to rethink it. That's because you train your mind on your responsibilities at shortstop, and it becomes second nature to you, and then when you go to another position, you're out of balance, because no position is like shortstop. You start to think, "OK, what is my job?" You sometimes forget what your role is.

My Eventful Final All-Star Game

I played my final All-Star Game in 2001, at Safeco Field, in Seattle. Tony Gwynn and I were honored that night, and the American League won 4–1. I hit way down in the order, deservingly so at that point, the last year of my career. Randy Johnson pitched the first two innings for the National League, and with two outs in the second inning I was on deck. It was twilight and hard to see, and Randy was throwing hard. I secretly rooted against Edgar Martinez, hoping he'd make an out, so I'd face another pitcher in the third inning—anybody but Randy. I came up in the third inning and, in my first at-bat in that ballpark, homered off of Chan Ho Park, on a ninety-five-mile-an-hour fastball, a good pitch to hit. Some people think he grooved it, but I don't know how you can say somebody grooved a ninety-five-mile-an-hour fastball.

I think people less remember my home run than when Alex Rodriguez, the American League's starting shortstop, suddenly started pushing me from third base to shortstop in the first inning. Alex goes, "Come on, go back and play shortstop one last time." And I said, "Are you crazy?" I don't like to be surprised, and it felt that it had been a long time since I had played short. Then I realized that our manager, Joe Torre, was in on it and everybody else was in on it. I felt like the dumbest person on the planet, because I think everybody but me knew they were going to ceremoniously put me over at short. I thought, "OK, now I'm forced to do this." So, I reluctantly went back over there. Now I'm on the stage, and I don't want to be embarrassed; I don't want to make mistakes. And it was kind of funny, because I started to feel the juices flowing, and everything went fine.

ALEX RODRIGUEZ
The Team and Player I Admired Most as a Kid

Growing up in south Florida, I watched New York Mets games on WOR. I'd feel Tim McCarver and Ralph Kiner were my teachers. I'd blast the volume, and my mom would always say, "Oh, turn that down! Turn that down!" And then she said, "Is it over yet?" And I said, "No, we have 'Kiner's Korner' coming up next," and I'd watch Ralph interview the star of the game. It was awesome. The Mets had great teams in the '80s, and I just loved them. My favorite player was Keith Hernandez. He was the best. Keith was always a great contact hitter and very good in the clutch. One year, he had twenty-four game-winning RBIs, when that was an official stat. But I think the element that made him very special was his leadership and presence on the field. He was like a pitching coach on the field. I'd never seen that before or since. He was fearless, and you don't have that type of player anymore. He's the reason I used to wear number 17.

It Was Time to Leave Seattle

I really, really enjoyed my time in Seattle. I spent part of seven years there under the tutelage of a guy who I consider like a father figure, Lou Piniella. Lou is a special person and a Hall of Fame manager if you think about what he brings to the table every day. Lou brings that Billy Martin–type attitude. "If you don't get it done, I'm going to choke you." And that was great. I loved it. It was exciting playing for Lou and with all the good young players in Seattle, despite not attracting many fans to the Kingdome those first few years.

In 1995, the dramatic divisional series between the Yankees and the Mariners gave me a little taste of what the postseason could be like, but there was so much at risk. If we didn't win that year, if we didn't make it to postseason, there was talk that we were going to St. Pete or even Nashville. And management kind of put that pressure on us, and we made up, I think, ten games in September to beat the Angels and win the division and reach the postseason. Then beating the Yankees in the division series was like being in a movie. We had to beat the greatest team—David against Goliath; there's no way we can beat 'em. On top of that, we're down 2–0, and how do we beat these guys? And somehow, Edgar Martinez hit that double off McDowell, and Griffey Jr. scored that winning run. That saved baseball in Seattle, no question. And they have that beautiful stadium in Safeco Field, and it's just a great home for baseball. They love their baseball up there in the Northwest.

I always point out that I got to Seattle as a seventeen-year-old boy and left there as a twenty-four-year-old man when my time was due. I knew that Lou was on his way out and that Edgar, Jay Buhner, and some of the veteran players were getting older. I said, "You know what? It's my time to move on." Going back was a lot tougher, because the fans hadn't forgiven me for going to Texas. I'd never really been greeted with that type of boos before. I mean, they were very angry boos. It was weird. You know the difference between playful, Hey-we-want-to-beat-you boos and those We-want-to-kill-you boos. The fans were very mad. But baseball's a business, and I needed to move on.

My Tribute to Cal Ripken Jr.

At the beginning of the 2001 All-Star Game, we took the field. I was supposed to play short, and Cal Ripken was supposed to play third, but this was going to be Cal's last All-Star Game, so with Joe Torre's permission, I pushed him out to short, his old position. That was a memorable moment for me. It's been the nicest moment of my career because it was a wonderful tribute to perhaps the greatest shortstop of all time and a great ambassador of our game. I called Joe up about five days prior to the game, and I said, "Joe, I have an idea. What about if the whole world gets to see Cal play shortstop one more time in the All-Star Game?" And he said, "Alex, that's a great idea. Let me run it through central New York baseball here, and I'll give you a call back." Joe calls me back two days later and says, "We're on board; keep it

104

under your hat. I'm going to let the right people know." I'm sure they let Tim and Joe Buck and everyone know.

When I went over to Cal, he said, "Get out of my territory. What are you doing? You're messing up my dirt." I said, "You gotta go to shortstop." He said, "I'm not going over there; there's no way." I said, "Look at the skipper," and Joe's telling him, "Hey, get over there. Get over there." So, then he tells Clemens, "Hey, Rocket, strike everyone out. I haven't been here in a long time." And Cal hits a home run, and it was like *The Natural*. I just couldn't believe he hit that ball out.

DEREK JETER
I Was the Second-Best Shortstop in My Family

I was brought up in Kalamazoo, Michigan. Our family time was spent at the baseball field. We lived behind my high school, which had a baseball field and a softball field, and we'd go out there—my parents, my sister, and myself. We'd take turns hitting a baseball, and then we'd get out the softball, and we played Wiffle ball. My sister, Sharlee, used to run circles around me. It's the truth. I'm not lying to you. She's the best shortstop in the family. Now, my dad will tell you he's the best, but he couldn't hit too well. My sister could hit. It was tough on her growing up, because anytime she played a sport like softball, they wanted to compare her with me, which wasn't fair. I'm so proud of her because she worked very hard and has been very successful at everything she has ever done. But I remember that Sharlee was a better athlete than me—by far.

105

Special Parents

I'm a little biased, obviously, but I think I have the best parents in the world. They were so supportive of me when I was younger. So many kids have dreams, and my dream was to play shortstop for the New

York Yankees, and I think a lot of parents would discourage that or maybe even laugh at their kids for having such a goal. But they said I could do whatever I wanted to do as long as I remained positive and worked hard. They said, "Well, it's not easy; it's going to be tough for you growing up. You're not going to be compared only with people in Kalamazoo, Michigan, but you're going to play against people from all around the world." So, they were very supportive but honest about my chances.

I worked hard, and I achieved my goal and my dream of playing shortstop for the Yankees. The draft is like a crapshoot, so how amazing it was to be a Yankees fan being selected as the sixth pick by the Yankees in the 1992 draft. Actually, I was supposed to go fifth to Cincinnati, and if that happened, I'd have been stuck behind Barry Larkin. So, I was real fortunate, not only because the Yankees drafted me, but also because Cincinnati overlooked me.

My parents and I were very close while I was growing up, but I think we've grown even closer as I've gotten older, as it is with my sister, Sharlee, and them. They treat us like adults now, but they're still our parents, and they're going to tell us what they feel is right and wrong. And that's good to know. They are at a lot of games and get a lot of TV time now, and they still get on me. If I'm struggling at the plate, my mom will be in the stands yelling at me. It's good to have people that you can go to for honest advice, because a lot of times when you're in a situation where people look up to you, they're only going to tell you what you want to hear. But my parents don't care; they'll tell me the truth. They've been honest with me ever since day one when I told them I wanted to play for the Yankees.

My Dad: Tino Martinez's Batting Guru

Every time Tino Martinez struggled and wasn't hitting as many home runs as he'd like, he talked to my dad and would hit a home run. One night before a game, I called home, and I said, "Tino, you need to talk to my dad." So, he got on the phone, and sure enough, he hit a home run. I don't know what my problem is: I talk to my dad every day, but Tino's hitting all the homers.

The Game I Pretended to Be Nomar

I got booed at the '99 All-Star Game, but I expected it because it was played in Boston. Nomar Garciaparra played shortstop for us the first three innings, and then Joe Torre let him take the field in the fourth inning. He thought that if I went out there when Nomar was coming out, the cheers would outweigh the boos, and, you know, they did for a minute. But once he got in the dugout, the boos picked up a little bit. They wanted to see Nomar instead of me, so I thought I'd give them a little taste of Nomar by imitating his routine when I came to the plate. The fans appreciated it, but it didn't work. I struck out, so I did something wrong.

Meeting My Heroes

Before the 1999 All-Star Game, at Fenway Park, the Players of the Century were introduced, and Ted Williams was rolled out in a wheelchair, and all the current and former players surrounded him and mingled. It was something special and extremely emotional. To be there with all those great players at the same time—I got the chills. I was a little bit afraid to try to even speak to anyone, because I was just in awe.

The same thing happened to us one year during the World Series, when we had all those great players come out there, and we were milling about. I had the opportunity to meet Hank Aaron. He actually approached me. He said that he had wanted to meet me! And I was speechless. I said, "You're Hank Aaron; you want to meet me?" I said, "I grew up watching videos of you, and you're a big idol of mine." I was overwhelmed, to say the least. Forget that I was a successful major leaguer playing in the World Series—I was just like any kid meeting his hero.

SEVEN

The Left Fielders

Stan Musial
Not Bad for an Ex-Pitcher

I was a good hitter in high school in Donora, Pennsylvania. I think I batted .400 or .500. But our coach or somebody else saw me as a pitcher, not a hitter. I didn't like to pitch, because I could always hit, but in high school if you have the best arm, they always make you the pitcher. The Cardinals signed me as a pitcher, and I pitched a few years in the minors. One year, I had a 6–6 record, and the next year, I had a 9–2 record. Then I pitched a full season and went 18–5. I was pretty good, but I was wild and walked a lot of guys.

I didn't have confidence when pitching, and that made it tough. But I could always hit, and here's what happened. One day when I wasn't pitching, I was playing in the outfield, and I dove for a ball and drove my left shoulder into the ground and hurt it. In those days, the Cardinals had so many players in their system that they didn't bother sending anyone to a doctor. The next spring, the pitchers went to the Cardinals' camp in Georgia before the hitters. Burt Shotten, who would later manage the Dodgers but was in the Cardinals' system then, said, "Is your arm bothering you, Stan?" I said, "Yeah, my arm is really bothering me. I hurt it the last week of last season." We had an intrasquad game, and Branch Rickey was watching when I hit a ball so far that he and Shotten decided to step it off. It went about 450 feet. So, they said, "From now on, you're not going to be a pitcher."

They sent me to Springfield, Missouri, Class C, and I was there three months. I led the league in hitting; I was hitting home runs; I was doing everything. Next I was shipped to Rochester, New York, Triple-A, for three months. I led that league in hitting, too. After our season was over, the Cardinals called me up. In those days, to be able to go from Class C to Triple-A to the majors in one season was remarkable. Harry Walker, my good friend, thought that was one of my greatest accomplishments. In my two weeks with St. Louis, I did very well. I hit .456. Not bad for an ex-pitcher.

I Switched from Outfield to First Base Without Realizing It

My signature position was left field, but a lot of people fail to realize that I played all three outfield positions, including almost three hundred games in center field. They forget that early in my career, I had great speed and was a good outfielder. I loved playing the outfield and expected to stay out there, but in 1946 our highly touted rookie first baseman, Dick Sisler, had trouble getting started. So, one day our manager, Eddie Dyer, came to me and said, "Why don't you take over at first base for a few days, until we get Sisler squared away." We went on to win the world championship, and would you believe that I moved back and forth between first and the outfield for the rest of my career?

110   I didn't like playing first base. First of all, it's a lot of work, whereas in the outfield, if the ball is hit to someone else, all you do is watch. At first base, you're jumping off on every pitch. You're making plays; you're backing up plays; you're charging bunts; you're taking throws— you're in on every play, more or less. But the main reason I didn't like playing first is I didn't like ground balls. They got to me a lot quicker at first than they did when I was in the outfield.

The Inside Pitch

For most of my career, we played without helmets. But we were knocked down and hit by pitches and thought nothing of it. It was part of the game. We understood that from a psychological standpoint, a pitcher had to throw inside, because if the batter knew you were going to pitch away every time, he'd have a great advantage. That's what goes on in today's game.

When he was managing the Dodgers and Giants, Leo Durocher used to yell to his pitcher from the dugout, "Stick it in his ear!" All the time. But it didn't bother me. The only time I got mad was when we were playing the Dodgers in a doubleheader, and in the first game, they started a pitcher named Ben Wade. I never hit singles off of Wade. It was always a double, triple, or home run. So, the first three pitches, he knocked me down. After the third one, I charged the mound for the only time in my career. I didn't know what I was going to do once I got out there, but, of course, they stopped me before I reached him. Mort Cooper was pitching for us, and he told me, "Stan, don't worry about anything. When Wade comes up, I'll let him have it." He sure did. He hit him right in the back of the neck.

My Crouch

My stance was very unusual, but it was very comfortable. It came about because I wanted to be a .300 hitter. I started a crouch to shorten my strike zone, because I usually punched the ball the opposite way, to left and left center, rather than pulling it. Although it was unorthodox, I always took a good level swing. The secret to good hitting is to take a good level swing and hit strikes. I had a good knowledge of the strike zone, and I always stood in the same position. That low crouch of mine really helped me. Naturally, I loved the low pitch. Most left-handed hitters like the low ball, and that gives us an advantage, because most pitchers try to keep that ball down. I was a low-ball hitter and a highball drinker.

111

My Most Unusual Record

I ended my twenty-one-year career with 3,630 hits, which remained the National League record until Pete Rose broke it more than twenty years later. What people find strange is that I got 1,815 hits at home and 1,815 hits on the road. The remarkable thing is that to even it out, I had to get my last two hits in my final game in St. Louis, against the Reds' Jim Maloney, who was a flamethrower. Warren Giles, the president of the National League, was there, and they wanted me to take the first pitch to get that ball. That didn't bother me, and I got a base hit, and then I got another base hit. And the odd thing about those two base hits is that I got them past Pete Rose, who was playing second base. He dove both times, and the balls went under his glove. Pete got three hits that day, so on the last day that I played, he was gaining on me.

Ralph Kiner
Meeting Babe Ruth

Babe Ruth was my idol when I was growing up in California, although he played on the other side of the country. He was the greatest athlete in America at the time, and you can't imagine the stature he had. I don't think anyone in the history of sports has been bigger, even Muhammad Ali. I got my only chance to meet Ruth when I was seventeen and still in high school. He was making *Pride of the Yankees*, the great Gary Cooper movie about Lou Gehrig. Babe Herman, who had been an outstanding player for Brooklyn and once hit .393, was trying to sign me for the Hollywood Stars, of the Pacific Coast League. He took me to Wrigley Field in L.A., which was serving as Yankee Stadium in the movie, and Babe Herman introduced me to the other Babe, George Herman Ruth. Ruth was wearing Yankees pinstripes with number 3 on his back. He had been out of baseball for a while and was heavy, but it was a thrill meeting him. He was still bigger than life. He called me "Kid," as he did everyone, and we made small talk about baseball, and he wished me luck.

112

That was the only time I ever met Ruth, and I'm sure he forgot about our meeting immediately. But after I hit fifty-one home runs in 1947, a year before he died, Ruth told the press, "That kid in Pittsburgh might break my homer record." That was extremely flattering, especially since I didn't think he knew who I was. During my career, I told people I didn't want to hit more than sixty homers and break Ruth's famous record. But in truth, I tried. The most I ever hit was fifty-four homers in 1949. Like a lot of others, I couldn't catch him.

Ted Williams Robbed Me of a Hit, with Dire Consequences

In the first inning of the 1950 All-Star Game in Chicago's Comiskey Park, I hit a long fly that Ted Williams made a nice catch on before running into the wall. He shook his arm afterward and stayed in the game nine innings. It was a great game that people may remember because of my home run off Art Houtteman that tied the game in the ninth inning—having never played in a World Series, that was my biggest thrill as a player—and Red Schoendienst's game-winning homer in the fourteenth inning. But Ted Williams would remember it because he cracked his elbow on that play and missed the rest of the season. Ted would play through 1960, but he told me that he never was the same after that play. He'd bat .388 one season and win two batting titles, yet he said he wasn't the hitter he had been. One time, I heard Howard Cosell talking about how Jackie Robinson hit that line drive on which Williams was injured. I said, "Oh, no, Howard, not that one—that's mine."

113

What's a Little Death Threat?

In 1952, I received a death threat. I showed the letter to a great Pittsburgh reporter named Les Peterman, who used to ghostwrite a column of mine called "Kiner's Liners." The letter went into detail about how I should place money underneath the seat of a cab, but I told Les

I thought the guy was a nut and didn't take it seriously. He took it seriously and contacted Branch Rickey, the Pirates' GM, who contacted the FBI. So, an agent who was my size put on my clothes and took my place in the cab and went through the whole operation, including leaving what was supposed to be a package containing $4,000 and inserting a homing device. But nothing happened.

This took place around July 4, and we played a doubleheader. Firecrackers were going off in the stands, and everybody thought someone was shooting a rifle. The players knew someone had threatened to kill me, and they wouldn't sit near me on the bench. After the doubleheader, I'm running off the field from left field, and George "Catfish" Metkovich, who was quite a character, was running off from center. He said, "I'm sure glad this day's over." I said, "Gee, thanks at lot for worrying about me." He said, "I wasn't worried about you; I was worried about me." I said, "What do you mean?" He said, "You wear number 4, and I wear number 44. What if that guy had double vision?" It turned out to be the visiting team's batboy, who needed the money to pay off his bookie. Rickey, a "wonderful" guy, made a passionate plea on his behalf, and he got off.

There Was One Man I Didn't Impress

In 1952, I hit thirty-seven home runs, to lead the National League, but the Pirates lost a record 112 games, because most of the players were what we called "Rickey Dinks," young guys who Branch Rickey paid the bare minimum. I was making $90,000 a year, the most in the league, and would have been satisfied to get the same amount in 1953. Instead Rickey offered me a 25 percent cut, the maximum allowable cut. Naturally, I held out. This went on for quite a while, and finally he came out to Palm Springs, where I lived in the off-season. He showed me my stats and said I didn't do this or that. I said, "Mr. Rickey, I didn't get any good pitches to hit but led the league in homers for the seventh straight year!" He said, "Son." I said, "Yes, sir?" He asked, "Where did we finish?" I said, "We finished last." He

114

said, "We can finish last without you." So, it was obvious that I was going to have to take the cut. The next year, he traded me.

Ty Cobb's Peculiar Letter

Ty Cobb was featured in an article for *Life* magazine in which he said that of current players, only Stan Musial and Phil Rizzuto could have played in his era, and that the rest of us didn't know what baseball was all about. When reporters asked me about his comments, I said that I didn't agree with him at all. So Cobb sent me a handwritten letter. He didn't begin it "Dear Ralph" or "Dear Mr. Kiner," but "Dear Kiner." He wrote that he'd been misquoted by the ghostwriter. But rather than deny what he supposedly said, he said it again, writing me that the players of his era were much better. And he didn't add me to the short list of current players he admired. I supposed he was trying to make a backhanded apology in his own way, but I didn't believe he had been misquoted.

I Date Elizabeth Taylor

When Bing Crosby was the minority owner of the Pirates, I got to play golf with him and a lot of other celebrities when I went home to California. One day in 1949, Bing asked me if I wanted to escort Elizabeth Taylor to the premiere of *Twelve O'Clock High*, with Gregory Peck. I said, "Sure!" So, I picked her up at her house that night in a Cadillac, which, as you know, is what home-run hitters drive, and we drove to Graumann's Chinese Theater in Hollywood. It was a star-studded premiere, but everyone was already inside, because we were late. So, we just dropped off the car with the valet in front of the theater and rushed in to see the movie.

Elizabeth was a sweet girl, probably only about eighteen at the time, and we were having a good time. When the movie ended, we came out, and there were many big stars outside waiting for their cars

115

to be announced. I told the valet announcing the arrival of the cars to ask for my Cadillac. We waited and waited, while everyone else drove away in their cars. I got impatient and went up to the guy again and demanded my car. He said to me, "Maybe your chauffeur fell asleep." I said, "I don't have a chauffeur." He pointed down the street to a huge parking lot. So, Elizabeth Taylor, who wore a fur coat and high heels, and I walked down the street till we got to the lot and then spent about half an hour searching for my car. She was a good sport about it, but I'm sure it wasn't what she expected on our date. I took her home and was too embarrassed to ever ask her out again.

DON BAYLOR
The Most Exciting Game I Ever Played In

No game I ever played in was as dramatic as Game 5 of the 1986 ALCS. How intense was it? The following year, the home-plate umpire, Rocky Roe, told me that about a month after that game, he was driving along thinking about it and had to pull off the road in a cold sweat; he couldn't drive again until he stopped shaking.

The Angels were up three games to one, so if we didn't beat them, we'd go home. Boston had such a splendid year as a team. Many players had great years; we overcame a lot of things. Over the years, the Red Sox had the reputation of being "twenty-five players, twenty-five cabs," but that year, everyone was together, thinking the same things. That day we thought about so many different things about the season. We're down to our last three outs in the top of the ninth inning, trailing 5–2. Mike Witt was still pitching because our only guy who was getting to him was Rich Gedman. I remember the fever pitch that was in the ballpark that afternoon when it seemed like the home team would win the pennant. I'd played with the Angels, and I'd never experienced anything quite like it. It was jarring just to see our dugout overrun with the California Highway Patrol. They were ready to hit the field after three outs when the fans started to cel-

116

ebrate. I looked over at the Angels dugout at Gene Mauch, who had never won a pennant, and there was Reggie Jackson next to their coach Jimmie Reese. And I looked up into the booth and saw Angels owner Gene Autry, who was anticipating his first American League championship.

There were a lot of things going through my mind that inning. What I try to tell guys is if it's your last at-bat, make sure it's a quality at-bat. So, guys, pitch in one more time, and see if we can do it. Bill Buckner led off with a single, and with one out, I hit a homer to left off Witt. That made the score 5–4, but after Dwight Evans popped up, we were down to one out. Gedman was the batter, and he had homered earlier, so Mauch took out Witt and brought in Gary Lucas. He threw one pitch and hit Gedman, who was the tying run. Then Lucas is out of the game, and Mauch brought in Donnie Moore to face Dave Henderson.

I remember seeing Moore's 2-2 pitch. It was a split-finger that was shoe-top high, a real good pitch. But Henderson went down and got it and homered to give us a 6–5 lead. For the moment at least, the celebration was off. The crowd was completely stunned.

But California tied the game in the bottom of the ninth and then had the bases loaded with one out. So again the crowd anticipated a victory. But Steve Crawford jammed Doug DeCinces, and he popped out to right, and Bobby Grich hit the ball back to Crawford, and we got out of that inning and went to extra innings. It was completely nerve-racking. In the top of the eleventh, I got hit by a pitch, went to third, and scored the winning run on Henderson's sac fly.

After the game, I looked at all the Red Sox's wives, and their mascara was running everywhere, and their corsages were dead. And the players were just as drained. But we knew one thing: once we survived that game, we were going to win Games 6 and 7. We had no doubt about that. There was no doubt in our minds. On the flight back to Boston, I talked to our scheduled starting pitchers, Oil Can Boyd and Roger Clemens, and they were confident. We just felt we would win. And we did, by large margins. It's an amazing memory.

117

The 1986 World Title Slipped Away

My wife still can't watch the clip of Mookie Wilson's grounder getting past Bill Buckner, and Ray Knight scoring the winning run for the Mets in Game 6 of the 1986 World Series. All the stars were lined up just right for them. In the bottom of the tenth, I was standing on the top step of Boston's dugout next to Tom Seaver, who was on our team that year but was on the disabled list. We were ready to run out and celebrate. I still recall that for a brief moment, there was a flash on the scoreboard that said "Congratulations" to the Red Sox for winning the championship. That was a bad omen that should have let us know right then that things would go wrong.

We had a two-run lead with two outs and nobody on base, but you have to get that twenty-seventh out, which we never did. You could truly *feel* the depression in the locker room after the loss. However, we felt our club would rally back and win Game 7 because we had come from three runs down in the ninth inning to win Game 5 of the ALCS and won the next two games, and had come so far to get to that point. We took a three-run lead in that game and let it slip away, too, but give credit to the Mets. They were a no-die bunch of guys, too, and they took advantage of breaks and got a lot of 0-2 hits when it counted. Ray Knight, Gary Carter—that whole group of guys wouldn't die. So many things happened on the field and behind the scenes that we'd never know about if Buckner had caught that grounder.

We Felt We Let Ted Williams Down

The Red Sox's slogan was always "Thirty-nine and drizzling," an answer to the question, "How's the weather?" After flying back to Boston after losing Game 7 of the 1986 World Series, I understood what that slogan meant, because it was cold and drizzling as we rode the bus back to Fenway Park. There were about fifty fans braving the weather to wait for us. I remembered the great sportswriter Dick Young writing, "Red Sox fans were put on this earth to suffer."

Ted Williams was on the bus with the team, and he was very disappointed, and when he got off the bus, he didn't want any fanfare. He pulled his jacket over his head and strolled away. He didn't want to be bothered. It really hurt me to see one of my all-time favorite ballplayers so upset that we didn't bring a championship to Boston. He tried himself but didn't have a good World Series in 1946, and he really thought our team would be the one to win the World Series forty years later. To see Ted in that state really added to our disappointment.

EIGHT

THE CENTER FIELDERS

LARRY DOBY
I Was Blessed to Have the Support of Bill Veeck

I never met anyone like Bill Veeck. I met him July 5, 1947, when I walked into his office to sign a contract to play with Cleveland. Right away I felt comfortable, because when I addressed him as Mr. Veeck, he said, "You call me Bill, and I'll call you Lawrence." His next statement was, "We're in this together." Here's a person I didn't know saying that to me. I didn't really know what I was involved in, becoming the first Afro-American to play in the American League. On Veeck's desk was a thick notebook full of information about me dating back to the day I was born in Camden, South Carolina, till I got off the train. It had the good stuff I'd done and the bad stuff. Thank God, there weren't too many bad things. After we went through the notebook, he said, "Now you have to go out and perform under difficult circumstances. Do you think that you can?"

I said, "Sure, baseball is baseball." I was twenty-two, and all I was thinking about was playing baseball, which I'd done all my life, in high school, college, semipro, and the Negro Leagues with the Newark Eagles. But I'd never given a thought to the history I was going to be part of. I'd learn what it meant over the years. To have Veeck with me most of the time to give me the courage and help me adjust to the different situations was a blessing. I lost my father when I was eight years old, and I have said many times that I would have liked my father to be the same kind of man Bill Veeck was.

Not only was Veeck the first owner to integrate the American League, but also, from a creative standpoint, he was ahead of his time. He was the first to have promotions at the ballpark, including the first funeral for a World Series flag. We won the Series in 1948, and we expected to win it again in 1949. But we finished second, so on Opening Day in 1950, he placed the '49 Series flag in a casket and had a hearse take it out to center field, where at the end of the ceremony, the casket containing the flag was buried.

My Troubled Teammates

Although I was five years younger than Jackie Robinson when we broke the color barrier in 1947, I don't think I had a harder time adjusting to life in the big leagues. I have often said it was harder on the Cleveland players who had never before associated with an Afro-American before. I was fortunate to grow up in a mixed neighborhood in Paterson, New Jersey. I played baseball, basketball, and football at Eastside High and experienced being the only Afro-American on the teams. So, I had some knowledge of the situation. I had more experience with the situation than the white players on the Indians, so I wanted to give them the benefit of the doubt.

I'm not a person to say that whatever is inside a person, I'm going to get it out. But by associating with each other, we could learn from each other. They could see that what they heard about us having tails wasn't true, because they saw me in the shower and I didn't have a tail. So, they learned that lesson. It was assumed that the Southerners were going to be the toughest on me, but sometimes I didn't buy it, because those Southerners who had Afro-Americans working in the fields or in their houses had to know something about us. Northerners might not know anything at all, because they never came into contact with Afro-Americans. Some of the Southern guys who didn't welcome me when

I came to Cleveland, and had racial prejudice, got to know and respect me over the years.

Three players did greet me when I arrived, and I will never forget them: Bob Lemon, Jim Hegan, and Joe Gordon. On my first day, I was given a locker with the other players, and some guys shook my hand, and some refused to do so. But the most embarrassing thing I had in baseball was that when we took the field and players paired off, I had nobody to warm up with. And Gordon, who had come over from the Yankees in the trade for Allie Reynolds, warmed up with me the entire 1947 season. I always thought of him as being a really good person. He, Hegan, and Lemon were the greatest people in the world.

How Good Were the Negro Leagues?

Some people doubted that Jackie Robinson and I had the talent to play in the major leagues, because they'd never seen the Negro Leagues. Talent-wise, the Negro Leagues were equal to the major leagues. The only difference between the Newark team that beat the Kansas City Monarchs for the 1946 Negro Leagues World Series and the 1948 Cleveland team that beat the Boston Braves in the major-league World Series is that we had nineteen players on the Eagles and we had twenty-five players on the Indians. If Hall of Famer Leon Day would pitch for us the first game of a doubleheader, he'd probably play in the outfield the second game, because we didn't have enough play-ers coming off the bench. That wouldn't happen on Cleveland.

The One and Only Satchel Paige

In 1946, the Newark Eagles played the Kansas City Monarchs in the Negro Leagues World Series. They had Satchel Paige and Hank Thompson and were managed by Buck O'Neil. We beat Satch 3–2 and 2–1, which meant we did a pretty good job, and won the Series.

Everybody really admired him, including me. He had long, lean fingers and threw from the top, from the side, from underneath—all with great control.

Satch was so famous that he could pick up $1,000 every time he pitched during the off-season. Sometimes he would pitch in three innings in three cities in one day—maybe Newark, Philadelphia, and Washington—and pick up $3,000. He needed that money to afford his private plane and chauffeur-driven Cadillac.

In 1948, Satch tried out for the Indians. Bill Veeck was good friends with Abe Sapperstein, the owner of the Harlem Globetrotters, and Abe brought Satch to the ballpark. I was there with Bill and our catcher Jim Hegan. Satch goes into his pocket and takes out a stick off gum. He opens the wrapper, puts the gum in his mouth, and lays the wrapper on home plate in front of Hegan, and he goes to the mound and throws a pitch that split it right down the middle. Veeck signed Satch, and he helped us win the pennant and draw huge crowds. His "hesitation" pitch, where he dropped his foot but held on to the ball, was so effective in throwing off the timing of batters that they outlawed it.

Sometimes you wanted to be like Satch because of his nature—to him, every day was a beautiful day. We were playing in New York one afternoon, and when I woke up, it was raining really hard. But I went to the park from Paterson, and the rain stopped, and we were able to play. In about the seventh or eighth inning, Lou Boudreau signaled for Satch to warm up. Mel Harder, the pitching coach, signaled back that Satch couldn't warm up. In fact, he wasn't even there. At the meeting the next day, they asked Satch what happened, and he said, "I woke up, looked out the window and saw it was raining, and went back to sleep."

On the road, we'd room together. After a day game, he'd go fishing and would come back to the room at night and cook his favorite dish, catfish, on a little electric stove he carried around with him. The odor in the room was unbearable, but he'd eat his fish and have his favorite drink, a sweet sherry. People always asked me how old he was, but I didn't know, because he'd never say. If I asked him his age, he'd say, "Larry, how old do you think I am?" If I said forty, he'd say, "Then I'm forty." If I said fifty, he'd say, "Then I'm fifty." He'd do that with every-one. He was quite a character.

I Would Have Been Better If I Could Focus Only on Baseball

I had a good year in 1948, a so-so year in 1949, a good year in 1950, a so-so year in 1951, and then three good years in a row. So, it took me a while to be consistent. I think one of the reasons is that I didn't feel I was part of the total picture on the Indians, as I'd been back in high school and college when I'd played on teams where I was the only Afro-American. Even in 1953, I still wasn't part of the whole structure of the team. I would have been a better player, particularly from a con-sistency standpoint, if I wasn't working to achieve that.

I'd work as hard as anybody to improve my game—practice was fun for me—but at the same time, I was trying to adjust to fitting into a certain part of our society, when some people didn't want me to fit in. So, I was trying to do two difficult things, and one of those things was bothering me, and my concentration wasn't what it should be. At the park, there'd be someone in the stands saying things that weren't acceptable. People would say not to let it bother you, or pretend you don't hear it, but every player hears the boos and name-calling. It would have been easier to play good baseball if some of those things were easier to accept, as far as race was concerned.

WILLIE MAYS
How I Became a Center Fielder

125

Without telling me, my father called the manager of the Birmingham Black Barons, Piper Davis, and said, "Look at my kid. He can play." At the time, I was fifteen years old. So Piper called me, and they played a special game in Birmingham to watch me. They put me at shortstop. The ball came so hard to me. In high school, the kids didn't hit the ball that hard. So, I said, "Hold on. Back up! Let me go out to center field." So I went out to center field and started catching everything that was hit out there and throwing out runners. So, Piper said, "That's your position. You're going to play center field for us." That was it.

I Was an Encyclopedia of Baseball Knowledge

I knew how to play baseball when I was young, but Birmingham was on another level. Piper Davis would sit with me on the bench, and we'd talk over every situation, so I knew all the angles of how to play baseball long before I played in the major leagues. When I played on the Giants, I knew how every guy on every team in the National League would hit, what he would hit, and where he would hit, especially under pressure. I knew all that because I was tuned to baseball, which was my life. I knew everything. I tried to tell a writer once, "I would call the pitches out in center field." He said, "How could you call pitches from out there?" I said, "I wouldn't call every pitch, just the pitch I wanted the batter to hit." I'd hold up a finger, like one for fastball, and though the pitcher could throw his curve or slider, or anything, he'd know that the fastball was the pitch I was setting the defense for." I said to the writer, "That's how we played baseball."

How I Became a New York Giant

Eddie Montague was a scout who came down to watch Birmingham and look at Alonzo Perry. We had an away game, and I went 4-for-5; we came back to Birmingham, and I went 3-for-4. I don't know if he started scouting me then. I was told that he was scouting for the Boston Red Sox and the reason he quit their organization was they wouldn't sign me. He went to the New York Giants and told the owner, Horace Stoneham, "I went to scout Alonzo Perry, but I saw another kid that you have to sign." I was a teenager and didn't know what was going on, but that's what I was being told. They talked to Birmingham's owner, Charlie Hayes, and said they needed me more than Alonzo Perry. So, that's how they signed me. They never signed him. He could hit, particularly the long ball, but I was ten or fifteen years younger.

Why I'm in the Hall of Fame

When I came up with the Giants, I didn't get a hit in my first twelve at-bats. I was sitting by my locker with Monte Irvin and started crying because I felt so bad. I was told Herman Franks went to Leo and told him, "Your boy's over there crying. You'd better go talk to him." He came over and didn't say very much. He said, "You're my center fielder. You go home; you come back; you're going to play tomorrow and every day after that." That relaxed me, and I got my first hit, a home run off Warren Spahn. He was a really good pitcher, and he beat us 3–1, but he threw a fastball that wasn't very hard and let me get a hit. The very first thing I said when I was inducted into the Hall of Fame was, "Do you see that little bald-headed guy over there? He's the reason I'm in the Hall of Fame." That was Spahn. I said to him, "Spahnie, I know you liked me, because you just grooved one in there, and you let me get a hit."

The At-Bat That Never Happened

In 1951, we were about thirteen and a half games out in August, and Leo called a meeting and told us we could win the pennant. You know how dramatic Leo Durocher was; he could make you believe anything. Fortunately, after his speech, we went on a tear. We had a long winning streak, lost a game, and then went on another winning streak. Leo was saying, "Keep going, keep going," until we caught them and forced a playoff. They moved me from third to sixth or seventh in the order because it was too much pressure for a rookie. I started hitting better after I was moved. Bobby Thomson was hitting in front of me, so every time they walked him, bang—I hit a home run. So, the move paid off.

127

I was batting behind Thomson in the final playoff game against the Dodgers and was on deck when he came to bat in the ninth inning against Ralph Branca. We were behind by two runs and had two men on base. Leo would do anything to win a game, and as I was kneeling down, I just knew that if Bobby got on base, he was going to pinch-hit for me, and that would kill me. Fortunately, Thomson homered to win the pennant.

Extra Meal Money

Leo Durocher had an adopted son, Chris Durocher, and he was my roommate on the road. I said to Leo, "Why are you making Chris my roommate?" He said, "It's for a reason." I didn't ask any more questions. We went to St. Louis and Cincinnati, and Chris had to stay with me in the hotels that allowed blacks. So Chris ate fried chicken, corn bread, and black-eyed peas. Chris went back to Leo and complained, and Leo said, "What are you giving my son to eat?" And I told him it was soul food, which is what I ate. He said, "Well, I want you to give my son a steak." I said, "OK, but I'll need a lot more money!" So, that's how I got a higher food allowance. I told Chris to go back and complain some more so we'd get some more money. And he did.

The Catch

My catch in the 1954 World Series wasn't my best catch, but it was important. Cleveland won 111 games that year and had a tremendous pitching staff, so my job was to make sure nothing in the outfield would drop, so they wouldn't take a lead. Vic Wertz hit the ball, and as I'm running toward the fence, I'm thinking, "There are two men on, so get the ball back into the infield." The Polo Grounds was so huge that a man on second base could score on a long fly ball to center field—and Larry Doby was on second, and he could run. So, I'm telling myself I have to make a quick throw, or a run can score. I catch the ball over my shoulder, stop, and throw, all in the same motion— I turned 360 degrees and ended up throwing the ball in the exact same spot where I caught it. That's very difficult to do, but I was young and didn't think of that. I just wanted to make the play and prevent the runners from advancing—which I did.

I Left My Heart in New York City

I hated to leave New York, because I had been killing the ball for a couple of years and was just making myself known throughout the country. Now we move to San Francisco, and the first thing I hear is, "Willie Mays is coming to our town, but we don't know if he's really that good." I'm thinking, "Wait a minute: I've played seven years—why do I have to show anything?" I made a mistake my first year out there. I said, "I'll show them," and I changed my whole game around. I hit only twenty-nine homers, but I batted .347, which was my career high. Richie Ashburn beat me out by two or three points for the batting title. The second year, I said, "Why am I changing my game for people who don't understand how I play?" I was disappointed in myself. So, the next year, I hit thirty-four homers and moved on and started playing my own game. It was OK to bat .310 or .320 with more homers instead of .347 with only a few.

Barry Bonds

I knew my godchild Barry Bonds would be a ballplayer, because he was hanging around Bobby Bonds and me all the time when we were Giants teammates. He was a really good kid, my godchild. Did I ever think Barry Bonds would hit seventy-three home runs in one year? Are you kidding me? No, no, never. Who thought of such a thing?

BOBBY MURCER
Why I Signed with the New York Yankees

I was signed to a professional contract by Tom Greenwade, the New York Yankees' scout who signed Mickey Mantle. I signed in May 1964, a year before the first amateur draft. Greenwade had a lot of bird-dog scouts reporting back to him, and one saw me play when I was in high school in Oklahoma City. He called Tom and said, "You should see this kid." So, Tom came and looked at me and became one of the scouts who wanted to sign me.

Until I graduated, teams could tell me they were interested in me, but they couldn't talk to me about money. I had my eighteenth birthday in May, and school ended at the end of May. I went from my high school graduation directly to my home, where representatives of the interested teams were waiting for me. My father was my agent, and not a bad one. Each team was given a ten-minute time slot to make an official offer. The Yankees offered me a small bonus, $10,000. The Dodgers offered me the most, $20,000. In those days, $10,000 was a significant difference. But money wasn't a big deal to me. Playing for the Yankees was the big thing. The Yankees were my team all my life, even though the Cardinals were the team we'd hear on the radio. The Yankees had mystique, and they had Mickey Mantle, who came out of Commerce, Oklahoma, and was a hero of mine. It made a difference that the scout who signed Mickey wanted to sign me. During the signing period, Tom had me come to Kansas City to work out with the Yankees, and I got to meet Mickey for the first time, Roger Maris, Elston Howard, Whitey Ford, and all the great players. Of course, that was the icing on the cake and made me want to sign with them immediately.

130

I had the business sense of someone who was barely eighteen, because in the back of my mind I was thinking I'd make up the $10,000 with World Series money. I guess I thought I'd go right to the Yankees and we'd play in the Series every year, as the Yankees had been doing since 1960. I didn't realize that after 1964, the Yankees would fall on hard times and not return to the Series until 1976.

The Worst Ballpark in Baseball

After being traded by the Yankees for Bobby Bonds, I spent 1975 and 1976 with the San Francisco Giants. I was not a lover of Candlestick Park. Like everyone else, I hated it. Every night, it was extremely cold and very windy, and that always was a distraction. I gained such admiration for Willie Mays, Willie McCovey, Orlando Cepeda, and all the Giants greats who toiled there for years and still had tremendous careers. Candlestick Park held sixty-five thousand, but only a couple of thousand die-hard fans would brave the elements each night. I got in trouble for something I said about our poor attendance. It was at the time Patty Hearst had been kidnapped by the SLA and everyone was looking for her. I commented that they should look in section 65, which was all the way in dead center field. I kidded, "They may be able to find Patty Hearst up there, because there hasn't been anybody up there for years." The Giants didn't take kindly to that.

My Final Memory of Thurman Munson

Thurman Munson and I were very close friends, and he spent the last weekend before his death staying with me in Chicago. I had told Thurman about a small airport outside Chicago that he could use during the Yankees' three-game series with the White Sox. After the series, I drove him back to the airport because he was going to fly his plane to his home in Canton, Ohio. My wife, Kay, and our kids were with us, and he asked us all to come on his brand-new plane and look at it. He showed us around the plane and talked for about thirty minutes. He then asked us to watch him take off. So we got in our car and drove down to the end of the runway. He taxied down and took off over our heads, and I couldn't believe that Thurman was up in that powerful plane all by himself, taking off in the dark. It was just an unbelievable sight.

He had wanted my wife and children to fly back to Canton with him. Then he wanted us to fly back and forth to New York, going there

131

for a game, and then returning on an off day, so that my family could spend time with him, Diane, and their kids. We didn't go with him, but we could easily have said yes. The next day, on August 2, 1979, he was killed practicing touch-and-goes at the Akron-Canton Airport.

A Miracle Win for Thurman

Four days after Thurman Munson's death, Lou Piniella and I were asked to deliver eulogies at his funeral in Canton, Ohio, where he'd lived with Diane and their children. Through those days leading up to the funeral, we were just exhausted and emotionally spent. I hadn't slept in forty-eight hours, because I'd been to Canton, where Thurman had been killed in the accident at the airport, gone back to New York, and returned to Canton. The funeral was draining, with many tears being shed, but there was still no time to sleep. Mr. Steinbrenner had chartered a plane, and the whole team flew back to New York after the funeral to play a nationally televised game against the Baltimore Orioles that night.

We got to the stadium about five hours before warm-ups, so we all tried to relax or take naps. I checked the lineup card and saw that my name was missing. So I went to Billy Martin and asked him why. He said, "You haven't had any sleep, so take the night off." I said, "Billy, I don't feel that I should take the night off. Something's telling me I need to play tonight." He said, "You really want to play?" I said, "I absolutely want to play." So he put me in the lineup.

I ended up driving in all five of our runs. In the seventh inning, we trailed 4–0, but I hit a 3-run homer off Dennis Martinez to cut the deficit to 1 run. But we still trailed 4–3 in the bottom of the ninth with two outs. We had Willie Randolph on second and Buck Dent on third, and I was due up. Their pitcher was Tippy Martinez, a very good left-handed reliever. I was left-handed, and in those days, they normally would have sent up a right-handed batter to pinch-hit for me with the game on the line. Under any other circumstances, I wouldn't have batted, but Billy let me face Martinez. He got two strikes on me, but then I lined the outside pitch the opposite way into the left-field corner. Both runners scored easily, and we won the game 5–4. The players ran out to greet me and celebrate, and everyone was so emotional as we headed into the dugout. We all had forgotten we were tired, because we were on a mission to win that game for Thurman. It really felt like he was right there with us.

MOOKIE WILSON
I Hit a Grounder to Bill Buckner

I often joke that if I had won the sixth game of the 1986 World Series by lining the ball off the wall in the bottom of the tenth inning, people probably would have forgotten it by now. But instead, the winning run scored when I hit a grounder that went through Bill Buckner's legs behind first base, and no one has forgotten that play. It has a place in history, and both Bill and I are proud to be part of history—of course, I'm the one on the good end of it, and I'm happy to still talk about it; if you're on the losing end, you don't want anyone to bring it up. But while it's gratifying, that one play has overshadowed what were two pretty good careers.

I played with Bill Buckner's brother Jim on the Tidewater Tides. Jim talked about his older brother, and when I came up to the Mets and we played the Cubs, I introduced myself to Bill. And we were friends after that, including after that play. Scorekeepers are kind of funny, and while I say I could have beaten Bill to the bag even if he caught my grounder, the scorekeeper and most people must have thought a borderline Hall of Famer should have made the play very easily. I'm not arguing that it should have been a hit rather than an error, because the only thing that mattered is we won.

Anyone who claimed to have been optimistic before Gary Carter got a two-out hit in the tenth had to be lying. I'm the eternal optimist, but with Boston scoring twice in the top of the tenth and leading 5–3 with no one on base and one out to go, I thought, "We flat-out blew it!" After Carter singled, we said, "Oh, well, it's a hit, but so what." But after Kevin Mitchell got a hit, too, we were thinking, "Maybe something's happening here . . ." Then Ray Knight got a hit, too.

133

The key to the whole thing was Calvin Schiraldi pitching for Boston to begin the ninth. When he came in, the atmosphere changed. We knew him very well, because he had been a Met, and we felt we had a chance against him. By the time Bob Stanley came in to face me, the score was 5–4, and we had men on first and third. Stanley almost hit me on a wild pitch that tied the score and allowed Ray to move into scoring position at second base. That set the stage for the famous play. I remember jumping out of the way on the wild pitch, but I remember nothing else in my ten-pitch at-bat other than hitting the ball. The rest of it is a blur. You may not believe this, but I've seen a tape of that play only once in all these years.

An Anticlimactic Game 7

Many people think that the World Series game in which we beat Boston on the ball I hit through Bill Buckner's legs gave the Mets the title. But that only tied the series 3–3, and we still had to play Game 7. Even people who remember we played that game might forget that we trailed 3–0 in the bottom of the sixth inning. Like most fans, the players didn't feel we were ever behind that game. There was just no way we were going to lose Game 7 after winning Game 6 the way that we did. To me, it was impossible. I was right. We came back to win and were the world champions.

The Great Game Many People Overlook

134   I don't want to take anything away from the 1986 World Series, but the NLCS against Houston was better by far. And there's no question that Game 6 of the NLCS was better than Game 6 of the World Series. Against Boston, we came from two runs down in the last inning; against the Astros, we scored three runs in the ninth to tie the score. I singled home the first run off Bob Knepper after Lenny Dykstra

tripled and my ball just made it over the glove of second-baseman Billy Doran when he leaped high off the ground. We were up in the series 3–2, but we had to win that game, because Cy Young winner Mike Scott was ready to pitch Game 7, and he had dominated us in two earlier games in the series and was into our players' heads. It would have been a lost cause, so we had to win. We managed to score three runs in the ninth to tie the score. Then we took the lead in the fourteenth inning, but with two outs in the bottom of the inning, Houston's Billy Hatcher tied the game with a home run. I can say this now: that was a game where you wanted any team to win, so you could start fresh the next day — because our nerves were shot. We had played a twelve-inning game the night before in New York and then took the three-hour trip to Houston, and then we had a 3 P.M. start. So, we were exhausted before the game started, and it went sixteen innings and well over four hours. Finally, we scored three runs in the top of the sixteenth, Jesse Orosco held them to two runs in the bottom of the inning, and we didn't have to face Mike Scott again.

She Asked for a Diamond

I married my wife, Rosa, at home plate when I played in Jackson, Mississippi. She said she wanted a big diamond, and you couldn't get any bigger than that baseball diamond. I dare anyone to top that!

A Man of Many Talents

In 1981, the players went on strike, and I took the job of maître d' at Joe's Seafood, on Roosevelt and 159th. I'd eaten there a couple of times for lunch and got to know the owner. I was doing nothing, so he joked, "Hey, if you want something to do, you can always come here and help me out." I showed up the next day. And I worked there for about two months.

Playing with Passion

Baseball's been my life. I grew up playing baseball, though I wasn't a fan who watched it on television. If I couldn't play it, I didn't want to watch it. Baseball was a game to me, and I was lucky to get paid for playing it. I loved the game with a passion, and my attitude was reflected in my play. Baseball is a very passionate sport; it's not golf or tennis, where everyone sits back and shushes other fans if they make noise. I've told young players that people should know they're on the field. Even if you go 0-for-10, they should still know you played that day.

I think Toronto acquired me from the Mets in 1989 less for how I performed on the field than my personality when I played. I never batted .300, I never led the league in anything but at-bats, I was probably the worst "leadoff" hitter in baseball, but I always got the job done. I brought energy, aggressiveness, and passion to what was already a good team, and it was infectious. That is why I was popular with the fans in New York and Toronto. You can't teach the passion I had, but you can teach the game, and hopefully players will develop passion through their knowledge of the game.

NINE

THE RIGHT FIELDERS

ENOS SLAUGHTER
How I Became a Major Leaguer

I was born in Person County, North Carolina, in Roxboro, just north of Durham. We'd go into Durham to watch the Bulls play, and that got me interested in baseball. In high school and with the team from the textiles mill where I worked, I was a pitcher and second baseman. At the time, Branch Rickey was the farm director of the Cardinals, and he had his bird dogs watch me play and come visit me. I decided to turn down an athletic scholarship to Guilford College, in Greensboro, and pursue a baseball career. Still, when I was finishing up high school, I never dreamed that I'd be in the major leagues just three years off my farm. But Fred Haney, the sports editor of the *Durham Morning Herald*, saw me play and told Oliver French about me. He owned the Greensboro farm team of the Cardinals. In September of my senior year, the Cardinals had a tryout camp in Greensboro, and they invited me up there as a second baseman. They said, "If you make good, we'll pay your expenses." I was hitting the ball very well, but they said, "You're so dang-gum clumsy, you're liable to break your neck making a double play." So, they moved me to the outfield, and that's where I stayed.

The next year, '35, the Cardinals trained in Asheville, North Carolina, up on the mountaintop. I can remember it just like yesterday.

The Cardinals had all kinds of players up there trying to get contracts. We were watched by guys like Wid Mathews, Joe Sugden, and Billy Southworth, who'd be my Cardinals manager when we beat the Yankees in the 1942 World Series. My number was 269. They didn't know you by name; you went by number. So, I checked the bulletin board, and there'd be a checkmark by my number to show I hadn't been cut.

Southworth and Craig Lammers, who would manage me that year at Martinsville, Virginia, in the Bi-State League, said, "You know, if we can't improve your running, the Cardinals are gonna let you go." So, we go to the outfield, and they ask me, "Has anybody ever tried to teach you how to run?" I said, "No, I'm just used to the south end of that mule and plow, down on the farm." They said, "We want you to practice running on your toes." So, I practiced running on my toes three or four days, and they could see improvement. So, I made the team and went to Martinsville, Class D; and then to Columbus, Georgia, in 1936; and Columbus, Ohio, in 1937; and in 1938, I was a St. Louis Cardinal. That day they told me to run on my toes was the turning point for my success in my baseball career, because I would stay around for over twenty years because I could run.

While I was in service, there was a doctor who came around. His specialty was muscles, and he had been one of Lou Gehrig's doctors. He took x-rays of people's legs, and he said to me, "You know, your legs from your knees to your hips are the most powerful that I've ever seen." He told me that running is the easiest thing you can do, because all you have to do is lean forward. In 1956, I was with the Yankees, and Lou Miller, of the *World Telegram*, in New York, wrote that I went from home to first in 3.6 seconds, which meant that at the age of forty, I was in the top twenty-five fastest runners in the majors. Even now, I don't have no problem with my knees or legs.

138

"The Mad Dash"

Being someone who always ran hard and never stopped hustling came in handy in Game 7 of the 1946 World Series between the Cardinals and Boston Red Sox. I scored the winning run in the bottom of the eighth inning, all the way from first base, on that famous play they call "the Mad Dash." The ball was hit to left center by Harry Walker. Well, it was an ordinary single, but the American League gave him a double. Walker headed for second, but when Johnny Pesky, Boston's shortstop, got the cutoff throw from the outfield and turned around, Walker headed back toward first. Only when Pesky saw me heading for the plate and threw home did Walker go to second. Pesky got blamed for hesitating before throwing home, but I blame their second baseman, Bobby Doerr, and third baseman, Pinky Higgins, for not letting Pesky know where to throw the ball when his back was turned.

To me, it was more a surprise play than anything else. People don't realize I tripled with two outs in Game 1 and might have had an inside-the-park homer. Our third-base coach, Mike Gonzalez, held me up, I got stranded on third, and we lost that ball game by one run. Our manager, Eddie Dyer, came straight to me and said, "From now on, if you think you got a chance to score with two men out, you gamble, and I'll be responsible." So, when Walker hit that ball and I rounded second, I knew I was going to try to score regardless of whether Gonzalez tried to stop me at third. I don't know if he tried, because I didn't see him. When I rounded third, I was expecting Roy Partee to block the plate. I'd hit a lot of guys, and it was going to be either Partee or me. Didn't matter, because the throw was up the line, and I slid in safely. The Sox threatened to score in the top of the ninth, but their men died on the bases, and we were the 1946 world champions.

I Played the Game Hard   139

When I reached the major leagues in 1938, I vowed, "I'm going to stay." I'd run out everything; I never took anything for granted. And if a pitcher knocked me down, that was OK with me. I didn't go out and fight him. What in the heck? I'd just say, "Well, if that's the way you want to play it, when you cover first with me coming down there, you'd better be ready, 'cause I'm going to be after you." That's just the way I felt. And if they blocked the plate, I got 'em out of the way. I can remember in the Polo Grounds after we sold Walker Cooper, I tried to circle the bases, and that big old mule jaw blocked that plate. He went one way, and I went the other, and I couldn't breathe 'til I got to the dugout. But that's part of the game. That was fun. Today you can't pitch inside, but boy, every time we played the Dodgers, if we didn't have three or four knockdowns, it wasn't a typical Cardinals-Dodgers game. One day, the umpire tells me, "You know, I think they're throwing at you." I says, "Heck, I just thought he was wild." I didn't care if he knocked me down. What in the heck? That's part of the game.

We didn't wear batting helmets in those days. In 1939, Branch Rickey tried to start with the helmet. He had us wear a little insert liner in your cap. I was the first player to try one in '39. Then they came up with a little piece that went all the way around. And I still have that little helmet at home right now. I don't think I could hit with these helmets on today, because they'd get in my way.

I Cried When St. Louis Got Rid of Me

What happened is that Augie Busch took over the Cardinals in 1953. Then on December 28, I went in to see him and signed my first contract with him. He said, "You're a credit to the game, and you'll always be with me." Two months later, I'm playing for New York. That's when I found out what a coldhearted game it was. I found out later that they'd been trying to get rid of me for five years. And I was driving in from ninety to a hundred runs a year! In '54, they had to get rid of me so Wally Moon could play. I had nothing against Moon, but if the Cardinals didn't sell me to the Yankees in '54, I don't think he could have beaten me out for the job.

It hurt me very bad to go to the Yankees. I cried, and I don't mind admitting it, because I had a tender heart, and I don't think anybody who ever put on a Cardinals uniform tried to give the Cardinals any more than Enos Slaughter did. That's why I can go back to St. Louis today and I think I've got as many friends in St. Louis as anybody that's ever played there.

I Play for the New York Yankees

Coming to the Yankees in 1954, I said, "Well, I'm in a new era." Casey Stengel was the manager, and I said, "Casey, I'd like to play more." He says, "My boy, you play when I want you to play and you'll be with me a long time." Well, what could I say? So, whatever he wanted me to do, I tried to do. I played right field some; I played left field some; I was a pinch hitter. I'll never forget I broke my arm in '54 by running into the wall in Yankee Stadium against Cleveland. I broke my arm in three places, but I told Casey not to put me on the disabled list, because my bones healed fast. But they put me on anyway, so I went down to my farm and baled hay for two weeks. It was no problem doing it with one arm, because a machine was doing the work. We used to cut wheat with a cradle, bale it up, and stack it. So, I did that and came back to the Yankees.

In 1955, the Athletics moved from Philadelphia to Kansas City, and the Yankees sent Johnny Sain and me to them. In return, they got pitcher Sonny Dixon, who had beaten the Yankees quite a few times. But Dixon didn't win a game with the Yankees, and I hit .315 with Kansas City. I was chosen the Athletics' Most Valuable Player, and they gave me a car the last day of the season. So, that was a bad trade the Yankees made.

The next year, the Yankees got in trouble. Joe Collins had a bad back, Norm Siebern had a bad leg, and they need a left-handed hitter. So, they called their shortstop, Phil Rizzuto, in and said, "Phil, we need a left-handed hitter, and we can get Slaughter back from Kansas City." He says, "Good; he can help us." "OK," they said. "We're releasing you and signing him." Phil didn't speak to me for ten years. But that's part of the game.

I didn't want to end his career like that, but I really helped the Yankees in '56. I came in on a Saturday night and against Detroit, which always was a thorn in the Yankees' side: I got a home run, a triple, a double, and two singles to help them sweep a Sunday doubleheader. We go to Chicago on Monday, and against old Dick Donovan, "Twin-kletoes," I hit a home run in the twelfth inning to win that game. And then in the '56 World Series, the Dodgers had the Yankees two games to nothing, and I hit a three-run home run off Roger Craig to bring us back—that was the first home run ever hit in a World Series by a forty-year-old player. I hit .350 in that Series, despite going 0-for-2 in Don Larsen's perfect game, and we beat the Dodgers in seven games. So, this time the Yankees held on to me, and I'd play in the World Series in the next two years as well, making it four world titles in five World Series. I ended my career in 1959 with the Yankees and Mil-waukee Braves. In 1985, I was selected to the Hall of Fame.

I Know All My Statistics

I'll tell you my statistics. I played in 2,380 games. I went to bat 7,946 times. I wound up with 2,383 hits, 413 doubles, 148 triples, 169 home runs, and a slugging percentage of .453. I scored 1,247 runs and drove in 1,304—I was the only player besides Pie Traynor to twice drive in 100 runs with less than 12 homers, in 1950 and 1952. I had 1,019 bases on balls and struck out only 538 times. I was a .306 lifetime pinch hit-ter. I had 152 assists in the outfield. I played in ten straight All-Star Games and hit .381. I played in five World Series and won four world championships. What else do you want to know?

The statistic I'm proudest of? Definitely my 148 triples. You know, I missed three years in the service. People don't realize Spahn, Williams, DiMaggio, Feller, Reese, Mize, and others spent three to five years for our country. People don't appreciate those years. I think Stan Musial wound up with 165 triples, but he spent only one year in service. I was hitting 12 or 13 a year, twice leading the league. So, if I had played three more years, I could have wound up with 180 triples.

142

I Remembered That Headline

I enjoyed playing baseball as much as anyone. The money I got meant nothing to me. I made $25,000 in '49, and the headline of an article by Bob Broeg in the *St. Louis Post-Dispatch* read "Why the Cardinals Lost the Pennant: Slaughter Ran Out of Gas and Only Hit .336." Musial hit .340, and Broeg didn't write a thing about him running out of gas. They had a celebration several years ago on the hundredth-year anniversary for the Cardinals, and they invited me back. They were honoring Bob Broeg, and I got up and told the two thousand people there about what he'd written. I didn't care that much about it, but it was the truth.

HANK AARON
My Modest Ambitions

We had a big sixty-fifth birthday party for me in Atlanta, and one of the people sitting next to me at my table was President Clinton. Can you imagine? Here's "a little kid who," as my mother said, "came all the way from Mobile, Alabama, and the president is coming to his birthday party." I felt I was in hog heaven. I felt like I finally had made it.

I didn't think that I was going to stay in the big leagues nearly as long as I did. All I knew when I first joined the Milwaukee Braves in 1954 was that I wanted to spend five years in the big leagues. The reason for *five* years was that I'd then get vested in the pension fund. It took five years in those days, and now I think it takes one day. I said, "Boy, if I could just stay five years, I might be able to help my kids and get a paid-up pension." Everybody worked like hell to get those years in. I remember some players talking about how they worried about getting hurt, because then they might get released. They'd have four and a half years in, and they'd say, "Oh, my God, I just need a half a year." I was very lucky avoiding injuries. In my rookie year, I broke my

143

ankle in Cincinnati, but after that, I was rarely hurt. So, I played much longer than five years.

What the Braves Could Have Achieved

I came along at the right time, because with the exception of Warren Spahn, most of the players on the Braves were young and had great careers ahead of them—Eddie Mathews, Del Crandall, Billy Bruton, Johnny Logan, Juan Pizarro, Carlton Willey; even Lew Burdette and Joe Adcock were fairly young. All of us grew up together. We could have gone to the World Series four years in a row, but we finished a game out to the Brooklyn Dodgers in 1956 and lost to the Los Angeles Dodgers in a playoff in 1959.

In 1956, we had a very good ball club and played very well, but we were young and inexperienced. As we headed into our last series with St. Louis, we heard that Jackie Robinson had said the Braves had a few playboys. He didn't name any names, so everybody started looking around and wondering, "Who could he be talking about? I wonder if he's talking about me. If my wife sees this in the paper, it's going to cause trouble." We did have a bunch of young guys like Wes Covington who probably did some flirting. But it was no big deal. What Robinson said was a very innocent remark that wouldn't have had any effect today. He was trying to put something into our minds so that we'd think about something other than baseball, and he succeeded in doing that. He was the master at doing that. We should have been concentrating on trying to beat the Cardinals, but we went out there that night and we were still thinking about it late in the game. And the Cardinals were out there doing business. They beat us two out of three. And meanwhile Jackie's Dodgers took three straight and won the pennant.

We did win the pennant the next two years and would have won both World Series from the Yankees, but in '58, they came back from a 3–1 deficit to beat us. In '59, we might have had our best ball club, but we got a little conceited and thought that we were going to walk

144

through September and nobody was going to catch us. And, of course, the Dodgers caught us again and beat us in a two-game playoff. I'm sorry about what happened. You know, you look back and say, "We could have . . ." That's why you can't let any day pass you by without doing your very, very best.

My Proudest Achievements

Recently, I told someone, "You know, I'm going to always be remembered most for hitting 755 home runs." He asked me, "But if that isn't the thing you most liked about your career, what is?" And I said, "The one thing I'd like people to remember is that I scored a lot of runs and I batted in a lot of runs." In fact, I think my major-league record of 2,297 RBIs is my greatest achievement. And another thing I'm proud of along those same lines is that I never struck out 100 times in one year. I was proud that I was able to do things other than just hit home runs.

When you look at a player's career, you ask, "What contribution did he make to his team?" In baseball, one player can't win a championship by himself. But if that one player is surrounded by good players, they can win a championship together. As a contributor to my team, I had four things that I wanted to do. My major goal was to go out and play as many games as I possibly could. Then I wanted to score 100 runs, drive in 100 runs, and hit .300. I felt that if I did those things, I could make a great contribution to my team.

Home runs weren't that important to me, though of course I'm proud of having set the record. Other than my 715th home run to pass Babe Ruth, the one that I am most proud of was the one I hit to win the pennant in 1957. The year before, we struggled at the end of the season, and the Dodgers beat us by one game. And the same thing was happening in '57. The Cubs had beaten us three out of four. Then we got back to Milwaukee and were playing the Cardinals. We went into extra innings, and I happened to hit a home run off Billy Muffett, who was a pretty good relief pitcher. That's the one home run that really

145

stood out, for obvious reasons: it clinched the pennant for the Braves and got us into the World Series.

As I Got Older, I Became a Smarter Hitter

Most of the time, I swung the bat as if I were chopping wood. Everything was down. It was just my way of hitting. That kind of swing can work against you sometimes, but I did all right. I hit a lot of home runs when I was thirty-eight years old, an age when most players were going the other way. I would say that in the last ten to thirteen years of my career, I really was a much more patient hitter and knew the strike zone a lot better than early in my career. I knew exactly the pitch I wanted and waited for it. And when I got it, I usually did something with it.

I saw the ball so well. I got so that I probably could read the ball about as well as anybody. Somebody said Ted Williams could count the stitches on a pitched ball. I couldn't do that, but I could pick up a curveball and a fastball halfway to the plate. The hardest pitch for me was the slider. It was hard to pick it up at certain times early in my career. Later on, I got the knack of it. So then I could read all the pitches. And I could do something even better: not all year, but during certain times of the year, I could pick up a pitch before the pitcher released it, even if he was hiding the ball in his glove. Somehow I just saw the grip on the ball in his glove and saw how he was going to hold it, and I would not be fooled by what he threw.

The other thing in my favor was that I was familiar with all the pitchers. The great pitchers didn't change teams in those days, so if I was going to play against the Los Angeles Dodgers, I knew I was going to face Koufax and Drysdale, and if we came into St. Louis, I was going to face Gibson or Carlton. We faced the same pitchers over and over again and knew what pitches they threw. What would bother me most about today's pitchers is that I wouldn't face them enough to know their pitches, especially if they threw many pitches. Since many of them today have specialty pitches, I might face five pitchers in a game who all have different stuff. I'm not saying that they're five good pitchers, but they might throw a lot of different pitches.

FRANK ROBINSON
My Opponents Were Not My Friends

How can you expect a base runner to take a second baseman out on a double play if he's talking to him before the game? If they were shaking hands and laughing and joking around, a runner won't be inclined to slide hard into a second baseman. And a pitcher isn't likely to push a batter off the plate if they had dinner together the previous night. Fraternizing, as it's called nowadays—I call it "sitting around and shooting the bull"—is something I couldn't do when I was a player. I didn't want to talk with my opponents, because I needed to focus on the things I needed to do to beat them, short of hurting anyone intentionally. I didn't want to be friendly with a pitcher so they wouldn't throw inside. Some pitchers used me as a dartboard, but that was part of the game and acceptable, as long as they didn't throw at my head. Getting knocked down just made me tougher.

Baserunning Was One of My Weapons

If I was on first base with less than two outs, it was my job on a ground ball to slide hard into second base to try to break up the double play. I didn't worry about getting hurt, because I needed to give my team an extra out. I wanted my team to score runs. I enjoyed scoring runs myself. That's why I made it from first to third or from second to home on most base hits to the outfield. I wanted to score, and I wanted to reward the batter with an RBI. I felt that if I did that, my teammate would do the same for me when I was at the plate.

147

I used to change my pace when running on the base paths. Some people took it as my not giving my all, but I knew when to turn it on. It was very deceptive to defensive players. I'd go into second base, and they'd see I wasn't going full speed, and then I'd turn on another gear and get to third base safely. I took pride in my baserunning and thought that was a big part of my game and part of my job. A lot of other guys who hit home runs didn't feel that way.

My Move to the American League

When I was traded to the Baltimore Orioles in the winter of 1965, for Milt Pappas and two other players, I was crushed. I had spent my entire career in the Cincinnati organization and had started to believe I would finish my major-league career with the Reds. I had hoped I would. But now I was going not just to another team but to my first American League team. It took me three or four days before I realized that I was going to a good ball club. The Orioles had been close to winning the American League pennant for a couple of years, so I figured if they played how they could and I had the type of year I was capable of, we had a good chance to win. That's what happened. We had such a great group of players there, and we just fit in together with no egos. I won the Triple Crown, but so many players made contributions on offense, defense, and pitching. The Orioles played the game the right way. We had a tremendous year and then swept the Dodgers in the World Series. That took the sting out of the trade.

I Wanted to Manage

I've always loved and wanted to be around baseball my whole life. As each job I've had in baseball ended, I'd figure out something else to do, always looking for a way to give back something to the game. I always wanted to help others, because there were so many people that helped me. I really enjoy working with young players, so it was rewarding to manage all those years in Cleveland, San Francisco, Baltimore, Montreal, and Washington.

When I was still playing, I knew I wanted to manage in the big leagues once my career ended, but I anticipated being told, "I'd con-

148

sider you if you had experience, but you don't have any." So, to prevent that, I managed in winter ball for six years. I was still playing in the majors, so that made my situation unique. It was tough, but I always was willing to work to get something; I never wanted anything given to me. I'm glad I did that, because I felt I was prepared to manage in the majors when the opportunity came in Cleveland at the end of the 1974 season.

I was proud to be the first black manager in major-league baseball, but I didn't set out to do that when I first went to winter ball. I just wanted to be a manager once I stopped playing. The Cleveland Indians chose me to be a player-manager for 1975 and '76. I said, "No, I just want to manage. Playing and managing are tough enough in themselves, so I don't want to do both." But I did what they wanted and was a player-manager those two years, and at times, it was very difficult. In 1977, I stopped playing and only managed, and the Indians fired me after less than half a season. When the Giants gave me my second opportunity, in 1981, I hadn't played in five years, and there was no question that I'd only manage from then on.

KEN SINGLETON

Two Hall of Famers Made Me a Good Hitter

I was worried about making the Mets in 1971 and was glad when they sent Ralph Kiner down to the Instructional League for about three weeks to work with me on my hitting. During our session, we concentrated on such things as getting the bat off my shoulder so I wouldn't drop my hands and turning my back leg and foot correctly to open up my hips and let my hands work through. He helped me quite a bit.

149

Then Tim Foli, Mike Jorgenson, and I were traded to Montreal for Rusty Staub, a typical Expos trade of a high-salaried player for three young guys who weren't making much money. Rusty was the team's star and the fans' biggest hero, so we didn't get much of a reception. But I got to play every day, which I hadn't done with the Mets, and benefited from working with Larry Doby, the Expos' hitting coach. I took things from Larry, who had batted left-handed, and incorporated what I'd learned from Ralph, who had batted right-handed, and I became a major-league hitter while in Montreal. I would become the answer to a trivia question. I just found out last year that I'm the player who hit the most home runs after leaving the Mets. Over thirteen years, I hit 222 home runs for the Expos and Orioles.

Eddie Murray's First Impression

It's often said that right-handed batters are better on the high pitch and left-handers prefer the ball down. I never thought there was a difference. Maybe that's because I'd been switch-hitting for so long and did some things with one hand and other things with the other hand, so both sides seemed natural to me. However, I'm sure that my former Orioles teammate Eddie Murray recognized a big difference, because he started to switch-hit only a year before he reached the major leagues. But he picked it up fast and became the greatest clutch hitter I ever saw, someone who always would get us the needed run from the seventh inning on.

We had never heard of Eddie Murray when he came to spring training. I was standing in the outfield with first baseman Lee May and outfielder Pat Kelly, and we were watching him rip the cover off the ball from both sides of the plate. They looked at each other and said, "Where does this kid play?" They said, "Let's watch him go into the dugout and see what kind of glove he picks up." So, we watched Eddie go into the dugout and pick up a first-baseman's mitt. Pat turned to Lee and said, "Oldie, you're in trouble."

150

Walking for Weaver

At the 1983 World Series, I told reporters, "A man once told me to walk with the Lord, but I'd rather walk with the bases loaded." I got that line from Earl Weaver. Outfielder Pat Kelly was like our team chaplain, a very religious man. One day, he was sitting in the Orioles' dugout next to Earl, which isn't a good place to be if you're religious. Earl was going off. Earl was upset that our guys were striking out with the bases loaded, and Pat said, "But, Earl, you can't get so upset that we don't homer every time up with the bases loaded. You've got to walk with the Lord." And Earl said, "Pat, I'd rather have you walk with the bases loaded, just to get us a run."

Earl was my manager for ten years, and he always appreciated that I had a high walk total. My first year in the minors with the Mets organization, I led the league in bases on balls. The way I felt at the plate was that if a pitch was too hard for me to swing at and hit, it had to be a ball; if I had to make too much of an effort to make solid contact, it couldn't be a strike. After a time in the majors, I got a reputation for not swinging at too many bad pitches, and the umpires were giving me some close calls. My teammates would be on me: "How can you take those close pitches, when the umpires call them strikes on us?" I'd say, "That's because you swing at everything." I wanted the count to go to 3-2, because that's when I had the pitcher where I wanted him. He's got to lay it in or walk me.

I stole twenty-five bases my whole career, but in 1975, I was Weaver's leadoff hitter, and Bobby Grich was his second hitter, because we were the two guys in the lineup who took walks. I stole only three bases, but I walked 118 times that year, and Grich walked 109 times. Earl was a great believer in the value of a high on-base percentage. He figured if we could get men on base, that could lead to his favorite play—the three-run homer.

DAVE WINFIELD
My Unheralded Hero

When you grow up, you tend to forget all your teachers, but you never forget your coaches. Not too many people know the name Bill Peterson, but he meant a lot to me when I was growing up in St. Paul, Minnesota. He was the director of the Oxford Playground on the next block, and he taught me baseball and basketball and helped shape me in life. Bill is probably one of the few guys who coached two Hall of

Famers—me and Paul Molitor. You see the way Paul plays? Well, that's the way we both played—headfirst slides, breaking up double plays, going all out. Paul and I would play on the same American Legion team and at the University of Minnesota, but not at the same time. I'm sure he'd say he was indebted to Old Bill Peterson, too.

I Chose the Right Sport

I was drafted by teams in the NFL, AFL, and NBA, as well as the Padres, out of the University of Minnesota. I was the first guy to be drafted by four different leagues, but I knew I wanted to play baseball. I enjoyed playing all sports as a kid, but there came a time I had to choose what I wanted to do as my livelihood. Football was fun and taught me about being tough and staying in shape, but I wouldn't recommend it to anyone as a way to make a living. Basketball was fun, too, and it was tremendous playing power forward at the University of Minnesota with seventeen thousand to eighteen thousand in the stands and being on national TV, but I loved playing baseball there even more.

When I pitched, I stood on the mound and felt in control of the game. When there was someone on the mound throwing the ball to me, you know how it feels to put good wood on the ball and run the bases. That's what appealed to me. I also appreciated that I wouldn't have to play in the minors. Back in those days, baseball players didn't have much leverage, but I told San Diego that if I didn't play immediately for the Padres, I'd go play basketball instead. So, they said, "OK, let's give the kid a shot." So, I went right from pitching in the College World Series, and being the MVP, to the Padres as an outfielder. If they had told me they wanted me to pitch, I would have been a big-league pitcher. But they told me they wanted me to play every day eventually, so I became an outfielder.

I played three months in 1973 and did OK, but they hadn't guaranteed I'd stay in the majors my second year, and they had me going to Triple-A in '74. But I came to spring training totally prepared, in

152

great shape, and running like a scalded dog. I was in midseason form and made the team. Then at the All-Star break, the manager, John McNamara, came to me and said, "We're going to put you in every day and see what you can do." My eyes got big with excitement, and I said, "I'm up for it!" And I ended up with twenty home runs and seventy-plus RBIs, and I went on from there. I never played in the minors.

Don't Disturb Bob Gibson When He's Reading

On my wall at the University of Minnesota, I had pictures of two major leaguers: Willie McCovey and Bob Gibson. Willie was a left-handed power hitter, while I was right-handed, but I loved how he hit the ball. Eventually we'd be teammates and become close friends. Gibson was bringing it and slinging it, and when I was on the mound, that's who I wanted to be like. I got a chance to meet him. He was sitting there reading a magazine, and I said, "Bob Gibson, I'm Dave Winfield, with the San Diego Padres." He looked over his magazine, scowled at me and grunted, and went back to reading. They didn't use the word *dissing* then, but that's what it was.

I was shocked. I didn't know he wouldn't fraternize with the opposition. I told myself that the next time we played, I was going to get this guy. I didn't play that series in St. Louis, but when the Cards came to San Diego, I was in the lineup. I go up to the plate; Gibson gets two strikes on me and then strikes me out with his slider low and away. I go through the dugout and into the tunnel, and everyone hears benches flying, and they're asking, "What's wrong with this guy?" I was still hot when I batted against him the next time: the same two strikes; the same slider low and away. This time, I went down and got it. Bam! I shot it out in left center and ran around the bases, staring at him all the way. I walked the last few steps to home plate and pointed at him, as if to say, "I'm here, too." I go into the dugout, and Cito Gaston and Nate Colbert say, "Man, are you crazy? That's Bob Gibson!"

153

The next time I faced Gibson, I came up all cocky, and his first pitch—zing!—went right toward my head. After I ducked, his second pitch—zing!—was right at my body, chest high, pushing me backward. Man, after the second one, I was bouncing like Muhammad Ali, not even thinking of digging in. I didn't realize he was that tough. But that's the way Bob Gibson was. Of course, now we're both retired and in the Hall of Fame—and good buddies.

I Was My Own Batting Instructor

In 1994, I tied Ty Cobb's record by getting five hits three times in a month. I was whacking that ball and running. When you're locked in, you can't wait to get to the park, and the ball looks like a balloon. I was hot and in a groove that month, but other times, I'd feel great and go 0-for-5.

Baseball is a game, a science, and a business. The science part came into play when I wasn't hitting. After a while in the majors, I knew how to self-correct, which was needed, because most coaches hadn't been on the team very long and didn't know what I did before they got there. I even put it on videotape, and I'd talk to myself as my own coach. On the video, I'd walk up to home plate and tell myself what I should do when I was at my hitting optimum. I'd walk up with an attitude, not with a big smile as if I were going to the ice cream parlor. I would have done my reconnaissance, scouting the pitcher ahead of time. I would know what pitches he has in his repertoire and what he uses on different counts. I'd factor in how he pitched me in the past, both early and late in the game. I would look where they were playing me—are they playing me to pull or to the opposite field?—because that would give me insight as to how they were going to pitch me. I would think up-the-middle and right-center first, rather than pulling the ball. But I had to stand the right distance from the plate so that I could wait longer to swing and adjust to the ball inside. When I went to the plate, I always was prepared.

154

I Finally Win a Championship

Some guys are fortunate, but for the most part, even if you give it your best—you give it your all—you need a team to win a championship in the big leagues. I was with a great team in 1992, the Toronto Blue Jays. I enjoyed my time immensely in Toronto—I was in a great city with terrific fans and a very talented team that had no discord whatsoever. The Blue Jays reached the World Series for the first time that year, playing the Atlanta Braves. I'd had only one previous opportunity to play in a World Series, in 1981, and I hadn't hit well with the Yankees, and we lost to the Dodgers. I prepared myself the same way all the time, no matter the situation, but it took me eleven years to finally get into another World Series.

Before the year began, I told the Jays' manager, Cito Gaston, "I've got to play, not DH all the time. Because if we get to the World Series and play in a National League ballpark, I need to be in the game, not on the bench." He smiled but said nothing. Fortunately, he played me 156 games that year, 27 in the outfield, so I was prepared to play the outfield in the Series. As it turned out, I drove in the winning run in Game 6 with a two-run double in the eleventh inning off Atlanta left-hander Charlie Leibrandt to clinch the World Series. That was Toronto's first title and Canada's first title. For me, it was the title I had waited for my entire career.

My 3,000th Hit

I got my 3,000th hit in 1993 playing for the Minnesota Twins, in my hometown. I got a long ovation from the Twins fans, and it was beautiful. Reaching 3,000 hits is a great milestone, because many people always said, "This is a big guy; he can't hit for average." I was proud to hit for average, and that many hits was important validation. My good friend Kirby Puckett, one of the best teammates I ever had, used to kid me, "Winnie, when you get your 3,000th hit, you're going to hit a chopper off home plate about two stories high, and you're going to have to run like a little chicken."

I told him, "No, I'm going to get a legitimate hit." And I hit the ball cleanly through the hole between short and third, and it was against the A's closer Dennis Eckersley, who's now in the Hall of Fame. Here I get the hit and drive in Kirby to tie the game, and my teammates, who were ready to run out and congratulate me on my 3,000th hit, look at each other and say, "That's Eckersley out there," and nobody ran out to greet me. The fans were cheering, but they were scared to run out because Eckersley was pitching, and it was a tie game. I said, "You guys are nothing, man! Where's the love?" We would joke about it afterward. It was a great day!

Tony Gwynn
A Baseball Historian's First Visit to Yankee Stadium

Being in the National League, I never got to play in Yankee Stadium. For years, of course, the Padres played the Mets in New York, and occasionally we'd take the bus past Yankee Stadium on our way out of town, and I'd look at that historic ballpark and dream of an opportunity to play there. Early in the '98 season, we went by Yankee Stadium, and guys were saying, "We're going to be going heads up against the Yankees in the World Series in that ballpark!" And I thought, "Boy, what a great thrill that would be." After we won Game 6 from Atlanta in the NLCS, I realized that my dream was going to come true.

On workout day before the World Series opened in New York, I grabbed my son, and we took the subway from downtown Manhattan to Yankee Stadium. We walked inside the stadium I'd seen on TV for years. While the rest of my teammates went to the clubhouse, my son and I went to the monuments. For about twenty minutes, I took pictures and read the plaques about Joe DiMaggio and Mickey Mantle and Babe Ruth and Lou Gehrig and all the great Yankees players. It overwhelmed me and humbled me. The World Series is a great event, but to me, it was almost as important getting a chance to read a little bit about the history of some of the greatest players who've ever played the game. My son and I talked about it in right field during batting practice. I put my arm around him and said, "Man, we're here in Yankee Stadium. Can you believe this? We're standing where Babe Ruth stood and where Mickey Mantle . . ." He was sixteen, and it just kind of bounced off of him, but I was really caught up in it.

The thing that really sticks out in my mind about Game 1 is the fact that I got to meet Bob Sheppard before the game. I was telling my son, "Boy, this is going to be great. Bob Sheppard's going to introduce me when I go out on the line today." He had no clue who Bob Sheppard was, so I explained to him, "That's the announcer. He's been here for a long time, and his voice is unique. There isn't anybody else like him." I was sitting in the dugout before the game with Keith Olbermann and Spike Lee, and we're talking about baseball and how great it is to be in Yankee Stadium. Bob Sheppard had heard that I was going to be thrilled to have him announce my name, and he came down to the dugout to meet me. I was, like, "Oh, my God! It's Bob Sheppard!" We sat and we talked for about five minutes, and he said, "Tony, is there any way you want me to say your name?" And I said, "No, just say it the way you would do anybody else. Just say my name." I had to regroup after meeting him and go back into the clubhouse to get my game face on. But running out to that line—I couldn't help but smile a little bit, because Bob Sheppard had already told me what it was going to sound like when he announced my name. It was a big thrill. It was just really one of the greatest experiences I've had playing baseball.

My one regret was not having my dad around to see me play in my second World Series. I was thinking about how great it would have been for him to have an opportunity to sit in a seat in Yankee Stadium. My son and I talked about it a little bit, and we knew he was somewhere watching.

We Lost to the Best Team

We were swept in the 1998 World Series by the New York Yankees, who won 114 games during the regular season. I don't think I've played against a better-balanced club in all my years in baseball, which makes what happened easier to deal with, believe me. Game 1 started out very promising. The Yankees took a 2–0 lead off Kevin Brown in the second inning, but we tied it in the third inning off David Wells, and then I put us ahead with a two-run homer in the fifth. I think my first at-bat in the first inning set up that homer. I put the hit-and-run on with Quilvio Veras on first, and Wells threw a great curveball. I don't know how I hit it, but I flipped it into left field, and Wells was not a happy camper. After that AB, I told Merv Retten-mund, our hitting coach, "After hitting a breaking ball like that, I gotta believe he's going to come in on me." So, the fifth-inning home run happened because I was expecting him to come inside, and the bat just caught up with the baseball, and it went flying out of the ball-park. That was a big thrill, because the game was tied at the time, and all of a sudden here we are, the lowly Padres, stepping into Yankee Sta-dium, and all of a sudden we've got the lead. It took everything I had not to smile going around the bases, because hitting a home run at Yankee Stadium was something I dreamed about but I never told any-body about. I was thrilled to death, but before I could even sit down, Greg Vaughn hit a home run down the left-field line. That gave us a 5–2 lead, but the Yankees scored 7 runs in the seventh inning to beat us.

Also in Game 3, we played our kind of game, where we had the lead late and went to the bullpen to close them out. But they rallied again and beat us. All year long, those were games that we won. The Yankees proved to me they were a great team, because we had 'em right where we wanted 'em and they still were able to recover, recu-perate, and win both those ball games. They did everything they had to do to win. The Yankees were truly the better team, and that makes losing the World Series easier to live with.

I'd Look Anywhere to Improve My Hitting

I was struggling one year, and my average had dropped to just above .300. I had batted over .300 sixteen years in a row, so I wanted to get my good swing back. We were playing the Mets, and a few of us went out to Shea Stadium for some early batting practice. When we got there, however, we were told we couldn't hit early because there was a minor-league game being played between the Hudson Valley Renegades, the Devil Rays' Class A team, and the Pittsfield Mets.

Instead of sitting around the clubhouse playing cards like I'd normally do, I decided to go out and sit on a dugout bench and watch those guys play. At Shea Stadium, you go down the stairs and then you come back up the stairs, and when you come out, you're in the dugout. And these guys on the Devil Rays' team look at me, and it's like, "Hey, you're Tony Gwynn—what the heck are you doing here?" I said, "Well, I'm gonna sit here and watch you guys play, 'cause I hope I can find something in one of your swings to help me out." And they're like, "Yeah, yeah, right." I got permission from their manager and sat there for four or five innings. He asked me to talk to them about hitting, so I told them how I really hadn't swung the bat the way I wanted to.

There was one player on the Mets' team, a right-hand hitter with a little power, who got my attention. The first time up, he hit a ball into right center field for a double. I told the guys who were on the bench, "See, that's what you should do. See how he got his foot down soft, and he took his hands right to the baseball. He didn't try to muscle it. He just put a good swing on it, and look at the result." When the guy was getting ready to bat again, I made sure I had a good seat so I could really watch him work. He got behind 0-2 and fouled a couple of pitches off before getting a base hit between short and third on a pretty tough forkball that was down. I said, "He fell behind but didn't give in. He battled. He got a tough pitch but got a base hit. That's what hitting's all about. Even when you're behind in the count, you still go up there battling. You still don't give up anything. You still try to get a good pitch to hit and put a good swing on it." Meanwhile I'm telling myself, "God, if I could do what he's doing, I'd get right back on track."

That night, Hideo Nomo started for New York. If you're in a slump, he is not the type of pitcher you want to face, because he's got a real long windup and a herky-jerky motion, and he's got a pretty good

159

splitter to boot. I fell behind 0-2 and got a fastball that was a little bit up. I didn't put a good swing on it, but it found a hole. The next time up, I hit a two-run homer. The next time up, I got a base hit off reliever Dennis Cook, who I really don't ever feel comfortable against. I ended up going 3-for-4, and I was thinking, "God, maybe I'm starting to turn things around." The next night, Al Leiter's pitching, and he's another guy you don't want to face if you're in a slump. But that night, I doubled to left and doubled to right and ended up going 4-for-5. Now I was thinking, "God, I'm really doing the things that I should be doing." Over eight games, I went 18-for-32.

I was telling guys on the club, "Hey, you know, I watched this guy hit on the Mets' minor-league team, and seeing him hit really got me going back in the right direction." When I told this to Merv Rettenmund, our hitting coach, he looked at me like I'd lost my mind. But, really, seeing that guy do it right gave me an idea of what I had to do in order to be successful again. For the rest of the season, I was trying to find out what this guy's name was. In the postseason, Tim McCarver told me his name was Robert Stratton. I owe him a big thank-you, because that run I was on after watching him was the best I swung until the World Series. If I ever run into him, I have to get him a bat or something, because he was the one who got me back on track.

GARY SHEFFIELD
Payback

After Milwaukee traded me to San Diego, I was excited that I'd finally get to bat against my uncle Dwight Gooden when we played the Mets. We'd been facing each other all our lives. Thanks to him, I'm used to being knocked down and getting drilled by pitches, because that's how he made me into a baseball player. I used to resent the fact that I had to play baseball. I didn't like it at all. I loved football and wanted to be like Tony Dorsett, but he made me play baseball. He pushed me into an area I didn't want to go. He'd make me play for hours. He'd hit me with his fastball, which is one of the reasons I didn't like playing. Then he'd make me pitch to him, and he'd hit the ball over the fence and make me go get it. I figured the only way I wouldn't have go get the ball was if I struck him out. So, I started to throw the ball hard to compete with him, and I became a good pitcher. Those confrontations with my uncle prepared me for the big leagues. People may have thought I was scared the first time I faced Nolan Ryan or Roger Clemens, but I really wasn't. I said, "I know you throw hard, I know you have the big overhand curveball, I know you're proud of your fastball, but I grew up hitting those!" Because I'd faced Doc Gooden when I was a teenager.

I still get mad at him when I think back at those confrontations. I remember telling him, "One day I'm going to get you back! I can't wait till I hit a home run off you!" Before the first game we faced each other in the majors, I told him I was going to homer off him, and he told me that I wouldn't get a hit of any kind. So, we had a bet going. The whole family was in town, so I really wanted to homer, but instead I got a single to left field on an inside fastball. When I got to first base, I was all smiles. It was the best moment of my life, getting a hit off my uncle at the big-league level.

We Like How You Play, So Let's Change Everything

I was a pitcher at Hillsborough High, in Tampa, Florida, but when I got to the minors, they handed me a fielder's mitt and said, "Go to short." I'm like, "I don't know how to play shortstop." In fact, the day I flew in there was a game, and they had to find me because I had gone to the bullpen thinking I was a pitcher. I played short wearing the new Nike pitching shoes my Uncle Dwight had sent me. Two years later, I'm in the big leagues and learning on the job. They changed the way I fielded the ball, and they changed the slot where I threw the ball from. And they changed my hitting style.

I was just nineteen when I got to the big leagues with Milwaukee in 1988, and they looked at my frame and my speed and said, "We want you to get on and steal bases." I said, "That's not my game." So, we had a dispute. They wanted me to hit for average and steal bases,

161

and I wanted to be a power hitter with speed. I looked up to Barry Larkin and wanted to pattern my game after his. He'd hit fifteen to twenty homers a year, and I thought that's how many I could hit early in my career and then get to thirty homers like I'd done in the minor leagues. But they stopped me from wiggling the bat, because they wanted me to hold it flat and try to hit the ball the other way. It was a learning process, because I hadn't been a hitter for that long.

Just imagine being my age and coming to the big leagues, and finding out that they wanted to change everything. It was very confusing for me. All I wanted to do was play baseball. My granddaddy used to say, "Just watch the veteran players and see how they go about their business. Just watch Robin Yount and Paul Molitor and see what it's like to go through a 162-game season." He told me to just be myself and pick up things from them, and I'd get good numbers. But the organization tried to change me, and if I complained, I'd get a bad label that would be very difficult to shake for the rest of my career.

How I Got My Bat Wiggle

When I first picked up a wood bat in the minor leagues, I grabbed the smallest bat so I'd have a quick swing. It was so light that I just started wiggling it all over the place. I was hitting balls over the fence, but I couldn't keep the ball fair. So, I grabbed a bigger bat and wiggled that, too, with weight behind it, and I was keeping the ball fair. So, that's how I got my bat wiggle at the plate.

TEN

THE RIGHTY ROTATION

ROBIN ROBERTS
How I Became a Pitcher

Not many major leaguers in my day were college graduates. After I got out of the army, I went to Michigan State on a basketball scholarship. I went out for baseball, and the coach said, "What are you doing here?" I said, "I can play the game, Coach." He said, "What position do you play?" I said, "What do you need?" He said, "I need pitching." I said, "I'm a pitcher." So, that's when I became a pitcher. At the time, I was really a third baseman. I loved hitting, but I never was as good as I should have been. I always lunged for the ball, because I was rusty. If I lasted a full game, I usually was pretty good my last time up.

When the Whiz Kids Won the Pennant

I pitched ten innings in the last game of the 1950 season. For the sixth time, I was trying to win my twentieth game, but more important, we had to win to clinch the pennant over Brooklyn. In the top of the inning, Dick Sisler hit a three-run homer off the Dodgers' ace Don Newcombe, and I shut them down to give us a 4–1 victory and the National League title.

The biggest play of the game until Sisler's home run came in the bottom of the ninth, when Richie Ashburn threw Cal Abrams out at the plate. Duke Snider had come up with men on first and second and nobody out, and I thought he might be bunting. But he ripped the first pitch right past me on the second-base side. I turned around, and Abrams was holding up because it was a line drive. I went to back up home plate, but I was surprised when their coach Milt Stock waved Abrams around third after he got such a bad jump off second. Whitey was playing a shallow center field, and he got to the ball quickly and made a perfect throw home to Stan Lopata to beat Abrams by ten to twelve feet. Abrams didn't even slide. I have no idea why he was waved home with nobody out.

We were still in a mess, because the runners moved up to second and third on the throw, and Jackie Robinson was the batter. My manager, Eddie Sawyer, came out and said, "Let's walk Robinson and keep the ball down on Furillo." So, I walked Robinson, and the first pitch I threw Furillo was face high. He popped it straight up. Then I got Gil Hodges on a fly to Del Ennis, and I was out of the jam. That set the stage for Sisler's homer that gave the Phillies their first pennant in thirty-five years.

Coming Up Short Against the Yankees

We had pitching problems going into the 1950 World Series against the Yankees. Curt Simmons was unavailable for the Series, and I was unavailable for the opener because I had pitched ten innings in the pennant clincher on the last day of the season. So, Eddie Sawyer started Jim Konstanty, who was the National League MVP that season as a reliever. He hadn't started ever before, and I couldn't believe how well he pitched. He got beat 1–0, on a double by Bobby Brown and two fly balls.

Then I pitched in Game 2, going ten innings again, and losing to Allie Reynolds, 2–1. Joe DiMaggio was 0-for-4 with four pop-ups before he batted in the top of the tenth. I was getting cocky, and he hit a real shot off a high fastball into the seats to give the Yankees a

2–0 lead in the Series, on the way to a four-game sweep that included three 1-run victories. I'm always "so happy" to see an old clip of that homer. Years later, I was at an old-timers game with DiMaggio, and we were in the locker room changing. Joe didn't say much, but he said, "I can still see that pitch you threw me." I said, "Joe, you oughtta see it from my angle. It doesn't look so pretty."

Back When Pitchers Finished What They Started

In my day, if you were pitching well and your arm wasn't falling off, the manager would leave you in the game. I'm proud to have pitched over 300 innings six consecutive seasons, and I'm told that at one time, I threw 28 complete games in succession. They used to ask me, "How did you do that?" I'd say, "Well, no one came out to get the ball. So, I just kept pitching." I didn't want anyone to come out there. I didn't want a crowd around me. I completed 305 of my 609 starts, just over half. Among postwar pitchers, that was the most except for Warren Spahn. Years later, Gaylord Perry made the Hall of Fame, and he looked at the list of pitchers with the most complete games. He had 303 games, and he joked it upset him emotionally when he found out he was only 2 short of my number. He said if he'd known, he would have stuck around for a while.

Adding a Second Pitch

Early in my career, I relied exclusively on my fastball and pinpoint control. I tried to throw a curveball, but I was a low-delivery pitcher, with my right knee touching the ground the way it would with Tom Seaver, and it's hard to throw a curve when there's no room to operate. When I tried to throw a curve, I'd pretty much stand straight up to do it, and that told batters a curve was coming. So, I gave up. Then in 1952, we were playing the Giants, and I watched Sal Maglie throw his breaking ball. He had two curves—one a little bigger than the other, but neither of them big. He just turned his hand over quickly,

165

and the result was a pitch with a terrific break. He beat us, and I decided I had to come up with that pitch. So, I worked on it in the bullpen before my next start. I'd give my wrist a little pop and release the ball, and I could curve the pitch with my low delivery. That's the year I won twenty-eight games, and using a breaking ball is what really helped me.

The Man Who Changed Baseball More than Anyone

In nineteen years, I won 286 games and made a total of $530,000. One year, I asked my owner for $50,000, and he said, "If I give you $50,000, my payroll will be almost three-quarters of a million dollars!" That was for twenty-five guys! Now when I look at the salaries of today's players, I laugh and grin. The man responsible for the big change was Marvin Miller. Jim Bunning and I were the ones who introduced Miller to the players in the mid-'60s as our choice to head the Players' Union. Before that, he had been a lawyer with the Steelworkers, and he knew everything about labor negotiations.

Under Miller, it got to the point where it was a battle between players and owners, and the fans weren't considered. I always felt bad about that, but it pretty much had to be that way, because the owners wouldn't treat him fairly after we elected him. They forced him to— let me put it this way— "use his education." And Marvin knew how to operate. I hope the players today understand why they have it so good. A lot of players stuck their necks out, and that took guts.

Every time the players struck, it upset me. When I brought in Marvin to be a candidate, I told him, "I'll back you if you promise never to strike baseball." Well, the first time they struck, in 1972, I rang up Marvin, and he said, "I've been waiting for your call." I said, "Marvin, remember our deal." He said, "Well, the players made me do it." I said, "I think that's a little strong." He told me he tried to talk the players out of a strike, and maybe I should have believed him. But I think he convinced them to do it. Anyway, they struck, and that's when the game started to really change for the players. I don't think

166

there's any doubt Marvin Miller belongs in the Hall of Fame. Babe Ruth changed the game by hitting home runs, and there was Jackie, Henry, and the rest of them, but nobody changed the game as much as Marvin Miller.

BOB GIBSON
I Was the One That Got Away

When I was at Creighton, the Yankees were one of the teams who wanted to sign me, but they didn't want to give me the $35,000 bonus I was asking for. At that time, if you signed for a bonus like that, the team had to keep you on the major-league roster rather than send you to the minors. Their scout asked, "Do you actually think you can make a major-league team?" I said, "Well, yeah." And he said, "Well, I don't think you can make a major-league team." So, I didn't sign with him. Seven years later, I beat the Yankees three times in the World Series. I wanted to know if he still felt that way!

I Expected to Be a Center Fielder

When I was at Creighton, I decided that I didn't really want to be a pitcher. I did pitch there, but most of the time, I played center field, or caught when they needed a catcher. I said, "I'm going to play major-league baseball one of these days, and I'm going be a center fielder." When I signed with the Cardinals, it was as a pitcher and out-fielder, but I didn't think that I ever was going to pitch. At Creighton, I had won a conference batting title, and I assumed the Cardinals wanted me to be a switch-hitting outfielder. But the Cardinals needed pitching at the time, so I stayed right there in Omaha on a Triple-A contract and pitched from the beginning. I *never* got a chance to play the outfield. If I got to do my career all over again, I'd probably do it the same way. But maybe, just maybe, I would play every day rather than pitch. What position? Center field.

Giving Up My Best Sport

Basketball was my first love, and I was better at it than baseball, which also was much harder for me. I could shoot, run, and jump. After playing at Creighton, I joined the Harlem Globetrotters for one year, in addition to pitching in the Cardinals' system. At the time, they went on a barnstorming tour where they played real, unscripted basketball against a College All-Star team. They had come into Omaha, and I played with the College All-Stars. In one quarter, I scored fourteen points, and that was one of the few games they beat the Globetrotters. That's when the Globetrotters asked me to play with them. I signed because I thought that was the kind of basketball we were going to play all the time. It wasn't. I didn't like that the games the Globetrotters played weren't real competition, or that every time down the court, they expected me to throw the ball to my roommate, Meadowlark Lemon, rather than shoot. But I loved the sport, and it paid good money.

The next winter, after the baseball season, Bing Devine, who was the Cardinals' general manager, said, "Bob, you can't concentrate on two sports at the same time." Wrong; I could have. He said, "You're playing basketball, and we really don't like it." I said, "Well, Bing, I play basketball in the winter, not only because I like it, but because I can make a lot of money playing basketball." And he said, "How much money can you make?" I said, "Well, I make $1,000 a month, and we play four months, so that's $4,000." He said, "If I give you $4,000, will you quit?" I said, "Yep." It was that quick. The Globetrotters wanted me to come back in '58, but I didn't re-sign with them. So, that was the end of my basketball career.

A Manager with a Big Problem

Solly Hemus was my manager when I first pitched for the Cardinals. Solly had a problem; he had a real *big* problem. Curt Flood didn't play, Bill White didn't play, and I didn't play. And *oddly* enough, we were the only black guys on the team. I *wonder* if that had anything to do with it. He said I wouldn't be a good major-league pitcher because I threw everything at the same speed. Hard. I threw too *hard* for him. He kept sending me down. One day in St. Louis, Bill was playing center field in a game I started. Naturally, I walked the first guy up. I always walked the first guy. The second batter hit a high fly to deep center field. Bill circled it, and it fell behind him. The hitter ended up on second, and the runner scored all the way from first base. Solly came to the mound, said a few words, and took me out. He then sent me back to the minors. Every time they sent me out, I would win three or four games in a row. Then they'd bring me back, and Solly would sit me on the bench.

Johnny Keane took over for Solly when he was fired in mid-1961. He was a super, super individual. He had been my first manager in professional baseball, when I broke in at home with Omaha. He had seen me pitch in college, so he knew what I was capable of doing. Johnny went to St. Louis the next year to coach for Solly, and when I got to St. Louis, he was there. Unfortunately, he was the coach and Solly was the manager. Once we got rid of Solly, Johnny managed the team, and we did well. Bill White played first, Flood was in center, and Lou Brock came in from Chicago and played left field and batted leadoff. And in 1964, we beat the Yankees in the World Series.

Curt Flood

Curt Flood and I were very close. We were together more than a married couple, because when we were on the road, we lived together and were with each other from sunup to sundown, day in and day out. At least when you're married, you get away from each other when you leave for work. We were together constantly, so I got to know him pretty well and love him like a brother.

Solly Hemus didn't love Curt and wouldn't play him in center field. Even Bill White played center back in the early '60s. Bill was a great first baseman, but nobody was going to move Stan Musial off first, so they put him in the outfield. Then White ran into the center-field wall. I believe that was the last time he was asked to play center field. He became our first baseman and a terrific player. Center field was open, but rather than give Curt the job in the spring of 1961, the Cardinals traded five minor leaguers for Don Landrum. Landrum played center and went something like 0-for-32. So, they sent Landrum out, and Flood finally became our center fielder.

I've never seen anybody go get the ball any better than Curt Flood. Nobody tracked down a fly any better or was better playing the fence. Now, you might think I'm crazy, because everybody knows about Willie Mays. Well, I think Curt Flood could go get the ball as well as Willie. Of course, after he got it, somebody had to run out and help him throw it in. He didn't have nearly the arm or the instincts of Willie. And he couldn't hit like Willie. But he was a pretty fair ballplayer.

Johnny Keane's Guarantees

In a game in Milwaukee, Johnny Keane told me to throw a breaking ball as my first pitch of the game. He said, "If the guy even swings at it, I'll eat my hat." Well, Roy McMillan led off, and I threw the curveball on the first pitch. He left the ground swinging and doubled down the line. And I looked over in the dugout, and Johnny was nowhere to be found. I said, "I'd better get him a straw hat, because the one he's wearing might choke him."

In the seventh game of the 1964 World Series between the Cardinals and the Yankees, we had a 7–3 lead going into the ninth inning. I was on the verge of pitching my second complete game in three days, when Phil Linz hit a solo home run with one out, and Clete Boyer followed with a two-out homer. Bobby Richardson was the next batter, and Johnny Keane came out to the mound and returned to the dugout. He later told reporters he left me in because "I was committed to his heart." That made me feel good. But he said something else people should know about *before* I went to the mound that inning. He said, "I don't want you to mess around with breaking balls or anything. Throw your fastball right over the middle of the plate." And in his gravelly voice, he added, "I guarantee you that they're not going to hit four home runs." So, I was throwing it right down the chute, and they were whacking it. After the second home run, I was wondering, "Are they going to hit four or not?" I would look in the dugout, and Johnny would be leaning over the watercooler with his back to the mound because he was scared to make eye contact with me. Luckily, Richardson popped up.

The Tailor

The Cardinals had a tailor come to our hotel to measure us for our uniforms. He was the same guy we'd use when we bought a new suit. Well, I'm standing there with my crooked arm, and he's trying to straighten it out. He says, "Here, pull it down." I said, "It won't go down. And when you pull on it like that, it hurts." He'd pull it down, and it'd pop back up because my muscles and tendons and everything else had shortened up after I'd thrown hard for such a long time. He wanted to send me to the hospital because I couldn't straighten my arm anymore.

Pitching Through Pain

I had my leg broken in 1967 by Roberto Clemente. Everybody says that he broke my leg with a line drive, but it was a one-hopper that skidded off the infield before there was an artificial surface at Busch Stadium. I thought it was an error. I always turned on my follow-through, and my leg had just come down and around, and I was looking behind me, more or less, which is why I didn't get a good view of that ball. And when I finally saw it, I put my hand down, but it was

171

too late, because the ball was hit so hard. After that ball hit my leg, I threw three or four warm-up pitches and then said, "I'm OK." I threw five more pitches. I walked Donn Clendenon on four high fastballs, and then I threw my fifth pitch to the next hitter, and my right leg popped. I broke it in half. That definitely hurt.

I came back seven weeks later and pitched the pennant clincher in Philadelphia and then pitched three complete-game victories over the Red Sox in the World Series. I guess you can talk about determination. You know that when you come back from an injury, there is always talk about Dizzy Dean pitching too soon after he broke his toe in an All-Star Game and never being any good again. Reporters would come up and say, "You know what happened to Dizzy Dean . . ." "Yeah, yeah, yeah." I was going to make sure that wasn't going to happen to me. I don't know if it made me pitch better against Boston, but I was determined to pitch despite the recent injury and be successful.

The Best ERA of the Twentieth Century

In 1968, when I had a 1.12 ERA and won the Cy Young and MVP Awards, I had a lot of fun. I felt like I could do anything I wanted to with the baseball, and I pretty much did. I could close my eyes and hit a corner. I think what made me so successful that year is that hitters don't like to give pitchers credit. They just didn't think I could hit that spot on the corner again and again, and I would. They took a lot of strikes, which is why I struck out over three hundred batters that year. I pitched over three hundred innings, and no one mentions that my control was so good that I hit only seven batters.

172   I threw thirteen shutouts and had forty-nine scoreless innings, until Len Gabrielson scored from third base on a wild pitch. Johnny Edwards was catching, and it was *not* a wild pitch. It was a sinker that sailed a little bit and got by him. The funniest thing is after the game was over, the reporters all asked me, "What happened?" And I said, "The jerk missed the ball." They all just looked at me, and then I started laughing. I said, "I threw the ball away; what do you want?" But

it was not a wild pitch. We won that game 6–1, and I threw a couple of more shutouts after that.

Nineteen sixty-eight didn't just happen. If you followed my career at all and watched me from '64 to '68, you saw that I was improving a little bit each year. And what really made me have that type of year in '68 is that right at the beginning of the season, Tim McCarver sat down with me and said, "Bob, I think we oughtta start backdooring the slider." Backdooring a slider to a left-handed hitter means that rather than throwing the slider inside, you throw it outside and let it break and nip the outside corner. And I said, "Nah, with the backdoor slider, if you miss with it, it comes over the middle of the plate." And Tim said, "I think you've got good-enough control where you can backdoor that slider and it will hit the corner." And he was the one who was instrumental in getting me to do that. I started throwing it, and I got a little bit more confidence. That's why I really had that good year.

Who Do I Sue for Lowering the Mound?

In 1968, there were seven pitchers who had earned run averages under 2.00. We had gotten to the point where we knew what we were doing. And then they lowered the mound five inches. My idea was to be the best pitcher I could be and one day be the best pitcher in the world. And I worked very hard at it. You get to the point where you perfect your trade, and they do something to take it away from you. That's the way I felt. They lowered the mound because the pitchers were too effective. Now, what kind of sense does that make? I guess now they're going to have to take bats away from hitters if they keep hitting home runs? They're too effective, so take that big bat away and give them little tweezers or a little stick and see if they can hit seventy home runs again! I say that although it didn't affect my breaking ball as much as it did some of those guys who threw straight over the top and had curveballs that went straight down. I threw the slider, and it didn't go straight down, but the guys with the best curveballs, like Nelson Briles,

173

no longer could get a breaking ball below the belt. The purpose was to improve hitting. I still feel like suing somebody.

Pitching to Hank Aaron

For years, we could never figure out how to pitch to Hank Aaron. I finally figured out that if I took a little bit off of the slider and kept it away—and it was a terrible pitch—I could get him to hit ground balls. I used to throw it all the time to him, and he'd hit one-hoppers to Dal Maxvill at second base. They would hit Dal in his chest, hit him in the ear, hit him all over. He complained, "Bob, why don't you have him hit that ball somewhere else?" I said, "We're getting him out. You just stand there and catch it." I don't know how many times he got hit in the chest with those hard one-hoppers skipping off the ground.

The Glare

If I'd realized how intimidating I was on the mound, I'd have been really nasty. I didn't "glare" to intimidate batters. I just couldn't see the catcher's fingers. Tim used to put tape and everything else on them, and I'd stand there trying to see. Half the time, I didn't even know who was hitting. I would be staring and trying to pick up the signs, and the hitter thought I was glaring at him. I guess that's part of my personality. Even now, people who really don't know me come up and ask, "Who are you mad at?" I say, "I'm not mad at anybody. I just look like this. What do you want from me?" "Are you angry?" "No! I'm not angry!"

There's one thing about baseball: if they label you, the label follows you throughout your life. I haven't played baseball in over thirty years, yet people come up to me and say that they heard how mean a ballplayer I was. After I wrote my book, I was in a New York bookstore signing copies, when I noticed a nine-year-old kid standing there looking at me. He finally walked over to me and said, "Bob?" I said,

174

"Yeah?" He said, "Give me *the* look. Give me *the* look." I said, "You better get outta here, or I'll give you *the* look."

The Decision to Retire

In 1970, I started out 0–5, and they were trying to sell me, trying to trade me, and thinking, "Let's get rid of him. Maybe we can get a bag of balls or something for him." But I had an ERA under 2.00, and I went on to win 15 or 16 games in a row and 20 games for the year. And in 1971, I pitched a no-hitter, which I never thought I'd do, because I was basically a high-ball pitcher, and batters like high fastballs.

I eventually left on my own terms. I'll tell you what prompted that. I was on the mound one day, and the bases were loaded, and the batter wasn't Willie Mays, although I'd like to think it was Mays, but it was a really good hitter at the plate. And I should have been concentrating on how to get this guy out, but I found myself thinking about my ex-wife, who I'd just divorced. I'm standing out there thinking about her, and I was not in the game. And I said right then, "It's over. It's time to quit." That's a true story.

Pitching to Today's Hitters

I'm often asked if I'd have a tough time pitching today because I pitched inside so much. I was a good-enough pitcher where I could adjust to what they have to do today. I probably would have a lot of problems at the beginning because of the way I pitched—inside, then away; inside, then away. When I was pitching back in those days, the guys didn't dive across the plate like they do today. I probably would hit a lot of guys and get kicked out of games for intentionally throwing at them, although it wouldn't have been intentional. I pitched inside because that's the way we were taught, and if a guy happened to get in the way of the ball, *tough*. But today, you can't do that anymore. I would adjust, but I wouldn't like it.

175

Batters today go up to the plate looking almost like the knights of old, with armor all over their bodies. How would I handle that? You ever been hit with armor on? I think it would hurt. I would have a ball trying to see if I could crack one of those things.

JIM BOUTON
World Series Memories

I started for the Yankees in Game 3 of the 1963 World Series against the Los Angeles Dodgers. Sandy Koufax had beaten Whitey Ford in Game 1 and struck out fifteen batters, and then Johnny Podres beat us 4–1, but Don Drysdale pitched even better opposing me. I gave up only four hits, but he gave up only three. The only run of the game came off me in the first inning when Tommy Davis hit a grounder that went off Bobby Richardson's knee into center field and Willie Davis scored all the way from first. I always tell Tommy that should have been scored an error. The Dodgers did get the bases loaded in the seventh inning. We got out of that jam when they had a baserunning blunder on a grounder to Richardson near first base and ended up with two men on first base.

Before that ball was hit, I had a little conversation with Joe Pepitone near the mound because I had given him the pickoff sign and he shook me off! Have you ever heard of a first baseman shaking off a pickoff sign? Can you imagine? He told me he didn't want to make any more mistakes, so he didn't want any throws to first. They won the Series the next day, when Koufax beat Ford again, 2–1. They scored the winning run when Pepitone lost a throw from third by Cletis Boyer in the white shirtsleeves of the L.A. crowd. So, I guess he knew what he was talking about when he told me not to throw over there.

We returned to the World Series the next year but lost again to the Cardinals when Bob Gibson beat us three times, in Games 1, 5, and 7. At least it was an exciting Series, and we got three victories, including my wins in Games 3 and 6. Both times, I opposed Curt Simmons. Game 6 was a blowout, 8–3, but in Game 3, the only two runs that scored through eight innings were driven in by Simmons and me. It was 1–1 going into the bottom of the ninth inning. Mickey Mantle was going to be leading off for us, so Johnny Keane took out the left-handed Simmons and brought in the right-handed knuckleballer Barney Schultz. Mantle got to bat left-handed for the first time in the game. Mickey didn't call his shots very often, but he said, "I'm going to take his ball right out of here."

We watched Schultz warm up, and his knuckler was breaking down. When Mickey batted right-handed, he would swing over the top of the ball—he'd chop the ball and hit vicious line drives. But left-handed, he had an underhand stroke and would hit under the ball. So, here was Schultz with a knuckler that dropped to the ankles, and Mickey could see what was going to happen. He walked up to the plate, and Schultz's first pitch came in knee high and dropped down to the ankles, and Mickey hit a 7-iron into the upper deck in right field in Yankee Stadium. As soon as he hit it, everyone knew the ball game was over.

My Friend Mickey Mantle

For the rest of my life, the thing I'll remember Mickey Mantle for is my first start in the big leagues in 1962. I shut out the Washington Senators at Yankee Stadium. It was one of the worst shutouts in the history of baseball. I walked seven guys, I gave up seven hits—I pitched the whole game from the stretch position. Ralph Houk said afterward, "Any more shutouts like that and we'll need a new bullpen." After the game ended, they interviewed me in the dugout, so I was the last guy to walk into the locker room. As I opened the door, I could see a path of white towels leading from the door all the way to my locker. Mickey was laying down the last towel, giving me the white-towel treatment.

Everybody loved Mickey. He was a leader, but a quiet leader who never stood up at a meeting or said anything, but just did it out on the field. We really enjoyed each other as teammates. I enjoyed his sense of humor, and I think he enjoyed mine. Once, he initiated a raffle. He was raffling off a Smithfield ham, and we all put in a couple of bucks. He has the drawing, and I win. I go to his locker to pick up my ham, and he says, "There is no ham." I said, "What do you mean? I have the winning number." He said, "That's one of the hazards of a game of chance."

I got traded from the Yankees after the 1968 season. In 1969, I pitched for the Seattle Pilots in their only season and the Houston Astros, and I wrote *Ball Four*. That was Mickey's final season, so when the book was published in 1970, my final big-league season before my 1978 comeback with Atlanta, Mickey had retired. I said nice things about Mickey in the book, and I also talked about a few other things, including the time he hit a home run with a hangover. Like a lot of players in those days, he occasionally drank too much. Mickey either read what I wrote or heard about it, and stopped speaking to me.

A lot of people thought Mickey was the reason I wasn't invited to the annual Old-Timers Games at Yankee Stadium. I told myself that if he was the reason, I certainly didn't want to go back if that meant he wouldn't show up. In 1994, when Mickey was battling his own health problems that would lead to his death a year later, his son Billy passed away. I wrote Mickey a note saying how badly I felt and that I had nice memories of Billy running around the clubhouse in spring training when he was a polite little boy. I also said, "I hope by this time, you're feeling OK about *Ball Four*." I sent it off to him and never expected to hear from him again.

Two weeks later, I walked into my office, and my secretary is standing by my answering machine. She said, "You're going to have to listen to this message yourself." I push the button and heard: "Hi, Jim, this is The Mick. I just want you to know how much I appreciate what you wrote about Billy. Thank you very much. I want you to know that I'm OK with *Ball Four* these days. And I just want you to know that I'm not the reason you're not invited back to Old-Timers Games. I heard that going around, and I would never say to anybody not to invite you. I wanted to clear that up. Thanks again for your note." I taped his message, and I still have it.

Pete Rose: Why Baseball Shouldn't Be Your Entire Life

Pete Rose and I broke in together in the New York–Pennsylvania League in 1959. And all through baseball, he was the model: "See that guy there? He eats, sleeps, and drinks baseball. And if you do that, you'll get to the big leagues, too." One of the problems with baseball being a player's whole life is that he becomes a partially formed person whose reality is only what happens on the field, in the clubhouse, or on the team bus. The rest of the world is a dim thing going on in the distance. One-dimensional people can't handle real life, so when you have a team of fourteen-year-olds in twenty-five-year-old bodies, it's inevitable that some of them are going to have problems. These guys are not prepared for reality, and they aren't good role models. You can copy a guy's batting stance or his pitching motion, but don't copy his lifestyle. At least in our day, the toys weren't as dangerous.

JIM PALMER
I Could Have Sold Dresses for a Living

My older sister, Bonnie, and I were adopted and lived in New York City. My mother had come from Omaha to put her youngest brother through the Juilliard School of Music. She had a little dress shop, and she met my dad, who had two dress companies. My mother was Catholic, my father was Jewish, and I was raised Presbyterian and Christian Scientist, which is probably why I've been confused from time to time. I never really played organized baseball until my father passed away when I was ten years old and we moved to Whittier, California, for a year, and then Beverly Hills. Then I got involved in Little League, and from there, it was Pony League, Babe Ruth, high school ball in Phoenix, Arizona—the whole deal. My dad loved sports, but he thought that was a profession beneath what a Jewish boy should have. According to a close family friend who I knew my entire playing career, he would have wanted me to take over his business and never allowed me to become a baseball player.

179

My Good Fortune to Play for Cal Ripken Sr.

I signed with the Orioles at the end of summer in 1963, two months before I turned eighteen. I went off to play A ball with Cal Ripken Sr., and we had quite a good team. We won fourteen in a row in spring training. Earl Weaver had a Double-A team in Thomasville, Georgia, and we used to handle them pretty quickly. We knew how to play the game. In A ball, the most you could make was $500 a month in your first year, which was about $410 after taxes. You're living in basement apartments, you're getting $3-a-day meal money, and you're taking fourteen-hour bus trips—but it's fun!

I know my life changed when I was young and played for Cal. We were taught the "Orioles Way," which was no different from the "Cardinals Way" or the "Dodgers Way." Everyone taught the fundamentals to win, but what Cal got us to understand—and I'm sure it's what Cal Ripken Jr. learned in order to play 2,632 consecutive games—is that you have to have fun and a passion for what you do, and you have to go to the ballpark every day trying to become a better player. It's easy to do that in A ball, because you want your salary to go up $100.

The One and Only Time I Listened to Earl Weaver

My major-league debut was against Tony Conigliaro, of the Red Sox, with the bases loaded. He didn't homer, and I would pitch 3,950 innings without giving up a grand slam. However, I did throw one in spring training to Freddie Patek, because I let the 5'4" guys have a good time, and one in Triple-A to Johnny Bench. I had hurt my shoulder, and at one time in 1967, I pitched for Earl Weaver at Rochester. I watched from the sidelines my first game with the team. We were supposed to play in Buffalo, but because of worry about race riots, they moved the game to some former football stadium near Niagara Falls. Bench was on Buffalo and had hit about twenty homers in thirty games, but I didn't know about that, because I just got to Triple-A. His first time up, he got jammed and had a looping single over second base. I casually asked who he was, and somebody said, "Aw, a ping-pong hitter."

The next night, I pitch, and I threw the ball over Bench's head, and he swung and struck out. Later, I had a 6–0 lead and walked the bases loaded, but before I pitched to Bench, Earl Weaver ran out to the mound. He hated walks under any circumstances and wasn't happy with my three walks, so he said, "Just throw the ball down the middle!" I was throwing only 80 mph, but I did what he said. When I last saw the ball, it was heading out to Niagara Falls. It went about 475 feet, the only grand slam I ever gave up in professional baseball. And that was the genesis of my relationship with Earl Weaver. That was the last time I ever listened to him when he came out to the mound.

Frank Robinson Joins the Orioles

I had heard a lot about Frank Robinson before the Orioles acquired him from Cincinnati for essentially Milt Pappas, before the 1966 season. But in those days, unless you played against a team from the other league in exhibition games, you didn't know that much about their players. So, I didn't know much about Robinson, other than that Reds GM Bill DeWitt had called him an "old thirty."

Baltimore had won over ninety games in finishing third the previous two years, including my 1965 rookie season, so, coming to spring training, I knew we had a good ball club regardless of how Frank would play. He was in Baltimore trying to get a house, so he missed the first week of spring training. We were having one of our intrasquad games, and we had a young former bonus pitcher from out of the Braves organization impressing everyone. His name was Steve Cosgrove, and he had a rising fastball and curve that dropped right off the table. Frank came up to face him, and it was the first time I'd ever seen him hit. I was sitting on the bench and watched Cosgrove get two strikes on him and throw him a curveball that went swoosh, straight down. Frank got right out on that front foot but kept his hands and his bat back and hit the ball with one hand down the chalk line in left for

181

a double. I turned to my roommate, Davy Leonhard, and said, "We just won the pennant." I was right. Frank won the Triple Crown, and because of him, we had a dynamic offense. The great thing about a superstar is that he elevates everybody on the ball club, and that's what Frank did for us as we won ninety-seven games and beat out Minnesota by eight games. We play Game 1 of the World Series, and both Frank and Brooks Robinson hit home runs off Don Drysdale, and we saw we had a chance to beat the Dodgers—which we did in four games.

Frank was a terrific all-around player. He didn't have world-class speed, but he was a tough base runner. The only other Oriole to break up double plays like Frank would be Don Baylor. He had intensity, even more than later Orioles Bobby Grich and Reggie Jackson. He played the game like you were supposed to play it. He didn't fraternize with players on the other team. Today during batting practice, you see guys from both teams, and they're so chummy that you think they're from the same family. But Frank didn't talk to anyone. He may have been a little surly and reserved, but that was all right, because I was making $7,500 and he was making twenty times that. It wasn't a mean surliness; it was his demeanor, his game face. We saw how hard he played every day.

In 1966, he led the league with forty-nine homers and 122 RBIs, and in 1967, he was on his way to an even better year before he slid into second base and hit his head on Al Weis's knee. He had twenty-two home runs going into early June, before spending a lot of time on the disabled list. I watched Frank Robinson play with the Orioles until 1971, and later, as an Orioles broadcaster, I watched Albert Belle. Albert was a great offensive player, but he didn't hit great pitching. Frank was so good that he could hit the best pitch any pitcher could make. I saw Frank take Dean Chance's low-and-away slider with one hand and hit it 390 feet over the bullpen. And I saw Catfish Hunter strike him out three times on high fastballs on a night I was pitching, and on his fourth at-bat, with a couple of men on, Frank took his high fastball right around the flagpole. Frank's R161 bat was thirty-five inches long and weighed thirty-six ounces, and it was heavy. But that's the one I used, because I figured he was going to the Hall of Fame.

I Pitch Against One of My Heroes

I came up to the Orioles in 1965, when I was nineteen, and pitched twenty-five or thirty games as a reliever and spot starter. In 1966, I was scheduled to go to Triple-A, but we had a rash of arm injuries in spring training, and I pitched in two exhibition games. I no-hit the Yankees through five innings—I still remember Frank Robinson hitting a two-run homer over the scoreboard at Miami Stadium against Al Downing. Then I pitched well against a good-hitting Cincinnati ball club, going against Jim Maloney, who had thrown three no-hitters and had a fastball that looked like a pea in those lights. So, all of a sudden our manager, Hank Bauer, starts me in the second game of the season.

I went on to win fifteen games, and we won the pennant. I hurt my shoulder painting our house, so it was a bit tentative that I'd pitch in the World Series. But I pitched Game 2 against Sandy Koufax. He hadn't pitched in Game 1 because he had to pitch to get them into the Series and needed the day off. I was twenty, making $7,500, with my first child on the way, and I was going against the pitcher of that decade and someone I'd greatly admired as a young Dodgers fan. I didn't really expect to win. At my age, I just didn't want to embarrass myself.

The Dodgers were about pitching and defense and Maury Wills manufacturing a run, and they were likely to beat you 2–0 or 2–1. I'd seen Koufax pitch in the 1963 and 1965 World Series, and he was virtually unbeatable. Sandy pitched extremely well against us, but Willie Davis dropped two balls in center, and he picked up the second one and heaved it into the stands, so we got four unearned runs early. We eventually got six runs. Meanwhile I became the youngest pitcher to throw a shutout in the World Series. Timing is everything, because that was the first shutout of my major-league career. Everybody knew that Sandy Koufax had arm problems, but he was only thirty and had won twenty-seven games that year, so nobody knew that would be his last game.

When This Pitcher Was a Pitchman

I did ads for the Money Store for years. Phil Rizzuto had been doing them, and they seemed to be directed to people who wanted to get out of jail and needed a bail bondsman. He did a terrific job, but they wanted a change. They went from $1.9 billion to $9 billion a year. I also worked for Jockey for nineteen years. I'd come up to New York on the Metroliner, a $35 round-trip. Pete Rose, Steve Carlton, Jo Jo White, Marquis Johnson, and some others were part of the original campaign. They had a luncheon and did the shoot while people were eating ham-and-cheese sandwiches, and they threw me a glove to make me feel comfortable and very slim underwear. Of course, Pete looked like a hockey player, so they gave him a T-shirt and boxer shorts. Pete missed his plane, and it cost him $5,000. He showed up late; I showed up on time. The next year, I was the only guy from the previous ads who came back. Steve Garvey and I went out to shopping malls. We looked alike, but they chose the taller of us. They tested the two of us, and I ended up being the victor. So I was on the famous billboard in my underwear. It was 46' by 96'. It was huge. I sent the billboard to my daughter when she went to Boulder, because there was a building outside her window. I said, "Kelly, if you miss me . . ."

184   My Special Relationship with Earl Weaver

People who think I had a contentious relationship with Earl Weaver are surprised that I spent my entire career with the Baltimore Orioles. We had our arguments, but they were tempered, because I had respect for Earl. We always would have a meeting at the end of spring training where he would say, "I'm taking the best twenty-five players in this organization back to Baltimore, and if we play together, and play the

'Orioles Way,' which is to play good fundamental baseball and be able to subjugate your ego for the team, then we have a chance to win." I played for Earl from 1969 through 1982, and he was right: we didn't always win, but we were in the race. That was a great thing and why I liked playing for Earl.

When I got in the Hall of Fame in 1990, I said, "Yes, he was a pain in the rear, but he gave me the responsibility to win ball games." He taught me to take responsibility. He'd run out to the mound and say, "Don't be looking out in the bullpen. There's nobody better out there." One game, I was pitching against Boston after they'd hit about sixty-six home runs in ten games. That's when they had George Scott, Fred Lynn, Jim Rice, Carlton Fisk, Carl Yastrzemski, Butch Hobson, and other good power hitters. In my previous start, also against the Red Sox in Fenway Park, I'd given up four home runs trying to hang on for a complete game, and lost, as it turned out. But this time, I was throwing a three-hitter and had a 4–3 lead through eight innings. I had pitched several complete games in a row and had thrown about 140 pitches, and I said, "Earl, I'm exhausted." He asked rhetorically, "Do you think I'm going to take you out and bring in Dick Drago?" So, I got out there. Yaz doubled down the left-field line, but then I got Rice to pop up. That brought up Fisk, who I had trouble with because he stood right on the plate and was a good fastball hitter. Fisk hit a ball to deep left, and it hit Pat Kelly's glove and bounced over the fence. So, from a 4–3 lead, it was now a 5–4 deficit. I'm saying to myself, "If Weaver comes out to get me now, I'm going to deck him. He may be only 5'6" and I'm 6'3", but he's going down!" But he was down the tunnel. I get the second out on a grounder. But here comes Butch Hobson. Kaboom! That game, I threw five home runs! So, in two consecutive starts against the Red Sox, I gave up nine home runs!

Ten days later, we go back to Fenway Park. I wasn't scheduled to pitch, and I'm thinking that's great. But Earl keeps me back the previous series just so I can pitch against the Red Sox. He knew that pride would make me pitch well. I won 8–1. Earl handled everybody differently. That was good. He knew that I was temperamental and knew how to push my buttons. He didn't want you to like him, because if he had a warm relationship with you, he thought it would prevent him

185

from managing like he wanted. So he never showed love, but I knew he had respect for me. He knew what my work ethic was. Once at Fan Fest, a fan asked Earl and me to describe the other with one word. I said, "Relentless." He said, "Talented." I was. I knew that if I pitched for Earl, he would do his job as manager and my teammates would do their jobs, so all I had to do was show up healthy and with a good attitude, and I was going to win a lot of games. That's why I ended up in the Hall of Fame.

Tom Seaver

I Realized the '69 Mets Were Special

In 1968, my second season, the New York Mets reached a milestone in that for the first time, we didn't finish in last place. In the last year before division play, we finished ninth, ahead of Houston, the other 1962 expansion team. In spring training in 1969, Jerry Grote said that we were going to win it all that year. And we looked at him as if he were nuts, because we'd only gotten out of the cellar. But being our catcher, Jerry knew what kind of pitching we were going to have on a day-to-day basis. There would be Jerry Koosman, who had a great year in '68, Nolan Ryan, me, and Gary Gentry, who was coming along. And at different times during the season, the players jumped on the bandwagon. For me, it was a game we were playing the Dodgers at Shea Stadium. It was a 1–1 game, and we had a single up the middle. Dodgers center fielder Willie Davis had a clear shot at the runner at home plate, but the ball went under his glove, and he couldn't make a throw. We had won another 1-run ball game, and at that juncture, I said, "We're going to win this thing."

Gil Hodges's Lasting Influence on Me

Gil Hodges became the Mets' manager in 1968, when we finally got out of the basement, and was the manager in 1969 when we won the

World Series. From a professional standpoint, he was the most important individual in my career. I was still trying to establish myself as a big-league pitcher, so early on, I didn't really understand the degree to which he was an analytical manager. Gil was the first manager I'd been around who in the sixth inning knew what he'd do in the eighth inning and in the fifth inning knew what might happen in the ninth inning.

He made me think differently as a pitcher and look ahead as I went through the batting order. For instance, I came to understand the importance of getting the eighth-place hitter out to end the eighth inning so that in the ninth inning, they wouldn't get to their fourth-place hitter with the tying run on base. I learned that the most important out might not be with a man on third and one out, but with nobody on and two outs—things like that. He had that approach and passed it along to me and the other players.

Gil never talked too much. He talked only when he knew it was absolutely the correct time to throw a firecracker underneath his team to get us off our rear ends and refocus. He was a mentor, a father figure, and a nice man, but I'm not sure I'd call him a best buddy. You knew what side he was on, but he was a very demanding individual, with an imposing physical presence and demeanor. He was a big man with huge hands and a reputation from when he was in the South Pacific in World War II. I had an immediate attachment, because we were both marines, and felt that was at least one thing I had toward equality with him.

One day in 1968, he called me into his office at Shea Stadium. You didn't want to go into his office, because you didn't know if you'd come out alive or with broken bones. I can joke about it now, but I was thinking, "My God, I hope he doesn't break my neck." I had pitched that day against Juan Marichal, who I'd seen pitch a few years before when my dad took me to Candlestick Park from our home in Fresno. I was ahead something like 7–1. As Gil said, I "got a little gay on the mound," because when I turned around, the score was 7–6. I held on to win, but Gil said, "Your approach today was very unprofessional." He gave me a professional piece of advice that I never forgot: "It doesn't matter if there are five thousand people in the stands or fifty thousand people; or if it's Tuesday night in L.A. or Saturday afternoon in Chicago; or if you're leading by one run or six runs; or if we're two games ahead or eighteen games behind. Your approach to your business is the same all the time. You must stay focused and professional, and maintain all those intangibles that go into consistency and a respect for your job." I'm fortunate that I got that advice in only my second season, because I would benefit from it for eighteen and a half years.

Evolving as a Pitcher

I benefited in that when I was young, I wasn't an overpowering pitcher, so I had to learn control and movement. I was 5'9" and 160 pounds coming out of high school, so I wasn't like a Dick Selma who came out of high school and threw 95 mph. But I grew, and as I developed physically, I could throw the ball with increasing speed. I had a really good fastball by 1969, '70, and '71, which was reflected in my number of strikeouts. So, I had the good fastball and still had enough confidence in my control where I could throw the ball to within an inch of where I wanted it. You have to believe in what you do and know where you are most effective.

There are two ways to pitch: to the batter's weakness or to your strength. I'd say that 98 percent of the time, I pitched to my strength. If my strength was going to a certain spot, and you knew I was going there, that was fine, but you had to prove to me that you could beat me before I would go someplace else. I felt when I made my pitch, nobody could hit it. My fastball had a lot of upward movement, and I'd usually get ahead of hitters on foul balls. They'd either hit it straight back or, if it was a left-handed hitter, hit it down the left-field line, because they'd be late on the ball. The fastball I threw on the first pitch wasn't necessarily the one I'd throw you with two strikes.

Early in my career, I threw my fastball at different speeds, and that was my equivalent of a changeup. I had a lot of trouble developing a changeup because of the energy I generated. I tried to develop it while I was a student at USC because Rod Dedeaux impressed on me the importance of it. But I was probably ten years in the big leagues before I had a decent changeup. I had an outstanding one toward the end of my career, and that allowed me to go on to win three hundred games.

My Proudest Achievement

The no-hitter I threw for Cincinnati wasn't even in the top ten things I'm proudest of in my major-league career. I think my greatest accomplishment was my consistency over a long period of time. I was able to accumulate three hundred wins, three thousand strikeouts, and other career numbers only because I had many good seasons along the way. Henry Aaron was, along with Sandy Koufax, my baseball hero, and what I took from him was a consistency of performance day in and day out, season in and season out; a real dedication; and a real focus on how to play the game correctly. My father, who played on the Walker Cup team in 1932, was like that with his golf game. The lessons that he passed down to his son were reinforced by Aaron. I incorporated them into the way I went about my business over my entire career.

On Each Team, I Had a Great Catcher

When I gave my induction speech at the Hall of Fame, I said, "Why was I so successful? Jerry Grote, Johnny Bench, and Carlton Fisk." 189 Grote was my catcher when I won my three Cy Young Awards with the Mets, Johnny caught my no-hitter and three-thousandth strikeout with the Reds, and Carlton caught my three-hundredth win with the White Sox. I was very close with all three personally. As a pitcher, how could you go wrong with them? They were among the best catchers of all time.

Bert Blyleven
My Curveball

I had a lot of confidence in my curveball. Growing up in southern California, I learned it by watching Sandy Koufax. It had a 12-to-6 type of break, and at that time, we called it a "drop." My dad was a huge Dodgers fan, and he remembered an interview he'd heard with Koufax during which Sandy, who had an arthritic elbow, said if he had a son, he wouldn't let him throw a curveball until he was fifteen or sixteen. My dad said with his Dutch accent, "Gosh darn it, if you don't wait to throw a curveball until you're thirteen or fourteen years old, then you aren't going to play baseball." Well, I loved baseball, so I didn't throw a curve until I was thirteen or fourteen, and I think that helped me avoid elbow problems until the strike of 1981. (Today's Little League should ban the curve, because kids do well throwing the curve there but a few years later can't even comb their hair.)

When my dad said I was old enough to throw the curve, I spent many hours in the side yard of our house, throwing it and throwing it, until I had confidence I could get it over at any time, on any count—and that didn't change when I came to the majors at nineteen. The curve was my best pitch, but, as young pitchers learn, it's effective only when you use the fastball to set up everything. I ran into Sandy Alomar one day, and he said, "You threw me a curveball with the bases loaded and two outs on a 3-2 pitch! It was a little Punch-and-Judy." I said, "Yeah, but you got a hit earlier, and I remembered you were looking for the fastball." I struck him out.

190   *I Should Have Started with the Second Batter*

I made my debut when I was nineteen years old. The first batter I faced was Lee Maye, and he homered off me. What a beginning that was! I see my manager, Bill Rigney, walking out to the mound, and I'm thinking, "That was the shortest major-league career in history." I thought he'd take me out and I'd be demoted. But he left me in, and that was the only run I gave up in seven innings. We won 2–1 because Ron Perranoski came in and pitched the last two innings for the save.

That was the first of many 1-run, low-scoring games I'd pitch in my career. In fact, I'd win fifteen nine-inning 1–0 games. Walter Johnson and Christy Mathewson are the only others to do that. I didn't get a lot of run support in Minnesota, so I just tried to do the best I could. For several years, I'd think it was my fault if we lost, even if I pitched well. Eventually I learned that if we lost 1–0, I shouldn't be so hard on myself.

I Wasn't Going to Leave a No-Hitter

In 1977, I pitched a no-hitter in Anaheim against the California Angels, which was kind of cool. I was with the Texas Rangers, and it was in September, and I'd just spent about a month on the disabled list with a right-groin injury. I wanted to pitch one more time that season, so I got a shot in my groin, and it was one of the worst shots of my career. I'd grown up in Garden Grove, and my mom and dad and brothers and sisters were in the stands. That made it even more fun as I pitched through seven innings without giving up a hit.

But I aggravated the groin in the eighth inning. My manager, Billy Hunter, asked me, "How are you feeling?" I answered, "Have you seen the scoreboard?" He turned around and walked away. I wasn't going to leave with a no-hitter on the line, but till the end of the game I could throw nothing but curveballs, because the pain was killing me. Somehow I made it through the ninth without giving up any hits. That would be my last American League start for a while. Texas probably figured nobody in the American League could get a hit off me and traded me that winter to the Pittsburgh Pirates.

ELEVEN

THE RIGHTY ROTATION II

(1977–present)

JACK MORRIS
Who Knew I Could Pitch in the Big Leagues?

I grew up in Minnesota and dreamed my whole life that I would go to the University of Minnesota and pitch on the baseball team. But when I was in high school, I recognized they didn't play a very good schedule, so I looked into other colleges. I ended up attending Brigham Young University, which isn't just a football school. I got to play against top collegiate baseball schools like Arizona, Arizona State, and Cal State Fullerton; we went to Hawaii; and we played in tournaments in California and Arizona, so it turned out to be a real good choice.

I didn't graduate, because I was drafted by Detroit, and there was my chance. I went home to Minnesota to kind of think about whether I should sign. I went to the ballpark to watch the Twins host the Angels and look at the big-league players and decide if I could fit in. Bert Blyleven, who was early in his career, and Frank Tanana, who was in his prime, locked up in a close, low-scoring game, and they were both throwing curveballs from outer space. Both had ten or eleven strikeouts. I looked at my mom and dad and said, "I can't play with these guys! They are so much better than I will ever be!" I thought to myself, "My goodness, if this is what big-league pitching is like, I have a long way to go."

The Bird Is the Word

I made my first start in Detroit on a day Mark "the Bird" Fidrych was supposed to pitch. The fans had come to see him, and this young pitcher they never heard of took the mound instead. I got a standing boo. There was no one more popular in that city than Fidrych. For one year, they said, "The Bird Is the Word." He was animated, and he did a lot of goofy things on the mound like talking to the ball and getting down to smoothen the dirt, but people don't remember what a good pitcher he was. He was nasty. He threw the ball on the black; he kept everything down at the knees. The reason he was so popular is that he won ball games.

My Lucky Day

I pitched on Opening Day in 1984 and two-hit the Twins in Minnesota. I came back on three days' rest in Chicago, on April 7, and threw a no-hitter against the White Sox. Quite honestly, I pitched better against Minnesota, but I had a lot of luck against Chicago. I walked four or five guys, but they didn't score because my teammates made some fabulous plays to rob them of base hits. The stars were lined up; the moon was in the right hemisphere. The last out came on a checked swing by Ron Kittle on the splitter. My splitter was working, and it was a cold day, and there were a lot of checked swings by Sox batters. It was great to finish that way, and we had a lot of fun after the game. There is nothing like the playoffs, but for one day during the season there's nothing more pleasurable than pitching a no-hitter.

My Secret Weapon

Early in my career, I was probably the only pitcher in the American League throwing a splitter. For about two years, I had total bliss throwing it, because none of the batters had seen it before. Nobody recognized it; nobody picked it up. Everybody was wondering, "What is that pitch? Is he throwing a spitter?" So, it was a lot of fun to throw it. Eventually I had some arm problems because of the splitter, some stress late in my career when I was with Toronto. But for years, nothing hurt, and it was really a devastating pitch.

Game 7 of the 1991 World Series

I feel so good inside that I had the chance to pitch the seventh game of the 1991 World Series for the Twins against the Braves. How many guys dream of playing in a World Series and never get the chance? I not only got to play in the Series, but also I got to live out my fantasy of pitching in the biggest game. I'd dreamed about it as a kid. In fact, I was so prepared for it because I'd lived it over and over so many times.

John Smoltz and I both pitched well, and neither team could score. Then it appeared Atlanta would break through in the eighth inning. After Lonnie Smith got a leadoff single, Terry Pendleton followed with a double on which Smith should have scored, but he went for a decoy at second base and got only to third base. And I pitched out of the jam, and he never crossed home plate. Lonnie shouldn't have been the goat, because Pendleton shouldn't have gotten a double. I felt I had Pendleton struck out, but the third-base umpire said he foul-tipped the pitch. He was 120 feet away, and I was about 58 feet away, and I knew he didn't tip the ball. But I had to pitch to him again, and he hit the ball in the gap.

That was certainly a key play in the game, because if Atlanta had scored 1 run, John Smoltz would be the hero. Instead he comes out

195

of the game, and we win it in the tenth inning on Gene Larkin's pinch hit off Alejandro Pena, and I'm the one who gets to win, 1–0, and be the hero. I got to see Smoltz one day when Atlanta was in town, and for the first time ever, we sat down and talked about that. To pitch ten innings and win Game 7 in front of my home fans . . . I've said many times that I wish everyone in the world could experience the feeling I had for one day, because I truly feel it would be a better world.

Ron Darling
The Bond Is Never Broken

I feel fortunate to be linked forever in time with the players of the 1986 world champion New York Mets. Hernandez, Strawberry, Knight, Mookie, Carter, the great pitching staff—it's a nice group to reflect on as you get older. You realize that you will never have the same feeling again in anything else you do. Having a baby is probably the closest you'll get to experiencing that kind of unbelievable, sincere love— because that's how you feel for teammates when you go through a championship summer. You end up loving these people. There's a trust: you have their backs, and they have yours. You invest in each other, and it pays off. My best friend on the team was Ed Lynch, and he got traded to the Cubs during the season. He had the best line ever; he said, "Getting traded in '86 was like being sent to a different family on Christmas morning." So, that's what it was like for him. And remember the Mets clinched against the Cubs, and Eddie was in their dugout watching.

My Dad Saved the Day

I'm from Boston, and in 1967, the "Impossible Dream" year, I fell in love with the Red Sox. So, I found myself pitching against Boston in the 1986 World Series and slated to start Game 4 in Fenway Park, with the Mets down two games to one. I had sixty friends and family there, and everyone's coming down to wish me well while I'm warming up. Well, my warm-up was as bad as bad could be. I was bouncing pitches, could not throw a strike, and threw one ball over the low fence into the other bullpen. That's how bad it was. I had lost Game 1, 1–0, and now I'm thinking that I have no chance in this start. Bobby Ojeda had pitched a nice game the night before when Dykstra led off with a homer, but this was another must-win game. I told our pitching coach, Mel Stottlemyre, who I loved dearly, "Let's just go to the dugout, and I'll try to regroup and figure out something."

So I start walking across the field. It so happened that my father was in the National Guard, and he was holding the flag that night for the National Anthem. I'm walking across; he's there, this man who taught me how to play baseball. I kind of sidle up to him and put my arm in his arm, and all my anxiety went away. It's all right; everything's going to be all right. As I walked across the field into the dugout, in my mind the game was over. I was going to win that game, which I did, 6–2. My father is a real macho guy, and we've never talked about it. But we know what happened on the field that night in Boston.

A World Series Win After a Close Shave

It's strange the thoughts that go through your head and the little things you notice during a game. In Game 6 of the 1986 World Series, Roger Clemens went the first seven innings and left with the Red Sox leading 3–2. This is no knock on Roger, but I'll never forget that they showed him on the giant screen, and he had shaved since he left the mound. I remember all of us thinking, "Boy, that's some hubris, right there, shaving and knowing you're going to be interviewed pretty soon." And that made us angry. However, when we were down to our last out in the bottom of the tenth, with no one on base and trailing by 2 runs, I'd have to say that twenty or twenty-one guys on our team thought that game was over and Clemens would be interviewed. Luck-

197

ily, Carter, and Mitchell, and Knight, and Mookie Wilson didn't think it was over, and that's why we ended up winning that game.

Roger Clemens
I Got to the Park in the Nick of Time

On April 29, 1986, I almost missed a start because I was stuck in traffic on Storrow Drive in Boston about two miles from Fenway Park. I was wearing jeans and boots, and I opened my trunk and took out a pair of tennis shoes. It was about twenty till 7:00, and the game was supposed to start at 7:05, so I was going to take off running. A motorcycle policeman saw me, and we looked at each other. He said, "Aren't you . . . ?" And I said, "Yeah." And he said, "Follow me." And he split the traffic and got me to the park. I was lathered up by that time.

Our pitching coach, Bill Fischer, was just about to name another starter. I threw my uniform on and ran to the bullpen. I don't know if I threw a strike warming up, and every time I bent over to grab the resin, I had the worst temple headache ever. I was a mess, and I'm sure Fish thought I'd be out of the game by the second inning. But I was about twenty-two at the time and went out and punched out twenty batters for a new major-league record. And I didn't walk anybody, which I was proudest of. Fish told me that I could come to the park any time I wanted from then on.

Me and the Babe

After warming up before a start at Yankee Stadium, I wipe sweat from my forehead onto Babe Ruth's bust in Monument Park to keep it nice and shiny. I don't want to say I'm superstitious, but I'm looking for a bit of extra luck. Also, it's kind of like bringing the past back to the future. I always respect the guys who did it in the past, and the Babe is the best for me. Like me, he played for Boston and New York and was a great pitcher before becoming a great hitter. To me, he is baseball.

DAVID CONE
Blessings in Disguise

After signing with the hometown Kansas City Royals, I spent six years in the minors. Finally in 1986, I got to pitch a few games in the majors, and I had hopes for 1987. Billy Gardner was taking over as the Royals' manager for Dick Howser, who was sick with a brain tumor and would pass away. Billy told me that I'd made the team and was the fifth starter. He had this expression, "Give 'em the glossy," which meant, *take his picture and put it in the program, because he made the team.* He said that about me. And the next day, I was traded to the New York Mets. I was devastated. I was leaving my hometown for a team that had just won the World Series, and I thought I was going to be sent back to Triple-A, because I didn't see how I'd crack their rotation. Little did I know it was a blessing in disguise, because I fell in with a great group of guys, particularly Ron Darling, who helped show me my way in my rookie year.

The Mets had a rash of injuries to starting pitchers—Darling, Dwight Gooden, Sid Fernandez—so I got a chance. I won two or three games in a row and got to feel what it was like to be in a major-league rotation. But then I had the misfortune of having my little finger on my pitching hand shattered when I squared around to bunt against the Giants' Atlee Hammaker. That was terribly discouraging for me. Being a rookie after spending so many years in the minors, I still didn't know if I had what it takes to stick in the big leagues. And I didn't know if I'd get another shot.

I missed a big part of the season, but I was able to come back. However, my finger was still crooked, so I guess the doctor didn't do too good of a job fixing it. Oddly, I was just an average pitcher until that happened. The old Three Finger Brown story comes to mind. I

199

came back the next spring, and my fastball started moving and cutting. I think the extra hop was from that crooked finger. I went 20–3 in 1988.

Paying Tribute to Two Teammates I Admired

Dennis Leonard and Keith Hernandez were two of the most stand-up guys I played with, which is why I wore their uniform numbers at different times in my career. Keith was a leader on the Mets in the late 1980s in the same way Don Mattingly was on the Yankees. He didn't have to say anything, but everyone saw how he prepared for a game and then played it in the right way. It was his mannerisms that struck me. If I was on the mound, I'd look over at him, and we'd make eye contact. He always was ready and was so into the game. He would pump his fist and would be so intense. He was so good with understanding situations and anticipating the flow of the game. He'd come to the mound in various situations—bunting situations, RBI situations with certain hitters up—and tell me what to throw. Gary Carter would join us, and they'd talk about how I should pitch a guy to not let him beat me. He'd get in my face, with that look and intensity, and whatever he was thinking was contagious. After I came to the Mets, I heard about how Keith ordered Carter to call only curveballs when Jesse Orosco pitched to Kevin Bass for the final out of the 1986 NLCS. That epitomized Mex.

Sometimes it was what he said; sometimes it was that look he gave you; sometimes it was just the way he swung the bat in the clubhouse preparing for the game. There was something about Mex. He had that intangible leadership quality that affected the entire team. After he left the Mets in the early '90s, I thought there was a big void in the Mets' clubhouse. In 1991, I switched from 44 to 17 so his presence would still be felt.

Dennis Leonard was one of the best pitchers the Kansas City Royals ever had, winning twenty games three times. I met him when I was still in the minors and hurt my knee. Because I was from Kansas City,

I was able to do rehab with the big-league club. I had the chance to rehab with Dennis, who went through a similar-type injury. He was true-blue, nice, and professional, and I learned so much from him. His final season was 1986, which was when I made my only appearances for Kansas City until I returned in 1993 as an established pitcher. That year, I wore number 17, but in 1994, I switched to number 22 to pay tribute to him. It worked, because I won the Cy Young in the strike-shortened 1994 season.

Leaving the Mets with Deep Regrets

When the Mets traded me to Toronto in late August of 1992, I had a mixed reaction. It took me a little while to realize what a great opportunity that was to be able to go up there when the Blue Jays were about to win their first of back-to-back world championships. The team was great, and the SkyDome's novelty hadn't worn off, and the team was drawing four million fans that year. The whole country was behind that team, hoping it would be the first Canadian team to win the championship. So, that was very exciting.

On the other hand, I was depressed leaving the Mets. The Mets teams that I played on since 1987 had underachieved, and I was disappointed that we hadn't done more. I got a taste of the playoffs in 1988, but we lost to the Dodgers in seven games and never really got back. I was waiting for another shot to redeem myself in the playoffs, but it never came. That's something that still bothers me about my days with the Mets. We could have done more; we should have done more.

Nothing but the Truth

I started Game 3 of the 1996 World Series, with the Yankees down to the Braves two games to none. There was a key point in the game. The Braves had the bases loaded, with Fred McGriff up. We had a lefty,

Graeme Lloyd, warming up, and Joe Torre got nose-to-nose with me and implored me to tell him the truth about how I was feeling. He said, "This is too important: don't lie to me." I said, "I can get this guy out! I can get this guy out!" I got McGriff out, and though I ended up walking in a run, we got out of the inning with a 2–1 lead, and we went on to win that game and the Series. I'll never forget that meeting on the mound. I don't think Joe has forgiven me, because in the postgame press conference, I made a bit of a faux pas when I said I had lied to Joe when I said I was OK. I was trying to be funny, but Joe took it a little personally. But we still joke about it.

David Wells's Perfect Game

Fourteen months to the day prior to my pitching a perfect game against Montreal on July 18, 1999, David Wells pitched a perfect game on the same mound, at Yankee Stadium. If you saw my reactions on the bench during the last few innings of his game, you would know that I was more nervous watching him than when I threw my own perfect game. I guess you try to channel your energies and get into a tunnel-vision mentality when you pitch, but when I was watching, I was biting my nails. I was pulling for Boomer so hard because I knew what it would mean for his career.

From about the seventh inning on, Boomer was pacing in the dugout. He was looking for someone to say something to him, but everyone was trying to avoid him, because they didn't want to make him more nervous. He came up to me—you have to know Boomer and what a crazy personality he is—and he said, "It's getting hairy out there." I didn't know what to say to him, so I blurted out, "Aw, just break out your knuckleball these last two innings and finish this off." And he burst out laughing. He had needed to hear something to break the ice and give him a release. He was appreciative of that. I think I took it a little too far, though, because after he got out of the eighth inning with his perfect game intact, he came back to the dugout, and before he hit the first step, I said, "You showed me nothing! You didn't throw the knuckleball!"

My Perfect Game

July 18, 1999, was "Yogi Berra Day" at Yankee Stadium, and Don Larsen threw out the first ball to Yogi to commemorate their being batterymates for the perfect game during the 1956 World Series. I remember vividly shaking Larsen's hand before he threw that first pitch to Yogi and watching their interaction and taking in the crowd's tremendous reaction to that first-pitch ceremony. I remember having a carefree feeling warming up in the bullpen and then on the mound, getting ready to face Montreal. I was thinking, "This just doesn't happen anywhere else." It was a true delight, and I made a point of telling myself to enjoy the moment. How many chances do you get to shake Don Larsen's hand and to see Yogi Berra come back to Yankee Stadium for the first time in fourteen years? The fans were so ready to see him, and they cheered as he rode around in a convertible. Who knows for sure, but I think what was taking place and my enjoying it helped me relax during the game.

I realized I was throwing a perfect game in the early innings. There was a rain delay around the fourth inning, which lasted about half an hour or forty minutes, and when I came back, I didn't even go to the mound to warm up. Instead I played catch with the batboy, little Luigi, right in front of the dugout. Everybody thought I was nuts. You should have seen the look on Luigi's face! I bought "Perfect Game"–inscribed watches after the game and gave one to Luigi for his assist. That was one of the great memories of the day, and Luigi and I still talk about it.

My arm still felt good. Then I had a really quick, six- or seven-pitch inning, and I said, OK, I'm feeling good, my pitch count is down, and nobody in Montreal's lineup has ever faced me before. Before the game, Joe Girardi and I talked about how Montreal had a lot of young

203

hackers, so my strategy was to throw them enough strikes to let them know I could throw strikes and then expand the strike zone, first to a couple of inches off the plate and then farther. And that's what I did. I had my Frisbee-like slider going that day, and the ball was breaking sideways with a sweeping action, maybe because of the wind, and the most free-swinging team in the big leagues was chasing it far off the plate. It was the perfect matchup for me, the perfect storm.

Before the ninth inning, I was sitting by myself in the dugout. I could appreciate what David Wells went through the last few innings of his perfect game in 1998, because I wanted someone to say something. Chili Davis was there for me. Chili put on full gear and warmed me up between innings one time. I was just lobbing it into him because he was an outfielder, and he yelled, "You can let it go now— I used to catch in the minor leagues!" That doesn't seem like much now, but when there's so much tension, you look for any little thing to break the ice.

In the ninth inning, I struck out the first batter, but then there was a fly to left that Ricky Ledee ran in for but didn't see, and at the last moment, the ball just found his glove, and he snapped it up. I couldn't believe it. Ricky almost had tears in his eyes when he told me later that he didn't see it and didn't know how it got in his glove. It was just part of an entire day that was mystifying, that proved there are ghosts at Yankee Stadium. At about this time, I could feel my hair growing. On my eighty-eighth pitch—with the number "8" painted on the wall to honor Yogi Berra—the last batter fouled out to Scott Brosius, and I had my perfect game.

Talk about being linked to someone—not only to Berra and Larsen, but also Joe Girardi. I collapsed on him after the final out before everyone piled on. I never thought being at the bottom of a pile could feel so good. But a lot of guys were going, "Enough already, get up!" They started pulling me up by my pants and giving me a wedgie. They pulled me off the ground, and I raised my fist to the crowd. I was thirty-six, and I knew it was the last chance I'd have to do something like that.

Yogi, who had planned on leaving about the fourth inning, and Don greeted me when I came off the field. I was so appreciative they stuck around. To give them handshakes and a hug was a true honor. It was one more thing to be thankful for.

It Wasn't Such a Bad Year After All

When I went 4–14 with the Yankees in 2000, a lot of people thought I was tarnishing my career by not hanging it up. But I was pretty proud of myself that year. I hung a lot of sliders and gave up a lot of homers, and at times, I couldn't get anyone out, but I took the ball from Joe Torre every fifth day and never backed down and never quit. Coming off that season, I made only one appearance in the Subway Series, pitching to Mike Piazza with two outs in the fifth inning of Game 4. Mike had hit a two-run homer earlier for both the Mets' runs, so Torre brought me in to replace our starter, Denny Neagle.

I threw Piazza a couple of sliders, and I think he was sitting breaking ball all the way. Instead I threw him what I had left at that point in that year, a mediocre fastball. But I surprised him and got it in a decent-enough spot inside, and he popped it up to second base. That kept the score at 3–2, and that would be the final score, to put us up three games to one. So, it was an important out. That would be my last appearance in pinstripes. To have that one last moment as a Yankee meant a lot to me.

A Memorable Pitching Duel

After I went 4–14 with the Yankees in 2000, I pitched the next season for the Red Sox. It was a great experience to be able to see the other side of what might be the greatest sports rivalry in the world. Fenway Park is a magical place, a great stadium to play in day after day, and the fans care so much. It's really a second religion, where they really do bleed Red Sox Nation red.

I won nine games with Boston in 2001, but one of my losses was the best game I pitched since my perfect game in 1999. It came in early September, and, fittingly, it was against the Yankees. Mike Mussina started for New York and gave perhaps the most dominating pitching performance I have ever witnessed. He was that good. He was literally one pitch away from throwing a perfect game. His perfect game was broken up with two outs in the ninth inning on an 0-2 pitch to Carl Everett.

We locked up in a 0–0 duel through eight innings, and I talked Joe Kerrigan into letting me go out to pitch the top of the ninth. Joe was Boston's longtime pitching coach until he replaced Jimy Williams as the manager a couple of weeks earlier. Had I thrown another goose egg, Mike wouldn't have gotten credit for a no-hitter or perfect game even if he had set us down in order in the bottom of the ninth. But I did my part and gave up a run, and that set the stage for him. He was still dominating in the bottom of the ninth. He got two quick outs and then blew two fastballs past Everett. But he tried to go up the ladder, and Everett tomahawked a humpback line drive to left field that fell in for our only hit of the night.

I never saw a pitcher as deflated as Mike was after giving up that hit and after the game. I was the losing pitcher, but I almost felt that I had won, because I got to throw into the ninth inning again and prove I still had something left. Mussina was the winning pitcher, and it almost looked like he lost. I knew how he felt. I had been so close a few times to throwing a no-hitter prior to my perfect game, and when you don't quite get there, you feel like it's a loss. I could tell by his postgame interviews and from talking to my former teammates on the Yankees that he was devastated. So, the next day, I sought him out. I emphasized to Mike not to let such a gem of a performance, a masterpiece, become a negative. And I told him that he is one of the best pitchers in the game and that one of these days he is going to get another chance to throw a no-hitter.

I Became a New Yorker

On a professional level, I don't think I'll ever find that emotion I felt pitching in New York—the emotion I felt when I threw a perfect game or when I pitched in the World Series or when I did not want to let down my teammates or the city of New York. I felt sometimes that the whole city was behind us during those postseason games. I feel so fortunate to have played the majority of my career in New York, six years with the Mets and six years with the Yankees, and winning four World Series rings. I had so many wonderful experiences, and my heart is still in New York.

I learned early on from Keith Hernandez, Ron Darling, Gary Carter, Wally Backman, and other teammates on those great Mets teams that when you play with heart and soul, and wear your heart on your sleeve a little bit, New Yorkers tend to feed off of that. They empathize with guys like that, as opposed to stoic players or ones they don't think are trying and are giving a lackluster effort. If you showed emotion like Paul O'Neil, they loved you. There was a whole section of seats behind the visitors' dugout where fans could peer into the Yankees' dugout and be thrilled when Paul whacked the watercooler with his bat—because it showed how much he cared. A key to success in New York is showing the fans that emotional, personal side of you.

It also helped that I had a good relationship with the New York media. A lot of players get into a defensive mode, where it's "us against them," but I always looked at it from a different angle. If you just make yourself available and don't hide in the clubhouse or in the trainer's room, and you are straightforward and honest, they will be more than fair to you. If there's a topic you don't want to broach, you just say, "I'd rather not get into that right now." That formula is so simple but works so well, especially in New York.

JOHN SMOLTZ
The True Story

I went through a tough time in 1991. Every player goes through tough times when they start second-guessing themselves and experience a "confidence slump," as I like to call it. I started the season 2–11, but Bobby Cox knew I wasn't that kind of pitcher and kept sending me out there. I spent time with a sports psychologist, Jack Llewelyn, and he helped me a lot. That story took on a "beast" of its own. I call it lazy journalism, because nobody ever wanted to know what really happened between us. I wasn't even aware of this, but Jack wore a red shirt when sitting in our dugout on days I pitched. I went 12–2 in the second half, to finish 14–13, so everyone made this big deal about his red shirt, saying I'd been hypnotized and when I saw that shirt, I'd go into robotic mode. The story kept getting bigger, and nobody took the time to ask me what we talked about or what a sports psychologist meant in my life. I sought help, and all of a sudden one reporter after another was saying how I was transformed into a mentally tough player by sitting on a couch and having him swing a watch in front of me. Two years went by, and I said, "Enough! If you want to know the true story, ask me questions about it."

What he helped me with was very simple and common, and he did it by rarely talking about baseball. When a young player has trouble, what he does is make things go faster, faster, and faster. When I see young struggling pitchers say, "Gimme the ball so I can throw it harder and faster," that was me in 1991. Jack allowed me to slow the game down and put a lid on the cup of emotions I had back then, and that helped me eliminate the one awful inning I'd been having every game that resulted in losses. He'd tell me that he didn't make me into a great pitcher, that I either had it or didn't, but he got me to trust that I was capable of slowing the game down. I love the playoffs and am 15–4, because that is the time the game slows down the most for me. That's when I have the most fun. I take advantage of the fact that all the batters I face want to speed things up, don't want to take walks, want to swing for the fences. I wish the season were shortened and there were more playoff games. That's what I would do if I were commissioner.

Bobby Cox Keeps Us Believing

You're not going to see another team win fourteen divisions in a row in any sport. What the Atlanta Braves have done will never be duplicated. But the media has to find something wrong, and the fact is we've won only one World Series ring, in 1995. It has been disappointing considering how many times we have been right there, but I could break down every World Series and show we've been in every one and could have won them all. The bounces and the execution just didn't go our way. It's been frustrating for the players, but we understand there has been a different formula every year. It's not like they took the same fifteen to twenty guys and said, "We'll get it right this year." We've had different rosters and different ways of winning. The only constant during my tenure in Atlanta has been Bobby Cox.

Our manager has been incredibly patient, and that has been rewarding. When you leave spring training each year, you believe his speeches. How many clubs can say they believe their managers' optimistic speeches when they break camp? The reason is that he seems to believe that we can win it all with the talent we have. Bobby keeps it simple. The only things he tells you to do are to be on time, wear headphones if you play music, don't wear earrings, and wear your hat correctly. That's basically it. He will instill confidence in players who don't have it, he'll defend and fight for you on the field—which results in half of his ejections—and he's a throwback who wears spikes like the players. That's why everyone loves him and wants to play for him. He's the reason I've stayed in Atlanta this long.

The Best Pitching Trio Ever

I agree with those who say Greg Maddux, Tom Glavine, and myself were the best pitching trio ever. If you consider the era in which we pitched, how long we were together on the Braves, the numbers we put up, and the six Cy Young Awards, I don't see how any other threesome can match that. It's fun for me to talk about us winning six Cy Youngs, because those two carried most of the weight. I got only one. I learned a lot being in the mix with two great pitchers, and we all benefited from playing for Bobby Cox, who is the perfect pitcher's manager. We played golf together and had a blast doing all the things you have to do to have a long career.

It was great when we all started, but during the 2001 season, the Braves asked me to switch to the closer role. We weren't winning the World Series, and they believed my relieving would make the team better. They also said they could afford to keep me only if I moved into the closer role. I told them that I didn't think we'd win a championship with me as a closer, because my value as a starter in the postseason spoke for itself. However, I said I'd try it and if I were wrong, I'd be the first one to admit it and I'd remain a closer.

I wanted to keep pitching for Bobby Cox, but another reason I agreed to become a closer was that I envisioned saving Maddux's and Glavine's three-hundredth victories. What a rush that would be. I really thought we'd stick together in Atlanta. I knew the economics were going to be difficult, but I thought we'd find a way. Once they left, it was difficult for me to remain in the closer role, which I thought was a secondary role. Three years came and went with me as a closer, we got knocked out in the first round each year and I never got to pitch in a significant situation, and my dream of saving Tom's and Greg's three-hundredth wins was shattered. So, I told John Schuerholz and Bobby Cox that I'd continue relieving, but if they picked up a closer, I'd be happy to go back to starting—and it worked out.

So, now Tom, Greg, and I are starters on three different National League teams. But we're still the best of friends and have set up a trip to Ireland to play golf. The timing never worked out during the season, but we always talked about doing that after we all had retired. It will be a monumental trip when we play golf and reminisce.

I Shouldn't Be Compared to Dennis Eckersley

I have never talked to Dennis Eckersley about how we both made transitions from starting to closing, and how people have compared us because of that. It's an honor to be compared to him, a Hall of Famer, but I think we're totally different. He is truly one of the greatest relievers ever in baseball and was a very good starter. But when he became a reliever in Oakland, it was because he was no longer an effective starter, and there weren't any other options for him. The difference is that I made a choice to go to the bullpen to help the Braves. I had fourteen great years as a starter and was still effective in that role. People would say, "Becoming a closer is going to get you into the Hall of Fame." No. If I never stepped into the relief role and continued as a starter, I believe my accomplishments would have spoken for themselves.

My Three Years as a Closer

Before the 2002 season, when I was going to be strictly a closer, I trained differently and had a different mind-set. I thought of starting as a marathon and closing as a sprint. I would be pitching only one inning, so instead of five pitches, I'd use only my fastball, splitter, and slider, and put aside my change and curve. I had to make myself believe I was a closer. Even on the eighteenth hole on a golf course, I'd try to finish it as if I were finishing a ball game.

During the off-season, I had to have surgery on my thumb. It was a hangnail type of thing, so I thought it would be simple, but I ended up having four different surgeries and numerous shots, and I couldn't pick up a ball the whole time until camp. Nobody knows it. I'm two weeks behind all the other pitchers when we break camp, and I wasn't one bit ready. But I had to fake it and go out there and pretend I was at the top of my game. My first game closing, I faced the Mets and gave up eight runs in two-thirds of an inning, and all the Atlanta fans started booing. That was my transition into Welcome to the Closing Role. All my buddies called me up and said, "Just think: only nine more scoreless games and you'll get your ERA under 3.00." The first month, I stunk. Who would have thought that at the end of the year, I would have saved a National League–record fifty-five games and finished sixty-eight games?

I tried to be even better the next year. I thought I could get my ERA down because it was high the first year only because of that awful beginning. In the last game, I had a chance to set a new record for the

211

lowest ERA, but I gave up two runs in the ninth inning to end that. I had another good year closing in 2004, but I never closed the door on starting, and on the side I always worked on the changeup and curve, the two pitches I'd eliminated when I became a closer. Leo Mazzone would say, "I know what you're doing. You're still working on your pitches in case you go back."

When I was finally presented with the opportunity to go back to starting, I took it, though once again, people told me I couldn't make the transition. I thought I'd earned the right for people to reserve judgment. In my first start, I gave up seven runs, and they said I was crazy. But at the end of the year, nobody said anything.

I learned so much being a closer. It was a total rush coming to the park every day thinking I might pitch, particularly in 2002 when I closed in on the saves record. I had crazy, crazy outcomes; in fact, players like Chipper Jones were apologizing for hitting three-run homers in the bottom of the eighth inning to take it out of a save situation. It was exciting. People don't understand how mentally tough closers have to be, year in and year out. I tip my hat to Mariano Rivera, Trevor Hoffman, and the others who have done it so well for so long. People think three outs is the same whether it's the second inning or the ninth inning. But getting those three outs in the ninth inning, night after night, is a hard thing to do. When I'd blow a save, I'd come into the clubhouse, and everybody would stare at me as if I had a booger on the tip of my nose. "You blew the game!" I found out quickly that reporters want to interview you only about four to seven times a season. That's about the rate I blew games, and those were the only times they wanted to interview me.

212

TIM HUDSON
When Size Doesn't Matter

The Oakland A's signed me as a pitcher out of Auburn although I batted almost .380 as an outfielder. I took away a few of Frank Thomas's Tigers records, which I tease him about, but my statistics were a bit deceiving; if you put an aluminum bat in my hands, I could swing with about anybody, but when we used wood bats in the fall, I'd hit about .180. I weighed about 155, and you had to be a big, strong guy to handle that wood. I'm bigger and stronger now, but I don't have the stroke I had back then. I've always had trouble putting on weight. I was always a small guy growing up, but baseball's a skill game where you don't have to be 6′6″ and 220 pounds to have success. I looked up to Pedro Martinez, Tom Glavine, and Greg Maddux, because they weren't just good, but the best in the game. They gave me hope as a small pitcher.

A *Friendly* Wager

Mark Mulder and I both were good hitters in college, but when you pitch in the American League, you don't get to bat very much. So, when we were on Oakland, we loved having the opportunity to take batting practice and swing against live pitching during interleague play. We'd always go back and forth about who was the better hitter. When we were traded at the same time to the National League, we were both upset, but a perk was that we'd get to bat every time we pitched. Naturally, we bet on who would hit the first home run. He beat me. After he hit his homer, he texted me and told me to put the check in the mail. He's one of those guys who make you sick: he's 6′6″, he's good-looking, he's single, he's a great athlete, and he makes a lot of money—he makes everyone want to hate him. But I have to admit he's a great guy . . . although, I'm a better hitter.

When the Sinker Doesn't Sink   213

As a sinkerball pitcher, I want my ball to be in and quickly out of the zone, to have depth. When I properly bring my front elbow to the hip, I will be on top of the ball and get the downward tilt that I want. When I have trouble with my sinker, it's usually because instead of bringing my front elbow down to my hip it will flare out and be perpendicular to my side. When that happens, my arm comes through at more of an angle and probably my right wrist hinges rather than staying in a straight, locked position. When I'm not staying behind the ball, the result is that the ball flattens out and tails toward the right-handed hitter. Instead of sinking across the outside corner, it might run back across the plate. If my sinker has more tail than sink and stays on the same plane, big-league hitters are going to be licking their chops.

TWELVE

THE LEFTIES

WARREN SPAHN
Apparently, I Needed an Agent

Lou Perini, the owner of the Boston Braves, went to Notre Dame with Fred Miller, the owner of the Miller Brewing Company, and they were very close. Miller was conscious of the success of the Milwaukee Brewers, the Braves' Triple-A farm club, because the brewery's head-quarters were in Milwaukee. So, he tried to talk Perini into moving his ball club to Milwaukee, to open up some Midwest competition with the Cubs. Perini had a construction company in Boston, so he didn't want to leave there. But in 1952, we drew only 400,000 people for the entire season in Boston, so Fred Miller's suggestion sounded much more enticing. Miller underwrote the move to Milwaukee and guaranteed Perini a new stadium and 850,000 people in attendance in 1953, and that's the reason the ball club moved there, which was the major leagues' first franchise move in fifty years.

I was a bit reluctant to make the move because I'd just opened a restaurant in Boston. That was perfect timing, right? But we go to Milwaukee, and the people there were so happy to have major-league baseball and a new stadium that they embraced that ball club with open arms. We had the nucleus of a good young team with Eddie Mathews, Johnny Logan, Billy Bruton, Del Crandall, Johnny

Antonelli, Lew Burdette, and Bob Buhl, and we finished second to Brooklyn and drew 1,800,000 fans!

Before the season, I was holding out, trying to get a better contract, because I was making peanuts—meal money, by today's standards. I wanted a raise in pay, and Perini offered me a base salary, which I think was around $27,000, plus ten cents on every ticket sold above 400,000 people. I rejected that deal because he couldn't guarantee we'd draw more fans than we had in Boston. I couldn't count on people coming to the ballpark in Milwaukee. If I'd taken it, I would have made ten cents on 1,400,000 tickets plus my salary. I'd have been the richest player in baseball at that time.

Three Frightening Hitters

It seems that every time I walked to the mound, Stan Musial was the batter. I threw him a million pitches, and I don't think he ever hit the ball off the end of the bat or on the handle. Everything was on the barrel! It was the same with Hank Aaron, who was on my team, fortunately. One year in the middle of June, Lew Burdette and I picked up one of his bats, a bat that he had used all year since spring training. That bat wasn't broken; it wasn't even chipping—all of the marks were on the fat part of the bat, in one place. That's kind of scary, isn't it? Even Mickey Mantle hit it off his fists on occasion. In fact, in the '58 World Series at Yankee Stadium, Mickey hit a ball inside the trademark on the handle, and it smashed against the scoreboard in left center field for a triple. At least a guy ought to hit the ball on a good part of the bat to make it go that far. They should have tied one arm behind him, because that's not fair. That's how strong he was.

216

Looking Down a Gun Barrel or Facing Ryne Duren

Everybody always asks if I felt pressure pitching in the big leagues. What's pressure? Pressure's self-inflicted. Did you ever have somebody stick a rifle in your face? That's pressure. But on the ball field, I never felt pressure. Never. Except, maybe, one time. Do you remember Ryne Duren?

Hank Bauer tells a great story about the time he was on deck and Ryne Duren was pitching for Kansas City. Ryne used to throw 95 mph pitches against the backstop and everywhere else just to intimidate batters about how wild he was, or pretended to be. Well, on this day, he wound up and knocked Bauer down in the on-deck circle! And Hank yelled over to Casey Stengel, "Buy that SOB and send him to Timbuktu." Well, Casey did buy him, and he became a good reliever for the Yankees. In fact, he pitched against us in the World Series. So, one game at County Stadium in Milwaukee, I came up to bat against him. It was late in the day, and the shadows were elongated between home plate and the mound, which made it particularly tough to see. It was hard to pick up the ball anyway with Duren, because he wore these big dark glasses that made you wonder if he was blind. It was as if he were looking through the bottoms of Coke bottles, and you didn't see his face, just his big eyeballs. And, oh yes, everyone heard that either he couldn't see or was an alcoholic. It turned out to be both.

So, Duren's out on the mound, and Yogi's behind the plate, and he's banging his glove in my ear. He tells me, "Watch out, Lefty. He's wild inside." Well, sure as hell, the ball was up and in. Red Flaherty was the umpire, from the American League, and I said, "Red, will you shut this dago up? It's tough enough trying to see this guy." And now Yogi's giving Red all this lip, and it was hard to concentrate. The count went to 3-and-2, and I made up my mind I was going to take; I didn't care where the ball was. And that stupid Ryne Duren walked me. Was I relieved! You talk about pressure in baseball? Well, that was pressure.

Good, Clean Fun

Back in the old days, we had a lot of innocent fun. My roommate for fourteen years was Lew Burdette, and we had so much fun together going out that it didn't matter we didn't make any money then. In fact, we had so much fun together off the field that one time when I was bored with the game, he convinced me not to quit. He was right-handed but still crazy, and when we stayed at the Chase Park Plaza in St. Louis, we'd go across the street to the zoo and agitate the gorillas. How many ballplayers would do that the day of a night game? But that night, we wouldn't feel the usual jitters before the game.

On our club, everybody agitated everybody else. Even the trainer got into the act. He used to agitate Hank Aaron. He'd tell Hank, "Look at that crazy Spahn—see what he's doing now." And I'd catch Hank watching everything I did, and I'd think, "What the hell? Have I got a bug on my nose or something?" And I'd be agitated. I found out that the trainer was the guy behind Aaron's watching me, so I decided to agitate him back. I was pitching one day, and I said to the trainer, "Hey, give my arm a rubdown." And he rubbed the heck out of my right arm. He forgot what arm I threw with. Twenty minutes later, I said, "That's good, Doc. Don't touch my left one. I don't want you to mess it up."

The Better Part of Valor

The Braves were a veteran team that policed itself and didn't need managers telling us what to do. Managers would get mad at us for not listening to them. During one game, Charlie Dressen got hacked off at us and started yelling at us in the dugout. He pointed at one player after another, saying, "I'll get you!" He went down the bench saying, "I'll get you, and I'll get you, and I'll get you." And then he came to Eddie Mathews, who was an ex-marine and strong as a bull. Eddie got into a lot of fights and never lost one of them. So, Charlie has his finger pointing toward Eddie, and he says, "But not you, Eddie." Eddie would have pinched his head off.

Dressen always was trying to catch us breaking curfew, but we usually managed to outfox him. Once, he hid in the bushes after midnight, and when he jumped out to try to catch us passing him in the dark, he was caught in an elaborate sprinkler system we had fixed up. By the time he dried off and checked our rooms, we were in bed. He got us back one night by giving the guy operating the elevator a base-

218

ball; he told him to get autographs of all the players who came back to the hotel after midnight. When the elevator operator gave him back the ball, he had proof of who had missed curfew. But that worked only once!

Taking On the New Gun in Town

As a boy, I'd play catch with my father in the backyard, and the things he taught me helped keep me from hurting my arm. For example, I tried to never throw across my body. Also, I always kept in shape because I had a cattle ranch back in Oklahoma that I worked in the off-season. I was slight of build and would go to spring training underweight so that I could drink all the beer I wanted all year and nobody would question me about gaining weight.

In 1963, I was forty-two years old and led the National League for the seventh consecutive year in innings pitched. I looked at it this way: at that advanced age, if I'd fallen back just a little bit, a younger pitcher was going to take my place. I was the senior citizen on the ball club, but I really didn't feel that old. On certain days, I threw the ball as well as I did when I was young, so I didn't feel any reason to *retire*. That was a dirty word. I had some aches and pains, but I didn't know what a sore arm was. I'd rub dirt on any place that hurt, and I'd go out to the mound.

That July, I pitched a famous game against the Giants. Their pitcher was Juan Marichal. He was only twenty then, a young pup, but he was already a great pitcher. It seemed like every time he got into trouble, he'd reach back for a little bit better stuff. We had good hitters, and they had good hitters—Mays, McCovey, Cepeda, Felipe Alou—but nobody could score. When you pitch against someone like Marichal or Koufax, if you get a run, you'd better hold it. But here we go three, four, five, six, etcetera, innings, and nobody scores. I remember that somewhere around the sixth inning, I hit a ball to right field that hit the top of the fence and almost went out. And I'm on second base with nobody out, and now we got the top of our order up. I felt pretty confident that we were going to score. We didn't get the ball out of the infield, proving how Marichal could turn it on when he wanted to. That game was so closely contested; neither of us gave an inch the whole way through.

Then it's the ninth inning, and it's still 0–0. I was getting pretty weary out there, but I didn't want to let anyone know, because I wanted to finish the game. Alvin Dark, the manager of the Giants, wanted to take out Marichal, but Juan said, "I'm not going to let that old man beat me." And that's why he stayed in there. Thank God it was cool that night. We both kept pitching, and the game went sixteen innings. We were the visiting team, and in the bottom of the inning, I threw a hard screwball to Mays. The funny thing about it is that when he hit that ball, I thought it was a routine fly to left field. But the wind always swirled at night in Candlestick Park, and when I turned around to watch Wes Covington catch the ball, I saw it fly out of the park. It's not that Mays didn't hit it well, but I was amazed that the wind had shifted and carried that ball so far. If I could have taken those shutout innings I'd pitched and divided them, I could have had two wins. But I lost 1–0.

I wasn't tired until about thirty minutes after the game, until after I'd taken a shower. Oh, then I was stiff from my toenails to the top of my head, which still had some hair on it at that time. I think losing that game made me even more tired. Still, it was a great ball game, no question about it. I see Juan every once in a while, and I tell him he was lucky that I didn't get up to hit more often.

WHITEY FORD
From Queens to the Bronx

It all began on Thirty-Fourth Avenue and Forty-Third Street in Queens. The name of the team I played on was The Thirty-Fourth Avenue Boys, and that's because there was a bar there that bought our first uniforms. I wasn't always a pitcher. When I was fifteen and sixteen, I was a hard-hitting first baseman. When I turned seventeen, I was a senior at Manhattan Aviation High School, training to be an airplane mechanic—which makes my wife laugh today, because if anything goes wrong with our house, she has to fix it. I continued to play ball, and my position was still first base. I tried out with the Yankees as a first baseman. When they saw how I hit, they said I should try to become a pitcher.

After I graduated, I played first for a sandlot team, but when one of our two pitchers got hurt, I'd pitch every other game. So, during my entire youth, I pitched only half of that summer. We ended up playing for the New York City Sandlot Championship in the Polo Grounds. There were scouts from several major-league teams there, and after we won, the Yankees offered me a "big" bonus of $7,000. The Giants offered me $5,000, and the Dodgers offered me $1,000, but I would have signed with the Yankees no matter what the price, because I'd been a fan all my life. So, instead of becoming a fireman, policeman, or bartender, or working for the Railway Express—which I'd do for a couple of winters—I became a professional baseball pitcher.

My Biggest Regret About the 1960 World Series

In the 1960 World Series against the Pirates, I threw complete-game shutouts in Games 3 and 6. But I wish I had started Game 1 so that I could pitch three times in the Series, including Game 7, which we lost on Bill Mazeroski's ninth-inning homer. I missed about a month of the season in July and August, but I finished up strong and was very surprised that I didn't open the Series. Art Ditmar started Game 1, and he'd had a great year for us, so if Casey Stengel and our pitching coach, Ed Lopat, decided he should start, that was fine. But I was surprised, and so were a few of the players. Casey told me that he wanted me to pitch the first Series game at Yankee Stadium.

In my shutout in Game 6, we scored a lot of runs, and it would have been a good idea if Casey took me out early so that I could come back the next game in relief. In Game 7, I went to the bullpen on my own and started warming up. I wanted to see how my arm was, and it felt all right. I could have gone. But when they saw me, they told me to sit down, and that was the end of it. We would have won that game, but a double-play ball hit something and struck Tony Kubek in the throat. We were up by three runs, so that play and Hal Smith's three-run homer cost us the game. Mantle scored the tying run in the top of the ninth, but Mazeroski homered over the left-field fence in the bottom of the inning to end the Series. Overall in the Series, we scored over fifty runs, and the Pirates scored only about half as many. That's the only time I ever saw Mickey cry. He felt really bad, because he thought we'd outplayed them.

Changing One Successful Pitching Style for Another

In 1961, Ralph Houk became our manager. I met with him at Madison Square Garden in January, and he told me that Johnny Sain was our new pitching coach and asked me how I'd feel pitching every fourth day. I said that I'd love it. If you started thirty-eight games with the Yankees and didn't win twenty games or have a good year, there was something wrong. They asked Ralph Terry and a couple of other guys, and they thought it was a great idea, too.

At spring training, Johnny Sain asked me, "Would you consider changing your way of pitching?" I thought I'd been pitching pretty good, but he got me to start throwing the slider and sinker, and I almost abandoned my curveball that year. I now threw just the sinker, slider, and change. Sain taught me how to throw a slider. He said to throw it just like a fastball but at the last moment to pull down with the index and middle fingers. I got it working pretty good, with a sharp break. A lot of hitters who had seen me for years throwing the curve were stunned the first time around. I won twenty-five games and the Cy Young Award in 1961 and changed my pitching style completely.

222

I Didn't Understand How I Could Break a Record of Babe Ruth's

I broke Babe Ruth's record of twenty-nine consecutive scoreless innings pitched in the World Series, in Game 4 of the 1961 Series. I'd already shut out Cincinnati 2–0 in Game 1, and in Game 4, I went six innings before I had to come out because twice I'd hit myself in the foot while batting. We were leading 4–0, and I'd gone thirty-two scoreless innings, and I went into the dressing room, and somebody told me, "You broke Babe Ruth's record!" I didn't know anything about it. I didn't know Babe Ruth had been a pitcher! That was the first time I ever heard that.

I Was a Better Hitter than Koufax

I started against Sandy Koufax twice during the 1963 World Series, in Games 1 and 4. I discovered his weakness: he couldn't hit. I told him, "I bet I strike you out more than you strike me out." So, we made a friendly wager, and I won. In Game 1, he broke the World Series record with fifteen strikeouts, but he didn't get me once. In Game 4, we lost 2–1 in Los Angeles, but he didn't strike me out then either. I struck him out a couple of times, so I won the bet. But I would rather have struck out and won those two games!

SANDY KOUFAX
When I Learned How to Pitch in the Big Leagues

For the first few years of my career, I threw extremely hard but was too wild to be effective. Norm Sherry, who was Johnny Roseboro's backup catcher, deserves some credit for my turnaround, just for getting through to my head. He was my roommate at the time, and during spring training, we flew to Orlando to play against the Twins. Two pitchers missed the airplane, so we had only two pitchers available. It was an insignificant "B" game, so Walter Alston asked Gil Hodges to manage. Gil was going to play first base, too, but he got hit in the head before the game, and Ron Fairly played first for the first time. So, Gil managed only, and he stuck a big finger in my chest and said, "Big Boy, you're going eight innings today whether you like it or not."

Norm was going to catch me, and he knew that if I was as wild as I usually was, I wasn't going to last eight innings. So, he talked to me

223

before the game and said, "Let's try to do something different today. Let's not throw hard, but make pitches. Every pitch, I'm going to give a location, and let's try and hit that." I was trying to hit spots, and I think I walked five or six guys, but I pitched a no-hitter for the eight innings. That night, I stayed out a little too late and got in trouble with Alston, but it was a successful day.

Norm got through to me that day, and for the rest of that spring, we talked about trying to throw strikes. More often than not, when I was young and wild, I'd blow it out early in the game, trying to throw harder than I was ready to do. I think nobody can go 100 percent physically. It may be 95 percent physical, 5 percent mental, or the mental part can be even higher. I had to find out where I was comfortable. Working with Norm, I learned to leave something for the mental, especially at the start of a game. As I went deeper into the game and had thrown a lot of pitches and my rhythm and timing was better, then I could increase the physical part and throw harder. That was my approach the last few years of my career when I had my success.

Searching for a Third Pitch

I was known for my fastball and curve and did well with just those two pitches, but people don't know that I tried to add a third pitch, any third pitch. For a long time, I tried to learn the changeup. The Dodgers taught the changeup in a certain way—it was the Dodgers' changeup—and I tried to learn it for ten years but never got the hang of it. I never liked my changeup, and I never wanted to throw it. One day, I was playing catch and started fooling around with the forkball, and it felt more comfortable to me. I said, "Well, I'm going to try this instead of the changeup." So, I started to throw it, but I only used it occasionally in games, because I didn't throw it hard enough.

I also threw the slider a couple of times. I threw the slider to Hank Aaron and Roberto Clemente, because I figured if it worked on those two great hitters, then I had something there. So, I threw it to Aaron and almost hit him in the face. He reached out to get it, and it came right at him. And I threw it to Clemente. You may remember that in

224

Forbes Field in Pittsburgh, there was a tower by where they used to park the batting cage. Halfway up, there was a bunch of transformers. Well, Clemente hit it off a transformer. I said, "Well, maybe I don't have a slider," and I gave it up. So, I never came up with a third pitch.

Pitching to Clemente and Aaron

For me, Roberto Clemente was the easiest guy in baseball to get two strikes on. The game would start, and I could get him to foul two balls over his team's dugout as easy as anybody. And then it got tough. At least I always knew what I was trying to do against him, although I might not have been successful. It was the opposite with Hank Aaron. When I went out to pitch against him when the game started, I had no idea what I was going to do. He was the only hitter I never figured out, especially in the days before his home runs mounted up. In the early days, he was particularly hard to pitch to, because he hit the ball to the opposite field. In Milwaukee, a lot of his home runs were to right and right-center. Later in his career, when he started pulling the ball to hit more homers, he gave up a little bit. But for me, he was still the toughest batter. I may have gotten him out, but he hit the ball hard, and my third baseman had bruises on his chest and legs from balls hitting him. Tommy Davis particularly got beat up one day—he claims he still has a mark on his chest!

JIM KAAT
Mimicking My Idol, Bobby Shantz

225

My dad was never a great baseball player, but he followed the game and stoked my interest. For some reason, he took a liking to Connie Mack, who owned the Philadelphia Athletics and managed them, wearing a suit and starched collar in the dugout, for a record fifty years. So, the Athletics became the team I admired, too. And because I was a little guy until I was eighteen or nineteen and grew to well over six feet, my hero was Bobby Shantz. He was a left-handed pitcher who was only about 5'7" and was quick off the mound and a great fielder. He was who I patterned myself after.

We didn't have games on television, but I listened to Bob Elson— "the Commander"—call games for the White Sox, and I'd have my radio on Sunday afternoons when Shantz would pitch against Chicago. Elson would say, "He delivers the ball, and he hops." He would hop to get into position. I would go in the backyard and throw a rubber ball against the back of the garage, and each time, I'd hop and be in position to catch the ball. I never actually saw Bobby Shantz, but I did what I pictured him doing from hearing Elson. I signed with the Washington Senators in 1957. In 1958, I had my first spring training, and I took part in the old PFP drills—Pitchers' Fielding Practice. I did about three drills catching the ball, and our pitching coach, Walter "Boom Boom" Beck, says, "Kid, you look just like Bobby Shantz."

Bobby Shantz should have won many Gold Gloves, but they didn't start giving out that award until 1957. By then, he was pitching for the Yankees and won the first Gold Glove ever given to the best-fielding pitcher. He'd win every year from '57 to 1960. Two years after his final award, I started my streak of sixteen consecutive Gold Gloves, picking up where my idol left off.

When They Started Noticing My Fielding

In 1962, the second year of the Minnesota Twins, I was pitching against the Detroit Tigers. They had two men on, and Bubba Morton hit a one-hopper that skipped off the wet grass. I thought I could make the play, but it was hit so fast that it hit me in the mouth. It knocked out six teeth, and I was lying on the grass with blood trickling from my mouth. Our third baseman, Rich Rollins, picked up the ball and threw it to Vic Power at first base. Vic came over to me with the ball, and it had fragments of my teeth in it. He bent over and said with his Puerto Rican accent, "You want to keep this as a souvenir?"

Oddly, if you're going to get hit in the face, you'd rather have it be in the mouth than the eye, like Herb Score, temple, or nose. I had to drink milk shakes for a month, but it didn't affect how I threw the ball.

In fact, four days later, I pitched again, wearing the old boxer's mouth-piece. Willie Tasby hit the first ball right back to me on one hop, and that cured me of any fear. That's also when I started getting attention for my fielding. I was a lot bigger than Bobby Shantz, but people could see I had quickness. I would win the Gold Glove in 1962 and every year through 1977.

The Senators Left Washington and Started Winning

In my first few years in the Washington Senators organization, I often heard that famous old quote about the team: "First in war, first in peace, and last in the American League." The Senators had been bad for years, and it didn't seem, at least to the fans who stayed away, that they would improve. In the fall of 1960, I was in the Instructional League in Florida. Then all of a sudden one day, we heard, "The team is moving to Minnesota." I hadn't established myself as a big leaguer in the city of Washington, so the move wasn't difficult for me. Most of the young players thought it was a good opportunity to go to a new area for major-league baseball. We had heard the stories about how well players were treated when the Boston Braves moved to Milwaukee a few years before that. They got cars to drive, and the community was extremely supportive. We were optimistic about going to Minneapolis, and it did turn out to be a terrific move. When I look back on it, I think that if we had stayed in Washington with the team we put together in the 1960s, the Senators probably would have become as big as the Redskins during that era. But the new Senators in Washington in 1961 were an expansion team and continued the losing tradition.

The team that we took to Minneapolis–St. Paul had a lot of Cuban players. When we first got to the Twin Cities, the logo on our cap read "TC." Very few fans around the country knew what that meant, so I'd tell people in Chicago or Detroit that it stood for "Twenty Cubans." I'd joke, "We have twenty Cubans on our team." Joe Cambria was our scout in Cuba, and he would sign a lot of players for us, and since they didn't speak the language, they probably got paid less than the $6,000

227

minimum. The Cubans who made big contributions in Minnesota were Zoilo Versalles, who was the MVP in 1965, Camilo Pascual, who won twenty games and was known for his great curveball, and Tony Oliva, who won the batting title his first two years, in 1963 and 1964. And Pedro Ramos was one of our top pitchers in 1961.

The team really came together in 1962, when we finished second, only five games behind the Yankees. In Minnesota, Harmon Killebrew emerged as one of the great power hitters, and we had a strong lineup with Bob Allison, Vic Power, Rich Rollins, Earl Battey, and later Jimmie Hall, Don Mincher, and Oliva. And I started winning some games, and later Jim Perry and Mudcat Grant joined Camilo and me in our rotation. In 1965, we reached the World Series against the Dodgers.

Sandy Koufax Was Even Better Than I Heard

Minnesota won its first game in a World Series in 1965, when we defeated the Los Angeles Dodgers at home, 8–2. Mudcat Grant threw a complete game to beat Don Drysdale. Sandy Koufax would have opened the Series for them, but it was the night before the Jewish holiday, and the Dodgers held him back a day. So, I drew Koufax in Game 2. I had never seen him pitch in person, not even in spring training. So, a couple of scoreless innings go by, and I sit down next to our pitching coach, Johnny Sain, and say, "John, if I give up a run, this game's over. There's not a man alive who can hit this guy." He had a fluid motion where his fingers almost hit the ground, and every 95 mph fastball and hard curve went exactly where he wanted.

We squeezed out a couple of runs off him, and they had to take him out for a pinch hitter in the seventh inning. Ironically, Drysdale pinch-hit for him. We scored 3 more runs against the Dodgers' relievers and beat Koufax, 5–1. I went the distance. I faced him twice more, but he shut us out in Game 5 and shut us out in Game 7. I can say that Koufax, along with Bob Gibson and Juan Marichal, may have been the greatest pitcher of all time. He had a combination of power and control that no one can match. It's not just that he struck out over three hundred batters a season, but in that year, he struck out three hundred more batters than he walked!

Johnny Sain Saved My Career

If there were a Hall of Fame for coaches, Johnny Sain would be in it. He and Eddie Lopat, who had been a crafty junkball-throwing left-hander for the Yankees, were the two pitching coaches who really helped me a great deal. Johnny helped me a lot in the mid-'60s with the Twins and with the White Sox in the early '70s. Johnny had a saying: "You never really learn how to pitch until you hurt your arm." I was a hard thrower when I signed to play professional baseball, but I hurt my shoulder when I was in Double-A ball when I was nineteen and had to learn to be a pitcher. So, every year was a year of adjustment.

In 1973, the Twins sold me to the White Sox because they thought I couldn't pitch anymore. I didn't blame them, because I wasn't pitching very well. When I got to Chicago, I told Johnny, "My arm doesn't hurt, I feel good, but I can't get anybody out. I'm backing up third every time I throw the ball." So, in his old Arkansas drawl, he said, "Well, we've got to get you a quicker release." I was slow because I was a "hooker," meaning that when my left arm went all the way back, I'd break my wrist, so the ball faced the sky. So we began to speed up the motion. We'd speed it up, speed it up, speed it up, and he still didn't think it was fast enough. So, I said, "Look, John, I'm going to imagine on each pitch that the bases are loaded with no outs and the hitter just hit a ground ball back to me. I'm going to field it and boom, throw it right back to the catcher so he can complete the double play in time. So I tried that, and it worked. I milked it and won twenty-one games in 1974 and twenty games in 1975, and I kept pitching till 1983.

229

When I Became a Reliever

In May of 1979, the Phillies sold me to the New York Yankees. I was in Los Angeles and took a red-eye to New York to be on time for an afternoon game the next day. When the plane arrived, I didn't have time to go to the hotel, so I told the cabbie to go directly to Yankee Stadium. I didn't know my way around New York at the time, and he got "lost" and rang up about a $50 fare, courtesy of the Yankees.

I still got there early on Saturday morning and walked into Bob Lemon's office. Lem said, "Welcome to the Bronx Zoo." He asked when I'd last pitched, and I said I'd pitched a few innings a couple of nights before. "Can you pitch today?" "Sure." So, I came in with men on first and third with one out and faced my old teammate Rod Carew. I get Rod to ground into a double play, and that was my first appearance with the Yankees. That's really when I became a relief pitcher.

My Biggest Thrill in Baseball

In 1997, I was sitting at home in Florida watching the Indians play the Orioles in the ALCS, and the trivia question was: *If Cal Ripken Jr. gets back to the World Series, it will be fourteen years between Series appearances. Who holds the record for the longest time?* I said to my wife, "I think I'm the answer to that question." It was a record seventeen years between my first World Series appearance in 1965 and my other appearance in 1982.

When the Twins got to the Series in '65, it was kind of a surprise, and we were just happy to be there. We were too busy performing, and lining up tickets for people, to fully appreciate how special it was to get there. You figured you'd get back there. But as the years went on, I said, "If I ever get back there again, I'm going to treat it with more intensity. Being there is great, but next time, I want to win." I finally got back to the World Series with the Cardinals in '82, and though I didn't play much of a part in our victory, it was fun being on that ball club and winning it all. This time, I savored it.

I remember sitting in the bullpen next to our bullpen coach, Dave Ricketts, during Game 7 against the Brewers and watching the end of the game. In those days, the closer would come in for two or three innings, and Bruce Sutter relieved Joaquin Andujar to begin the eighth inning with a 4–3 lead. We added 2 insurance runs in the bottom of the eighth, and Sutter took a 6–3 lead into the ninth. With two outs, Gorman Thomas was hitting. They had all the policemen and dogs lined up, and they came into the bullpen and told us, "If you want to go to the dugout and beat the rush of fans, go right now!" I said, "I'm not moving. I'm going to sit here and enjoy every bit of this." Sutter struck out Thomas, and we were champions.

That's when I had thoughts going as far back as the bus rides in the minor leagues and of all the near misses since then, and at the age of forty-three, I really appreciated what it meant to get a World Series ring. It came in the twenty-first year of my twenty-two years in the majors, and it was the highlight of my playing career.

A *Telltale Sign That Your Career Is Over*

Steve Carlton threw one of the best sliders ever. In fact, before games, Tim McCarver and his other catchers would tell the first-base umpire to "be alive" because Lefty would get so many right-handed batters to go around, trying to check their swings when his ball broke. I got to see that when Tim and I were his teammates in Philadelphia. But I was with Carlton in St. Louis near the end of his career, and batters were no longer fooled by that sharp break and no longer checked swings. They would almost spit on the ball as it slowly went by and would say, "I can take that slider now."

I have my own story about losing something on the slider. I was forty-four years old, and Cardinals manager Whitey Herzog sent me in to face Claudell Washington, a left-handed batter. Joe Torre was managing the Braves, and he countered with Bob Watson. The "Bull" always gave me trouble. I got him 2-2 and decided to throw him my hardest slider on the outside corner. He swung and missed. The next day, I was at the batting cage, and he came over to me and asked, "When did you come up with that changeup?" The point is that as you get older, you lose the tilt on your slider, and it becomes the equivalent of a mediocre fastball. When Watson thought my hardest slider was a changeup, it was the telltale sign that I was through.

Tom Glavine
Pitching with a Calm Demeanor

I was in control of my emotions even early in my career. The game has never overwhelmed me, and I don't know why. I guess part of the reason is my parents and my upbringing. My dad, who was a heck of an athlete growing up, has a good work ethic, and my mom is the same way. They've always been even-keeled about everything. There was always the sense that whatever was going on, we could handle it. I got a lot of that attitude from them, and from some of my minor-league pitching coaches. Mudcat Grant was one of my pitching coaches, and I always have remembered him telling me, "When you're out there on that mound, you need to act like you've got everything under control, whether things are going well or not, because you don't want the other team to think there's a chink in the armor."

For some reason, that always stuck with me. So, when things are going well, I try not to do anything to rub the other team the wrong way and make them want to beat me any more than they already do, and if things are going poorly, I try to maintain an air of confidence so that the other team can't sense that I'm struggling with a particular pitch or am uncomfortable being in a bad situation. That's the way I've always been. In pitching, you really do have to keep your emotions in check, because if you start giving in to tense situations, you'll start doing exactly what you do not want to do. You can't worry that the bases are loaded with two outs and the tying run is on base, because you need to stay focused on getting the batter out. The more you can keep your emotions out of it, the better off you'll be.

Baseball and Hockey?

Growing up in New England, I played a lot of hockey as a kid. I was a center and shot left-handed, and a lot of people will tell you—and I agree, to an extent—I was a better hockey player in high school than a baseball pitcher. You wouldn't find too many street hockey games while I was growing up in the '70s where someone wasn't wearing a Bobby Orr jersey. He was as close to a sports idol as I had. I didn't really idolize athletes too much—I idolized my dad more than anybody—but I enjoyed watching athletes and always knew I wanted to be a hockey player or a baseball player. Back then, I didn't care which sport I'd play, as long as I did one.

When I was in high school, the biggest decision I had to make was which college I'd go to. I had three or four big baseball schools recruiting me and a bunch of big hockey schools recruiting me, but there were few schools that would allow me to play both. I wasn't ready to give up either sport at that time.

I was drafted by the Los Angeles Kings of the NHL as well as by the Atlanta Braves, and once that happened, it became more of a business decision, thinking about a career. The Kings called me up and said they'd watch me play college hockey and talk to me in a couple of years—college hockey was pretty much like a minor-league system. The Braves called me up and said they wanted to sign me and put me into their system immediately. I knew there would be more of a fast track in baseball. And being a left-handed pitcher, I felt I possessed an advantage in baseball that I didn't have in hockey. And baseball could give me the money that made it possible to give up a four-year scholarship that was in my back pocket and was very important to me, and still afford to go to college if my baseball career was brief. So, with my dad as my agent, I chose baseball.

I think I'm as good a hitter and bunter as I am, and a good fielder, because I was a good hockey player. Hockey is so fast, and the reactions are quick, and I carried over from hockey my hand-eye coordination. It is such a competitive game, and every time there is a shift,

233

every time you're on that ice, it's so intense and so competitive. A lot of that carries over to my style of pitching. I'm very competitive, and I don't give in very much, and a lot of that comes from my hockey background. My composed demeanor isn't totally at odds with hockey. You have to keep yourself in check in hockey, too. Being a hockey player is about tempering the physical side of your emotions; being a baseball pitcher is about the cerebral side of your emotions.

My Best Performance

The best game I ever pitched, because of the circumstances, was Game 6 of the 1995 World Series in Atlanta, when we clinched against Cleveland. I gave up one hit over eight innings, and Mark Wohlers pitched the ninth inning for the save.

My Braves teammate Greg Maddux would talk about going out and pitching a "perfect game," not a statistical perfect game, but a game in which you throw every pitch as you want to. In my mind, it was as good as I have ever thrown. There weren't many pitches that didn't end up where I wanted. A pitcher devises a game plan and wants to execute it with very few mistakes, and that game, I did. I had to pitch well, because we won by a score of 1–0. The game's only run came on a home run by David Justice, who was in trouble with the fans that week for getting on them for not being vocal enough and supporting us. To his credit, David was never afraid to speak his mind. Then he went out and walked the walk, as they say, hitting the big home run. The fans stopped booing him when he did that. It turned out that was the only run I needed.

234

Atlanta's Big Three

Anytime people start talking about you as being part of the greatest something, it's got to be good. I don't know if Greg Maddux, John Smoltz, and I were the best pitching threesome in history, as some people have told us, but it's flattering enough just to be mentioned with some of the great trios there have been. We won a lot of games, but all I know is that it was fun pitching with those guys. It was a rare thing. We had such a great relationship on and off the field. It was a great time for a long time. We'd feed off each other so much while we pitched that I'm sure we brought out the best in each other and made us even more competitive. And when we were away from the diamond, we'd talk to each other about pitching to various hitters while we played golf.

We played in many World Series together, and though we won only one of them, so many of them were pitching rich on both teams. I think about the NLCS in 1996. After John, Greg, and I swept the Dodgers in the division series, we found ourselves down three games to one to the Cardinals. And then we just annihilated them in the next three games, allowing them only 1 run. John started a game we won 14–0, Greg won 3–1, and I started Game 7, which we won 15–0. We had the momentum going into the World Series against the Yankees and took a two-game lead in Yankee Stadium when nineteen-year-old Andruw Jones started hitting home runs as if he were a veteran. Coming home with a two-game lead and our staff, it's hard to believe we lost four games in a row, one in which we led 6–0. That was the one Series that I thought we let get away, that we didn't lose to a better team.

I Was Forced to Change My Pitching Style

I did change my style a little bit because of QuesTec and baseball's desire to change to more of a rule-book strike zone. It went from being an east-to-west strike zone there had been since I broke in to the league to more of the rule book's north-south strike zone. I now am unable to expand off the outside corner and get a strike call. A pitcher has to find seventeen inches of the plate somewhere, so I'm trying to get those inches back by pitching inside. I've tried to expand the zone up and down, but that's hard for me to do. I have had a little more success down, because a guy whose fastball tops out at 88 or 89 mph can't really pitch up in the zone. Pitching inside has definitely helped me get back a workable strike zone. That's best for me.

Al Leiter
A Secret Admirer

My father was a merchant seaman who was gone six months at a time. It was hard to sustain a marriage under those conditions, and my parents split when I was in the ninth grade. So, my father wasn't around after that. He wasn't around when I made it to the major leagues in 1987 with the New York Yankees. After my father passed away, my oldest brother, John, went to collect his possessions. He found that my dad had a lot of Yankees posters and scorecards that he'd taken from *Yankee* magazine, which he could have gotten only if he had been to Yankee Stadium. Apparently, he had been going secretly to games to see me pitch and put those things up on his refrigerator, like a proud father. I had always hoped that even if we didn't reconcile, we could be friends, because I never knew him as an adult. It upset me that it never happened. He was a proud man who didn't want me or my brother Mark—who reached the majors three years after me—to think that he was coming back on the scene in order to enjoy the fruits of the hard work we had done to have success in baseball. It's sad that he stayed away.

What's Proper No-Hitter Etiquette?

On May 11, 1996, I threw my only no-hitter at home against the Colorado Rockies. That came a year before the Florida Marlins won their first World Series and was the first no-hitter in team history. We scored 6 runs in the first inning and won the game 11–0, so the only suspense was whether I'd give up a hit. I walked two and hit a batter, but we had a couple of double plays, and I faced only one batter over the minimum. I threw inside all night long, using my cutter, striking out six, including Eric Young, who went down swinging to end the game. I'd seen no-hitters before, and they always ended with big celebrations on the mound. But after I struck out the last batter, I didn't know what to do. My catcher, Charles Johnson, walked toward me, and I was kind of standing there with a sheepish grin. I didn't know if I was supposed to jump on him or if Charley, a big guy, was supposed to leap on me. And all we did was embrace, kind of a casual hug. Then the other guys gathered around for a lot of high-fives and rubbing and patting my head. Later guys told me that I didn't seem that excited. And I'd tell them, "I didn't know how to respond."

I Was Ready for Game 7

I pitched well for the Florida Marlins in Game 7 of the 1997 World Series against the Indians. That's because I learned a lot pitching in Game 3, which was played in thirty-degree temperatures in Cleveland. We won that slugfest 14–11 by scoring 7 runs in the ninth inning, but I was out of the game by the fifth inning after giving up 5 runs. It was a bad game, and I went back to the drawing board and watched how Andy Pettitte and David Wells, of the Yankees, had pitched against the Indians in the division series. I came to the conclusion that I *must* throw more curveballs to slow the batter down in front, which would make my cut fastball more effective.

Game 7 begins, and I tell my catcher, Charles Johnson, that I'm going to throw a curveball on the first pitch. I didn't even know who the batter would be. It turned out to be Omar Vizquel. During my warm-ups in the bullpen, I couldn't throw one curve over the plate — they were bouncing all over the bullpen. But I still threw it as my first pitch. Eddie Montague calls, "Strike!" That set the tone early. The opposing bench saw a first-pitch curveball, and they realized I wasn't going to be as predictable as in my previous start. Going against Jaret Wright, I went six innings, striking out seven and giving up two runs. Five relievers held them scoreless after me. We caught them at 2–2 in the bottom of the ninth, and then Edgar Renteria won it in dramatic fashion with a single in the eleventh inning to give us the championship.

THIRTEEN

THE BULLPEN

ROLLIE FINGERS

Growing Up in California, I Became a Baseball Player

I don't know how much baseball I would have played if I'd grown up where I was born, in Steubenville, Ohio. I'm sure I would have played some, because my father, who taught me the game, had played in the minor leagues and was even a roommate of Stan Musial's when he pitched in the Sally League. After his career ended, he worked in the coal mines and steel mills in the Ohio Valley, but one day in 1955, he came home and said, "That's it; we're outta here." He was tired, so we sold the house — and I remember my mom showing me the $1,500 in cash we got for it — and my dad went off and bought a '54 Buick, and off to California we went. We didn't have the money for hotels or motels, so we slept on the side of the road, with me and my brother in sleeping bags. When we arrived in California, my dad couldn't find a job, so ironically he ended up working in the steel mills there, too.

I grew up in Cucamonga, and that's where I had the opportunity to play a lot more baseball. From the age of nine or ten, I played baseball all year-round and became a good hitter and good pitcher. In 1964, I hit about .450 in American Legion ball to lead the nation, and my Legion team in Upland, California, went to the World Series in Little Rock, Arkansas. I played left field and pitched the final two games, and won them.

I signed with Kansas City as an outfielder/pitcher after turning down the Dodgers as a pitcher. The Dodgers wanted me real bad and offered me a $20,000 bonus, which was a lot back then, but I looked at their starters—Koufax, Drysdale, Osteen—and thought I might be stuck in the minors forever. So, I took only $13,000 to sign with Charlie Finley, the owner of the A's. I gave my dad $3,000, bought my mother a sewing machine, and got myself a '56 Chevy for $700.

My Scariest Moment

I was the starting pitcher for Birmingham on Opening Day in 1967. In about the third or fourth inning, I threw a slow breaking ball down and in to Fred Kovner, a young left-handed hitter in the White Sox organization. Thinking he was going to pull the ball, I relaxed, and he hit a sinking line drive right up the middle. I threw my arms up, but the ball went right through and hit me on the right side of my face, below the eye. It shattered my cheekbone, broke my jaw, and cost me several teeth. I couldn't see out of my right eye for a couple of days before the vision started returning. I was in the hospital for nine days with my mouth wired shut, and I was allergic to the medicine and kept vomiting. I went from 205 pounds to 168 pounds.

I was back on the mound in two or three months and even faced Fred Kovner in my first appearance. I worked my way through the rest of the season. It was tough coming back after something like that, because once you get hit in the face, you're always flinching after throwing a pitch. However, I was young and wanted to play, so I got over it. After something that dramatic, however, I made sure my glove always was in position. I'd be hit all over my body, but never again in the face.

240

How Reggie Jackson Eluded Fate

Reggie Jackson had signed for a big bonus out of Arizona State and joined us in Modesto in midseason. He stayed at a hotel in downtown Modesto. I shared an apartment with Steve Colker, a right-handed pitcher, and every single day, we'd drive through town, pick Reggie up, and drive to the ballpark. One particular day, Reggie was standing on the corner, and I drove right by him. Later I found out that he was jumping up and down, screaming. But I went past him, and two blocks later on a highway overpass, a car ran a red light and hit us right where he would have been sitting. We got rolled, and the roof collapsed down to the seats. We were off to the hospital, and if Reggie had been where he should have been, I doubt if he would have made it. He got to the ballpark and was upset and saying, "Where the heck is Fingers? He was supposed to pick me up!" Then he realized that the wrecked car that he'd passed in the cab was mine. So, he lightened up on me.

I Became a Hall of Fame Reliever by Default

Coming up through the minor leagues in those days, you got to the majors by being a starting pitcher. I had a few good starts for Oakland, but it got to the point where I couldn't get out of the second or third inning. I couldn't get anybody out. So, in 1971, I was on my way out of baseball.

About midway through the season, we played the Yankees. Our manager, Dick Williams, had already told me in the bullpen that I was going to be the mop-up man. We were getting beat about 11–3, and all of a sudden it's the eighth inning and we're winning 13–11. And I'm the only guy left, so he has to use me unless he throws a coach out there. So, I came in and pitched two shutout innings and got a save. The next night, he brings me in again, and I pitch another two innings and get another save. So, he calls me into his office and says, "From now on in game situations, you're going to be my closer." So, from the All-Star break till the end of the season, I saved seventeen games, and that's how it all started for me. I just happened to be at the right place at the right time.

241

Pitching in Relief Cured My Insomnia

When I was a starting pitcher, I couldn't sleep. It was the worst thing. So how could someone not sleep as a starter and be able to come into pressure situations as a closer? It was because as a starter, I knew when I would pitch, and that wasn't a good thing. I knew that if I got knocked out in the second inning, I'd have to wait four days to start again. I knew what day I would pitch, and I would think and worry about that, including at night when I was lying in bed. As a reliever, I never knew when I was going to pitch. I didn't know I was going to be in a ball game until the phone rang in the bullpen. I liked that situation a lot better, because I didn't worry.

I was more suited to relieve. I had pretty good control, and as a closer, that's probably the biggest asset to have. If you're a little wild and you get behind hitters, you won't be a good closer. I liked coming into pressure situations. I had an arm where I could throw a couple of innings in six or seven games in a row, and it wouldn't bother me—I rebounded real fast. I had thirty-seven or thirty-eight saves where I pitched three innings or more. That's the way it was back then. All the closers who pitched in my era—Bruce Sutter, Goose Gossage, Kent Tekulve, Dan Quisenberry, Sparky Lyle—usually went more than an inning, and when I hooked horns with those guys, I knew I was in for a three- or four-inning stint because they weren't going to give up any runs either. Nowadays, there are setup men, and closers go one inning. Back then, you were your own setup man.

The Stingiest Man Alive

In the mid-'60s, Charlie Finley picked up many scouts, and they covered the entire country. He picked up the best ballplayers he could possibly find. That's when he signed Catfish Hunter, Gene Tenace, Joe Rudi, Vida Blue, Sal Bando, Reggie Jackson, me, and some others who would be the nucleus of the world championship teams of the '70s. We all came up through the minors together and hit around 1969. We won titles but didn't make a whole lot of money.

In 1972, I was making $29,000. Oakland won its first pennant, and we beat the Reds in the World Series, and I saved two games and won one game, and he gave me a $1,000 raise. I called him up and told him what he could do with his raise, and I slammed down the phone. I got an agent and never spoke to Charlie Finley again.

He was a beauty. He's the only owner in the history of baseball not to put a diamond in the World Series ring. We beat the Mets to win the '73 Series, and the following spring we were given our rings; they were pieces of junk, and guys wanted to flush them down the toilet. Everybody blasted him in the newspapers, but he didn't care. All he cared about was saving money. Everybody was upset.

We opened up in Oakland that year, and my roommate, Kenny Holtzman—who hated Finley—and I were shagging balls in right field before the game. I spotted Finley sitting in the third-base dugout watching batting practice. I said, "Holtzie, let's put a couple of balls in our back pockets, and on the count of three, we'll fire them into the dugout." One, two, three: we fired them toward the dugout and immediately lay down and started doing sit-ups, so by the time the balls were rattling around him in the dugout, he had no idea who threw them. That was the last time he came down to watch batting practice. That year, we won our third consecutive World Series, beating the Dodgers, but our team salary in 1975 was only $1.1 million—that's for all twenty-five players. A year later, there was free agency, and eventually everybody who had been so badly underpaid went to other teams.

The Mustache Gang

In 1972, Reggie Jackson came to spring training with a mustache and wouldn't shave it off. So, all the guys got on him because at the time, there was no facial hair in the big leagues, but he wouldn't shave. So one day I was sitting around in the outfield with Catfish Hunter and Darold Knowles, and we decided to grow mustaches, too. We figured that when Dick Williams saw our mustaches, he'd tell us to shave them off, and he'd have to tell Reggie to do the same thing. Charlie Finley got wind of what we were doing and thought it was a great idea, and as crazy as he was, he told everybody that if they had a mustache on Opening Day, he'd give them $300. So, I grew my handlebar mus-

243

tache for a lousy three hundred bucks—but back then, it was a week's salary. I just happened to grow a handlebar because no one else was growing one, and I just wanted to see what it looked like. Many guys grew mustaches, and we started winning at the beginning of the season. Ballplayers are pretty superstitious animals, so we kept them. And then we started growing long hair, and we wore colorful uniforms with white shoes, and when we went on the road, we'd pack ballparks. We started winning titles, and it was hard to shave them off after that. Even Dick Williams grew a mustache.

The Fighting A's

On the A's, it was almost like picking straws to see who was going to fight that day. It would be over piddling things. One guy would use another guy's name on a pass list, and the other guy would get upset, and the next thing you know they'd be going at it on the floor. We had guys with short fuses. Mike Epstein got into a lot of fights with teammates; Reggie Jackson fought with Billy North; I got into a fight with Blue Moon Odom before a World Series game. That night, the guys who'd wrestled with each other in the locker room were out having dinner together. That's what we were like. Once the game started, don't have a different color of uniform on, because we played together, and we were going to beat you.

Dennis Eckersley
Frank Robinson Gave Me My Start

When I got to the big leagues, I felt lucky to be there. I had been drafted by the Indians, and people reacted, "Aww, Cleveland." But that was my ticket to the big leagues. If I'd been drafted by the Dodgers, I might have hung out several years in the minors, but Cleveland needed pitching. I'll never forget Opening Day in 1975, because there were sixty thousand people and media galore at Municipal Stadium to see the debut of baseball's first black manager, Frank Robinson. It was Gaylord Perry against the Yankees' Doc Medich, and Frank homered his first time up for the win, and I'm thinking, "God, this is great; this is the big leagues!" For the next game, there were five thousand people. But I was thrilled to be in the majors, and it was because of Frank.

I was only twenty, but Frank liked what he saw in spring training and fought to keep me. Luckily, he had a lot of clout. I bided my time in the bullpen for a couple of months, and when they traded Jim Perry, I became a starter. In my first major-league start, here I was, a kid from the Bay Area facing the Oakland A's. It was a dream come true. They had a nice team, which was coming off three straight world championships, but I threw a three-hitter and shut them out.

An Eventful 1978 Season in Beantown

I wasn't happy being traded by Cleveland to the Boston Red Sox in 1978. I didn't want to leave Buddy Bell and all the other friends I'd grown up with. And I'd disliked Boston when I'd visited as a road player. But when I became a Red Sox, it was a perfect fit. The Red Sox had an all-star team with Fred Lynn, Jim Rice, Carl Yastrzemski, Carlton Fisk, Rick Burleson, Luis Tiant, Mike Torrez, and Bill Lee, and I loved the passion there. We had a great year in '78 and took a fourteen-and-a-half-game lead in July. What happened is that we lost Burleson for a couple of weeks, and we took gas for a while.

Meanwhile the Yankees were incredible. They changed managers, from Billy Martin to Bob Lemon, and then took off, playing .800 ball. We had to win our last six games to force a playoff, ending with ninety-nine victories. So, it wasn't so much our collapsing as it was the Yankees' playing so great. Even though we lost on Bucky Dent's homer off Mike Torrez, I figured we'd be in the race every year. But it never happened.

Making the Transition from Starter to Reliever

After a couple of bad years with the Cubs, the timing was right for me to go to Oakland. I'd watched Tony La Russa from a distance from the other dugout. I'd say, "Look at this guy! Who does he think he is with

245

that long hair?" He didn't like me either, for the most part. I think I'd knocked down a couple of his players in spring training. When I got over there, I thought I was going to start, but when I walked into his office, he said, "I'll let you know what you're going to do. Why don't you go down to the bullpen for a couple of weeks, and we'll figure it out." Well, we would figure it out, but when he said that, it was definitely a slap in the face. But the secret to all the good that would happen is that I accepted what was asked of me. If I'd balked, and bitched and moaned that I should start, it would have been a different thing. At the time, I was changing my life on a personal level, so I was willing to change in baseball, too, and pitch in relief and make the most of it.

And my fastball came back—hello! My arm had been a bit dead starting with the Cubs, and it just got stronger throwing only fifteen to twenty pitches in relief. I also was doing isometrics and all the boring, preventive stuff you have to do so your arm doesn't fall off. I was just blessed with an arm that was resilient. Before, when I'd start, they would throw up nine tough left-handed hitters; now when I'd come into a game, the first guy up was a right-handed lamb. I'd think, "I can get this guy out. I can get any right-handed hitter out." I still had that intensity and was aggressive as hell, and I could paint the corners. I was confident, and that allowed me to "let it go." And the success started building, and the next thing I know I was becoming a reliable closer. And I was so grateful. People thought I was cocky and too demonstrative, but deep down inside I was as humble as anyone, because I was thrilled to be in that position. I was blessed to hook up with Tony. Now we're the best of friends.

246

Dealing with a Brutal Defeat

All games you lose are brutal, and some are even worse because of the importance of the games. I'm proud of how I reacted after giving up the two-run walk-off homer to Kirk Gibson in Game 1 of the 1988 World Series, patiently and honestly answering all the reporters' questions at my locker. I didn't plan to do that, that's for sure! But it was just the right thing to do. It was kind of an instinctive reaction. You know somebody's got to be the guy to take responsibility for a loss, yet that's not so clear when it's the last pitch and you're the guy who threw it. But I told the reporters that I threw the slider, and he hit it.

That game was so intense, and I never thought he'd hit a home run off me. I don't think anybody thought he would. More than anything, I will never forget walking off that field while the Dodgers celebrated. I couldn't make eye contact with any of the players. It was like I had the plague. I looked around Dodger Stadium, and everyone was so ecstatic, and then I walked into our dugout, and still no one would even look at me. I could just go back to that right now, it's so vivid.

You know, it helped me that I went through that, and I reacted the way I did because I was at a state of being so grateful. I was just coming off saving four straight games against the Red Sox and got the MVP of the ALCS. Sure I was upset, but I had peace at that moment knowing, "You're lucky to be here, pal." I was thirty-four, and I was finally in my first World Series, so if you can take the good, you've got to take the bad. I'm glad I did. We never rebounded from that loss, because Orel Hershiser was on a roll. He had a great postseason against the Mets and A's after coming off throwing fifty-nine consecutive scoreless innings. He was just so perfect, and watching him be so perfect would drive me nuts. Not even a hair was out of place! I don't mind getting beat, but it was perfection to the nth degree.

Fear Was My Biggest Motivator

I said that fear was a big motivator when I pitched. That's not something you should admit to anyone when you first get to the big leagues—I think I had twelve or fourteen years in before I said it—but it's the God's honest truth. Anyone who says there isn't fear in baseball is lying. I knew how precious my job was, especially closing, and that fear made me go. If a player is uptight and can't channel that fear, that's a big difference. As a closer, the intensity builds as the game comes to you. You're fighting all that negative stuff anyway, thinking, "I don't want to blow this." But that fear was in everything I did. That fear was in me when I was running. I'd run tons of miles, a marathon to pitch one inning. It was like, "I'm going to beat this thing; I'm going to be ready." So it motivated my whole being.

A Split Career Helped Me Get to Cooperstown

It was incredible to be voted into the Hall of Fame. As a kid, I was a Giants fan, and my heroes were Willie Mays and Juan Marichal—who I got my high leg kick from—and I couldn't believe I was now with them in Cooperstown. What a thrill that was.

I was the third reliever to be elected to the Hall of Fame, following Hoyt Wilhelm and Rollie Fingers. I guess I represented the new wave of relief pitchers who throw only an inning to close out a win, although before I did that in Oakland, I pitched longer in relief. But it was the combination of being a starter who won two hundred games and a reliever who saved three hundred games that got me into the Hall of Fame. John Smoltz also has had a career split between starting and relieving, with Atlanta. You don't just go from closing back to starting. You can always go from starting to closing like I did, but going the other way is unheard of! I didn't have the stuff he's got—he throws 95 mph and probably has the best slider in the game—and if he keeps doing what he's doing, I think he will be in the Hall of Fame, too.

DAVE RIGHETTI
When My Knees Shook

248

My best memory in baseball was winning the pennant against the Oakland A's in 1981. It's funny how things work out. I grew up in the Bay Area and went to World Series games at the Coliseum in the mid-'70s, and Oakland was a favorite place of mine. After their dynasty ended, the A's fell on hard times, but they finally started winning again under former Yankees manager Billy Martin, who would be my future manager when he returned to New York. Pitching against Oakland that day was the first time I felt nervous in a big-league game. My knees were shaking. I was back home, my parents and all my buddies were in the stands, and the entire Bay Area was watching. And the mound is so far away from the dugouts in Oakland that I felt I was on an island. It was a bit uncomfortable, but we managed to get through that one. I went six innings, Goose finished up, and we won 4–0 for a three-game sweep that put us into the World Series.

My Brief World Series Career

I played in my only World Series as a rookie in 1981. We took a 2–0 lead over the Dodgers in New York, and when we headed west to play the next 3 games, the whole organization felt pretty good, because the Yankees had won big games in L.A. in both the 1977 and '78 World Series. In Game 3, I was matched up against Fernando Valenzuela, which was kind of neat, since we were the two leagues' Rookies of the Year that season. I remember going out to warm up, and Graig Nettles came running up and grabbed me. He said, "Hey, your folks can't get into the game!" I said, "Well, I can't do much about it now." So, I was thinking about that. I think my father got hold of Tommy Lasorda in the L.A. clubhouse, and my parents got in through the Dodgers. The game itself was a total blur. I didn't pitch well. I gave up three runs in the first inning on a homer by Ron Cey—which gave them momentum—and lasted only two innings, though I didn't get the loss. They ended up beating us 5–4 and would win the next three games as well, to win the Series. That would be my final time in the postseason.

249

Using Disappointment to Fuel a No-Hitter

In 1983, I wanted to go to the All-Star Game, but since I was scheduled to pitch on July 4, a day before the break, I wasn't selected.

There was some rule that said you had to be able to pitch in order to make the staff. Ron Guidry had a bad back, so he withdrew from the All-Star team. He said, "Let Righetti go." But they still turned me down. They picked Tippy Martinez instead, because the American League had lost eight games in a row and wanted an extra arm. I was very upset. I didn't understand why I couldn't be on the team without pitching, because the roster was so huge.

I called my agent and told him to show up at Yankee Stadium the next day because I was going to do "something." I didn't know if it was going to be good or not, because Boston had creamed us three days in a row. It was Sunday, July 4, and it was hot. The day before, I'd been sitting on the steps outside the dugout, which I never did, because if you look up in the stands, somebody would punch you in the back of the head, and our DH, Don Baylor, told me to get out of the sun to save my energy to pitch the next day. That night, our whole team was a guest of Willie Nelson's at his concert in the Meadowlands, and there were three million people there, and it was so hot that people were taking off their shirts. I left early to get home and get some rest, and got lost and wound up driving through the Lincoln Tunnel and onto a packed Forty-Second Street. Maybe all this made me relax for the game.

Against Boston, I had no game plan, just a first-inning plan to go out to the mound and make everyone know I was there. My intention was just to go as far as I could in ninety-six-degree temperatures. It was a nutty day in which they had raffles and other on-field things going on. But I struck out Wade Boggs with two outs in the top of the ninth and had pitched the first no-hitter in Yankee Stadium since Don Larsen threw the perfect game against the Brooklyn Dodgers in the 1956 World Series. It was very exciting!

How I Became the Yankees' Temporary Closer, Permanently

I don't think I was ever fully appreciated as a stopper in New York, because in all the years, the Yankees themselves never said how much they loved me as their closer and every year brought up the possibility I'd return to starting. I had done well as a starter from 1981 to 1983, when I threw my no-hitter, and I didn't want to go to the bullpen after Goose Gossage left the Yankees. But there was a precedent set in 1979, when Goose broke his thumb in a fight with Cliff Johnson, and Ron Guidry agreed to go to the bullpen while he was out. If Guidry could do that after going 25–3 and winning the Cy Young Award, it was hard for me to turn it down. I knew there weren't a lot of free-agent stoppers out there.

Until George Steinbrenner acquired a closer like Bruce Sutter, we needed someone to fill the void. I know Guidry turned down the job, because he told me. And the next phone call went to my house. Yogi Berra, who replaced Billy Martin as manager, called me. I trusted Yogi and believed he'd take care of me. I was the one who made it very hard on Yogi, because I went to the bullpen every day ready to pitch. Maybe I wasn't going to be as good as Goose, but I had the same mentality in regard to being available every game. When I said *yes*, I meant it. It wasn't going to be just a test in spring training, but a commitment. I thought it was going to just be a one-year thing, and I think the Yankees really believed it, too. But we had a good year and seemed to be on track to improve as a team, so nobody wanted to tamper with the bullpen. The Yankees never would say the move was permanent, but I'd never start another game for them. In fact, I wouldn't start again until 1992, when I got four starts with the Giants in my final season.

Part of the Yankees' Relief Legacy

A writer walked up to me one night and couldn't wait to tell me the good news that Mariano Rivera got his 224th save as a Yankee. He said, "Hey, Rags, what do you think of Rivera breaking your record tonight?" I said, "He tied it! He's never going to break it!" Of course, I was joking. I'm now out in San Francisco as the Giants' pitching coach, so I guess it will be fun to have my name mentioned for a while along with Rivera's back in New York.

Goose Gossage was a huge name in New York before I got there, and Sparky Lyle was there before him. When I became the Yankees' stopper after having been a starter, I didn't know what I was supposed to do or how I was supposed to act, so I think it was an accomplishment for me to save more games than they did. But I never had a chance to pitch in the postseason after my rookie year, 1981, and never as a stopper. I didn't get to show what I could do and make my name and leave my mark. Obviously, Mariano Rivera has done that. He has been one of the best playoff and World Series pitchers ever. He's up there with the greatest, so if I get mentioned with him, that's wonderful.

MIKE STANTON

A Great Moment in Atlanta Braves History

There are many moments I've experienced in my career that I will file away and later tell my grandchildren about. At the top of the list is the seventh game of the 1992 ALCS between the Braves and Pirates. Pittsburgh scored a run in the first and another in the sixth off John Smoltz, but we couldn't break through against Doug Drabek. I pitched in the seventh inning and then sat in the dugout. I was just a fan at that point, and it was so nerve-racking. Fulton County Stadium had a wall in the dugout, and I was so nervous that I squatted down behind the wall, not wanting to watch but still watching. It was kind of like trying not to watch a scary movie but peeking through your fingers.

Drabek carried a shutout into the ninth inning. Then Stan Belinda came in, and we finally scored on a sacrifice fly. With two outs, we had the bases loaded and trailed by one run. So, it all came down to our pinch hitter, Francisco Cabrera. He singled past Jay Bell into left field, and we scored the tying and winning runs that got us into the World Series.

Sid Bream, who wasn't a fast runner, scored from second when Barry Bonds's throw was a bit up the first-base line. In 1995, I played with Stan after being traded from Atlanta to Boston. That play was the first thing he brought up when he saw me. He didn't say, "Hi"; he didn't say, "How ya doin'? Welcome to Boston." He said, "How does Sid Bream not get thrown out at home plate?"

Setting Up the Greatest Reliever in Baseball

I had the pleasure of watching Mariano Rivera for six seasons when I was his left-handed setup man for the Yankees. He is by far the most incredible thing I've seen in my life. He actually changed the way he pitches. In 1996 and 1997, he was a high-fastball pitcher. He had the one little stumble when Sandy Alomar homered to the opposite field to beat us in the 1997 division series against Cleveland. From then on, he started pitching inside, and that's when he picked up the cut on the fastball. It was amazing watching him throw that pitch on a daily basis, and seeing batters know it's coming but still not hit it. All of us pitchers get hit; we all give up hard hits. Except for him.

If you beat Mariano Rivera, you beat him like Arizona did in Game 7 of the 2001 World Series. If you remember, that entire Series, including the three games in New York only a few weeks after 9/11, was so emotional and dramatic. To me, it was like a dream. We lost because of Curt Schilling and Randy Johnson: we took the approach that we could scratch out a run or two against them in the four or five games they'd pitch, but we couldn't. Those two beat us, but the hit that gave them the Series win was by Luis Gonzalez—a broken-bat one-out single off Mo *over* a drawn-in infield. If Jeter had been playing in his normal position, it would have gone right to him. That was the only way to beat Mariano Rivera.

We tease Mo about the last out of the 2000 Subway World Series against the Mets, when he got Mike Piazza to fly out to center field. If you look at the tape, you'll see that when Mike hits the ball, Mo puts his right arm up and ducks, although the ball is fifteen feet over his head. At night in Shea Stadium, the ball doesn't travel to center field, which is fortunate, because Mike hit it really well. When he hit it,

253

everyone in our dugout went, "Oh, no." Mo thought Mike got it all, too, but then we saw Bernie Williams slow down in center field and catch the ball well in front of the warning track. And we won the World Series.

JOE TORRE
On Mariano Rivera

In 1997, when we went to Game 5 of the division series against Cleveland, we were four outs away from going to the next level and playing Baltimore in the AL Championship Series. We felt at that point that we were there. If you need four outs and you've got Mariano Rivera, who was in his first year as our closer, you've got to like your chances. And we lose on Sandy Alomar's opposite-field homer. That loss made us better the next year, because the players thought we were better than Cleveland and should have gone further. Mariano, I think, came of age with that home run.

Despite his failures in the 1997 division series against Cleveland, the 2001 World Series versus Arizona, and the 2004 ALCS, Rivera has been the best postseason reliever in history, as well as the dominant closer of this era. I'm as amazed as anybody that a guy who throws one pitch, at one speed, can be as successful as he is. All he throws is a fastball—but it can be a two-seamer that goes down, a high four-seamer, or a cutter. The reason for his success is movement. I think, toward the end of the '98 season, Mel Stottlemyre worked with him on his grip, and his movement got even better. So Mariano has this fast pitch that's devastating to left-handed hitters. Normally, you'd pinch-hit a left-hander against Rivera because he gets the steam from the other side of the plate, but that pitch goes into the left-hander and away from the right-hander. One goes away from the fat part of the bat, and the other one sort of goes out toward the end of it. So, either way, it's tough. And if you try to take the ball up the middle, Mariano is like an extra infielder. He's such a good athlete that he could play center field.

254

I've had a number of successful relievers—John Wetteland, Lee Smith, Tom Henke—and I loved them all, but they all made you bite your fingernails a little bit. Rivera comes in and throws strike one. Then he's not consumed with striking out people, which I think has been his biggest attribute. When he comes in, you expect to win. As a manager, I spend the entire game figuring out how to get to him. The trust I have in Mariano Rivera is enormous. He has earned that trust.

INDEX